EUROPEAN CS DEMOCRACY?

European Company Law - Towards Democracy?

CHARLOTTE VILLIERS

Ashgate
DARTMOUTH
Aldershot • Brookfield USA • Singapore • Sydney

Published by
Dartmouth Publishing Company Limited
Ashgate Publishing Limited
Gower House
Croft Road
Aldershot
Hampshire GU11 3HR
England

Ashgate Publishing Company
Old Post Road
Brookfield
Vermont 05036
USA

British Library Cataloguing in Publication Data

Villiers, Charlotte
    European company law - towards democracy?. - (European
    business law library)
    1.Corporation law - European Union countries
    I.Title
    341.7'53'094

Library of Congress Cataloging-in-Publication Data

Villiers, Charlotte.
    European company law : towards democracy? / Charlotte Villiers.
        p. cm.
    Includes index.
    ISBN 1-85521-603-5
    ISBN 1-85521-614-0 (pbk.)
    I. Corporation law - - European Union countries. I. Title.
    KJE2448 .V55 1998
    341.7'53 ddc21   98-31355
                                                           CIP

ISBN 1 85521 603 5 (Hbk)
ISBN 1 85521 614 0 (Pbk)

Printed and bound in Great Britain by MPG Books Ltd, Bodmin, Cornwall

Contents

List of Abbreviations

AG	Aktiengesellschaft
AktG	Aktiengesetz 1965
CA	Companies Act 1985
CBI	Confederation of British Industry
COREPER	Committee of Permanent Representatives
DGV	Directorate General of Employment, Industrial Relations and Social Affairs
DGXV	Directorate General of Internal Market and Financial Services Sector
DTI	Department of Trade and Industry
EC	European Community
EC Treaty	Treaty of Rome 1957
ECOSOC	Economic and Social Affairs Committee
EEC	European Economic Community
EEIG	European Economic Interest Grouping
EFTA	European Free Trade Area
ETUC	European Trades Union Congress
EU	European Union
GmbH	Gesellschaft mit beschränkter Haftung
GmbHG	Gesellschaft mit beschränkter Haftung Gesetz 1892
IASC	International Accounting Standards Committee
IOD	Institute of Directors
LAC	Ley de Auditoría de Cuentas 1988
LSA	Ley de Sociedades Anónimas (1951 or 1989)
LSRL	Ley de Sociedades de Responsabilidad Limitada (1953 or 1995)
RRM	Reglamento de Registro Mercantil 1989
SA	Sociedad Anónima
SRL	Sociedad de Responsabilidad Limitada
TUC	Trades Union Congress
UNICE	Union of Industrial and Employers' Confederations of Europe

Preface

In a recent Consultation Paper on Company Law the European Commission claimed that the harmonisation programme has to some extent been a success. At the same time, however, the Commission recognises that the harmonising power under Article 54 EC Treaty is limited and that it has become necessary to create uniform legal instruments of co-operation and integration between European businesses so as to enable them to derive the greatest possible benefit from the establishment of a single market.

The Commission also observes that the Community institutions have had few discussions on company law in recent years. This does not mean that the company law programme is no longer relevant. On the contrary, the fact that the draft Fifth Directive, the draft Tenth and Thirteenth Directives and the proposed European Company Statute have been stalled in the Council, amid newspaper coverage of heated debates between the Member States in the negotiations concerning these proposals, suggests that company law is a very controversial and important field of European activity. Companies are major employers across the European Union and their activities have an enormous impact on the economies of the Member States in which they carry out those activities. The European laws affect significantly what the companies will do and where they will operate.

This book has four separate aims: first, to provide an account of the development of the European company law programme and a description of the legal provisions adopted since the programme began in the early 1960s. Secondly, the book aims to introduce readers to the company laws of a Member State whose legal system is little known in the UK. For this reason Spain has been chosen as a comparator against the implementation measures of the UK. The Spanish legal system also represents the continental tradition and Spain entered the Community later than the UK, a factor which may have encouraged a different response to the European provisions.

The book is also concerned with the problem of democracy both at European level and at the level of the company. These two levels require different forms of democracy. At the European level, democracy will be representative and at the company level democracy may be more participative. A number of democratic theorists claim that representative democracy at the wider level may be made more effective by participatory democracy at the local level. This book's third aim will therefore be to explore the problems of representative democracy in the European Community, using the company law programme as a case study by which to assess the quality of the Community's representative democracy. Finally, the book will also explore the arguments for and against participatory democracy at the level of the firm. The book will present an argument that suggests that it is possible to establish democracy in the company and that this will be necessary for the future progress of the European company law programme.

The description of the European company law provisions is kept relatively brief and is limited to the mainstream measures, partly because detailed descriptions and analyses already exist in other helpful texts. Similarly, the description of the development of the measures through the different legal procedures has been selective because the provisions explored are representative of a general category of provisions, in particular of the generations of directives which may be identified by the date at which they were adopted and the procedure by which they were enacted.

In writing this book I have been fortunate enough to have benefited from the assistance of many individuals and institutions. I would like to thank the following in particular: The Nuffield Foundation for funding the research of the Spanish law (ref: SOC (100)974); my publishers, especially John Irwin and Valerie Saunders for their encouragement and patience; Apostoulos Iakomides of DGXV; Heinz Kröger, of UNICE; Anthony Murphy, UK Permanent Representative, DTI; the Spanish Permanent Representative; the Universities of Sheffield and Oviedo, Spain; the library of the Colegio de Abogados of Oviedo. I also wish to thank a number of individual colleagues, including Geraint Howells, who invited me to write this book for the *European Business Law Library Series*; Lorna Woods, with whom I have worked on ideas developed in Chapter 6; my colleagues in Glasgow who responded in a lively manner to my ideas in a seminar and helped me on to a clearer path; and my father who has discussed some of the ideas in the book with me on several occasions.

The months I spent in Oviedo are an unforgettable period in my life. I learned not only about Spanish company law but, through my friends, I enjoyed all the beauty of Asturias, from the mountains to the cider and the folk songs. I thank warmly for their hospitality and kindness, Alicia de León Arce; Carmen Moreno-Luque Casariego; María Isabel Alvarez Vega; María Dolores Palacios González; Angel Luis Bernal del Castillo; María Isabel Huerta Viesca; María José Fernández Antuña; María Luz García García; Graciela Martínez Fernández; Margarita Fuente Noriega; Ana María Sanz Viola; Luis González Morán; Amparo and José.

Fraser Davidson read an earlier draft of this book and he stopped me from jumping without a parachute. I have learned enormously from his criticisms. Finally, special and warm thanks are due to Tony Prosser who not only read more than one draft, but, like on our real mountain climbs, has encouraged me all the way.

This book states the law up to November 1997.

1 Introduction

1. SETTING THE AGENDA

The European Community was established in 1957 to 'promote a harmonious development of economic activities, a continuous and balanced expansion, an increase in stability, an accelerated raising of the standard of living and closer relations between the states belonging to it'.[1] The two principal means of achieving these aims were by 'establishing a common market and progressively approximating the economic policies of the Member States'.[2] In this respect, the primary aim of the Treaty of Rome was to create an economic area for the founding six Member States of the Community capable of guaranteeing the free movement of persons, goods, services and capital. The creation of a common market would necessitate the elimination of disparities between the national laws of the Member States.

Central to the modern economy are capital companies through which business tends to be conducted.[3] Thus it is no surprise that the company laws of the Member States within the European Community became a key focus of attention. The activities of the European Community in the company law field have been important to the creation and development of the Single Market. Two principal objectives were to allow companies freedom of establishment in other states and to combine and merge with other companies within and across national frontiers. In order to achieve these objectives it became necessary to break down national barriers that created discriminatory restrictions. The European Community took steps to 'approximate' the laws of the Member States in order to facilitate the creation and functioning of the common market[4] and aimed at providing equivalent protection for shareholders and third parties in each Member State.[5] This has evolved as a

---

1   Preamble to the EC Treaty.

2   Art. 2, EC Treaty.

3   Eric Stein, *Harmonisation of European Company Laws – National Reform and Transnational Co-ordination* (Bobbs–Merrill, Indianapolis, 1971), at p. 23. See also Robert Drury, 'A Review of the European Community's Company Law Harmonisation Programme' (1992) 24 *Bracton Law Journal* 45–51, at p. 45.

4   See in this respect Art. 3(h) EC Treaty. For a discussion of the terminology see Ignaz Seidl-Hohenveldern, 'Harmonisation of Legislation in the Common Market and the Heritage of the Common Law' (1962) *JBL* 247–252 and 363–372, esp. pp. 247–8.

5   Art. 54(3)(g), EC Treaty.

European Community company law which now influences fundamentally the national company laws of the Member States.

The primary focus of this book will be the company law harmonisation programme. The book will discuss the Community legislation adopted and proposed under the programme. The discussion will be limited to the 'mainstream' company law directives and regulations[6] and will not consider the legislation concerned with specialist companies or stock markets,[7] although their relevance cannot be denied.

Since it was established, the European Community has gained overwhelming economic and political importance for the activities of its Member States and citizens. The commercial laws of all the Member States are hugely influenced by the policies and legislative provisions of the European Community. The Community involves itself with policies on competition and industrial and economic co–operation and expansion, it affects imports and exports within and among Member States and beyond the European market, it both enables and restricts economic activity and it impacts on taxation policy. As Snyder puts it: 'law matters: it has effects on political, economic and social life outside the law.'[8]

The weight of the European Community's influence on economic activity requires its own institutions and processes to be justified. Thus, a second complementary concern of this book will be democracy in the European Community. Indeed, democracy is regarded by some as fundamental to the European Community. For example, Ress remarks: 'the principle of democracy as a constitutional principle of every Member State has to be regarded as a general principle of the Community itself, and that the principal structures of a representative democracy must be transferred to the Community level.'[9] In this way, representative democracy provides a

---

6   See Chapters 3 and 4 for a description of the Directives and Regulations that will be examined in the book.

7   For example, the banking directives and directives on co–operatives.

8   Francis Snyder, 'The Effectiveness of European Community Law: Institutions, Processes, Tools and Techniques' in T. Daintith (ed.), *Implementing the EC Directives*, (Wiley, Chancery, Chichester, 1995) 51–87, at p. 51.

9   George Ress, 'Democratic Decision–Making in the European Union and the Role of the European Parliament' in Deirdre Curtin and Tom Heukels (eds), *Institutional Dynamics of European Integration – Essays in Honour of Henry G. Schermers*, Volume II (Martinus Nijhoff, Dordrecht, Netherlands, 1994), 153–176, at p. 158. See also Deirdre Curtin and Herman Meijers, 'The Principle of Open Government in Schengen and the European Union: Democratic Retrogression?' (1995) 32 *Common Market Law Review* 391–442. For a contrary view see G. Federico Mancini and

basis of legitimacy for the European Community. Thus, the official publications of the European Communities make frequent claims to democracy as an achievement of the Community.[10] For example, the Commission claims that the 345 million people of the Community 'enjoy democratic freedoms and living standards which are matched by few other countries' and that 'the Community will not be able to claim to be a true union if it does not reinforce its structures and rationalise its decision–making procedures, which must be both efficient and democratic' and that the Community 'has soldered together democratic Europe'.[11]

Democracy was also a key aspect of the negotiations for the Maastricht Treaty on European Union.[12] Article F1 of the Treaty on European Union states that 'the Union shall respect the national identities of its Member States, whose systems of government are founded on the principles of democracy'. The European Court of Justice has also recognised democracy as a principle of the highest order.[13] Democracy featured as a primary focus of debate in the recent Intergovernmental Conference.[14] Yet despite these

---

David T. Keeling, 'Democracy and the Court of Justice' (1994) 57 *Modern Law Review* 175–190.

10　For example, *From Single Market to European Union* (European Commission, Brussels, 1992).

11　*Ibid.*, especially at p. 6 and p. 18.

12　See eg Deborah Z. Cass, 'The Word that Saves Maastricht? The Principle of Subsidiarity and the Division of Powers within the European Community' (1992) 29 *CMLR* 1107–1136, especially at p. 1122.

13　Case 139/79 *Maizena v Council* [1980] ECR 3393 at 3424; Case 138/79 *Roquette Frères v Council* [1980] ECR 3333 at 3360. See also George Ress, 'Democratic Decision–Making in the European Union and the Role of the European Parliament' in Deirdre Curtin and Tom Heukels (eds), *Institutional Dynamics of European Integration – Essays in Honour of Henry G. Schermers*, Volume II (Martinus Nijhoff, Dordrecht, Netherlands, 1994), 153–176, at p. 158. For a contrary view see Judge Thijmen Koopmans who argues that courts 'are not designed to be a reflex of democratic society': T. Koopmans, 'The Roots of Judicial Activism' in *Protecting Human Rights: The European Dimension*, Studies in Honour of Gérard J. Wiarda (Carl Heymans, Köln, 1988) 317 at p. 321, quoted by G. Federico Mancini, 'The Making of a Constitution for Europe' (1989) 26 *CMLR* 595–614, at p. 612.

14　See eg *Commission Report for the Reflection Group: Intergovernmental Conference 1996* (European Commission, Brussels, May 1995) and *Commission's Opinion: Reinforcing Political Union and Preparing for Enlargement* (European Commission, Brussels, February 1996). It is also interesting to note press reports that the European Union and the United States, in the year of the 50th anniversary of the Marshall Plan and the 40th anniversary of the Treaty of Rome, have an awards programme to

claims the European Community is frequently criticised for its 'democratic deficit'.[15] For example, the Council tends to be regarded as too powerful and the European Parliament not powerful enough in the decision–making process.[16] Lack of transparency has weakened the cause of the European Community, a problem exacerbated by the complexity of legislative procedures and the fragmented development of the Community.[17]

The company law legislation will serve as a case study of how the European legislative process functions and will provide a basis for evaluating the democratic claims of the European Community and its legislative and decision–making procedures. Thus, for example, we might ask if company law harmonisation was created through democratic procedures. To what extent did Member States and interested parties participate in shaping the legislation? Who voted and how? The book will therefore consider the different procedures used for introducing different aspects of the company law programme, including the consultation procedure, the co–operation procedure and the co–decision procedure.

The book will also evaluate the company law Directives by comparing the experiences of two Member States: the United Kingdom and Spain. These two states will provide an interesting comparison since neither Member State was an original member of the Community but each entered the Community at different times. The United Kingdom entered at the time of the first enlargement of the European Community with effect from 1 January 1973[18] and Spain entered with effect from 1 January 1986 in the second enlargement.[19] The two Member States also have quite different legal systems. The United Kingdom has a common law system. UK company law is therefore based primarily on some important Acts of Parliament, but this statutory regulation is supplemented by a significant weight of case law. Spain, having a codified system with a written constitution, adopts a more rule–based approach. Another interesting difference between the two states'

---

encourage communities, individuals and non–governmental organisations at the local level to promote across the continent of Europe peace, prosperity, democracy, human rights and open, market–oriented economies: DN: IP/97/456, 29 May 1997.

15   See eg B. Boyce, 'The Democratic Deficit in the European Community' (1993) 46 *Parliamentary Affairs* 458; J.C. Piris, 'After Maastricht, are the Community Institutions More Efficacious, More Democratic and More Transparent?' (1994) 19 *ELR* 449.

16   See eg Stephen Weatherill, *Law and Integration in the European Union* (Clarendon Press, Oxford, 1995) esp. Ch. 3, pp. 58–96.

17   *Ibid.*

18   Under the European Communities Act 1972.

19   Under the Spanish Treaty of Accession of 12 June 1985.

company laws is that the United Kingdom's legislation tends to apply generally to both public and private limited companies whereas the Spanish law has separate company laws applicable to specific company types. These differences may have affected the manner in which each Member State implemented the company law Directives and the practical application of their provisions in each country. Indeed, the process of implementation of the directives took different forms in each of these Member States. The United Kingdom's implementation provisions have been largely fragmented, owing to the early entry of the UK into the Community. Spain, on the other hand, with her later entry into the Community, was able to introduce a more wide-ranging programme of company law reform, although later reforms became as fragmented as those of the UK because of their piecemeal introduction at European level. It might be argued that Germany would have been a more appropriate comparator Member State than Spain. This argument has some force since much of the company law programme was influenced by German law. For this reason, a description of the German company law will be provided. In any event, Spanish company law has itself been influenced by the German company law. Spain is a relatively new democracy and little has been written in the UK on Spanish law. This study provides the opportunity for an introduction to the Spanish legal system.

The discussion will proceed in the following order. The first part of the book will provide a description of the company law directives. A number of 'generations' of company law Directives are identifiable starting with detailed and prescriptive legislation and ending more recently in 'framework' legislation.[20] The characteristics and practical consequences of these legislative 'generations' will be considered. The second part of the book will critically assess how the directives were created at European level. The democratic claims of the Community will be evaluated by examining the institutional arrangements and the legislative processes by which the European company laws have been elaborated. This part will therefore be

---

20 Commentators overseas speak in terms of 'generations' of EC legislation: see eg Aurelio Menéndez Menéndez, 'El Anteproyecto de Ley de Reforma Parcial y de Adaptación de la Legislación Mercantíl a las Directivas de la CEE En Materia de Sociedades' in Angel Rojo (ed.), *La Reforma de la Ley de Sociedades Anónimas* (Civitas, Madrid, 1987) 13, at p. 19 and Rafael Guasch Martorell, 'La Armonización en el Marco del Derecho Europeo de Sociedades: La Obligación de Resultado Exigida por las Directivas Societarias a los Estados Miembros' (1994) 596 *Revista General de Derecho*, 5651–77. UK lawyers make reference to 'new approach directives': see eg Noreen Burrows and Hilary Hiram, 'Legal Articulation of Policy in the European Community' in Terence Daintith (ed.), *Implementing EC Law in the United Kingdom: Structures for Indirect Rule* (Wiley, Chancery, Chichester, 1995) Ch. 2.

concerned primarily with representative democracy. The book's third part will compare the experiences of the UK and Spain of the company law programme and how each such Member State implemented the European provisions. It will explore the effects of the European provisions on the national laws and on companies in the European Union and through this discussion the book's third part will consider to what extent 'harmony' between the company laws of the Member States has been achieved.

Finally, the fourth part of the book will again be critical. One area of exploration within this theme will be the extent to which the company law programme has altered the structure of corporations and whether or not it has created greater opportunities for participatory democracy within those enterprises. It will be argued that the company law programme would have been strengthened by a more democratic agenda, not only for the procedural level of law–making but also for the practical operation of the rules created. It will be argued that a democratic aim would have enabled the programme to achieve a more convincing level of harmonisation and would have created more effective companies and economic activities in Europe. This would also have provided an opportunity to improve the representative democracy aspects of the European Community.

For the purposes of the argument put forward in the book the remainder of the introduction will set out a model of democracy against which the European processes and eventual effectiveness of its laws may be evaluated.

2.   A MODEL OF DEMOCRACY

Within the short space available it is impossible to elaborate a full theory of democracy. This section will therefore seek to identify the central characteristics of democracy and will attempt to construct a model that is workable within the European context.[21]

---

21   There is a vast literature on democratic theory to which the reader may refer. Many of these references discuss the earlier liberal democratic theories. See for example: Anthony Arblaster, *Democracy* (2nd ed.) (Open University Press, Buckingham, 1994); Ross Harrison, *Democracy* (Routledge, London, 1993); John Hyland, *Democratic Theory* (Manchester University Press, Manchester, 1995); Alain Touraine, *What is Democracy?* (Westview Press, Oxford, 1997); Joseph A. Schumpeter, *Capitalism, Socialism and Democracy* (Routledge, London, 1994); C.B. MacPherson, *Democratic Theory* (Clarendon Press, Oxford, 1973); C.B. MacPherson, *The Life and Times of Liberal Democracy* (Oxford University Press, Oxford, 1977); Robert A. Dahl, *Democracy and Its Critics* (Yale University Press, New Haven, 1989); Robert A. Dahl, *A Preface to Economic Democracy* (University

The most basic definition of democracy is 'decision–making by the people' or alternatively, 'government by the people'. Perhaps in its purest form this involves direct participation in decision–making by all those who are to be bound by the decisions. In Ancient Greece the Athenian city state operated a model by which citizens participated personally and directly in the government of the city. Every member of the citizen body, excluding women, foreigners and slaves, was entitled to attend the assembly, which took final policy decisions and met ten times per year. Offices of government and administration of the laws, including the courts, were held for a limited period by citizens who were chosen by lot.[22]

In a modern context this direct democracy model is unworkable. Nations are generally too large and the people too widely dispersed for them to be able to partake consistently and continuously in politics. These problems for direct democracy have long been recognised and in the eighteenth century the concept of representative democracy had established itself as the most realistic model of democracy. Thomas Paine, for example, stated that 'simple democracy was incapable of extension, not from its principle but from the inconvenience of its form. Simple democracy was society governing itself without the aid of secondary means. By ingrafting representation upon democracy, we arrive at a system of government capable of embracing and confederating all the various interests and every extent of territory and population...'.[23]

Representative democracy entails indirect participation of citizens in the political system by voting in rulers and holding such rulers accountable. Within this framework the characteristics of representation may vary. Thus it is possible to adopt a Burkean form by which once they are elected the representatives are required to be independent of their electors and make their own decisions.[24] Alternatively, the representation could be more radical, by which the representatives seek instructions from their electors and speak with the voice of those electors.[25]

---

of California Press, Berkeley, 1985); Carol Pateman, *Participation and Democratic Theory* (Cambridge University Press, Cambridge, 1970); Peter Bachrach and Aryeh Botwinick, *Power and Empowerment – A Radical Theory of Participatory Democracy* (Temple University Press, Philadelphia, 1992).

22 For a brief description of the Greek model of democracy and a bibliography, see Ross Harrison, *Democracy* (Routledge, London, 1993), Ch. 2.

23 Thomas Paine, *Rights of Man* (Penguin, Harmondsworth, 1984), p. 180.

24 Edmund Burke, 'Speech to the Electors of Bristol', 3 November 1774 and discussed by Arblaster, above note 21, at p. 80.

25 For example, see Aneurin Bevan, *In Place of Fear* (Quartet Books, London, 1978), p. 35, discussed by Arblaster above note 21, at p. 81.

Representative democracy dominated democratic theory during the eighteenth, nineteenth and early twentieth centuries. Yet the different possible forms of representative democracy have bequeathed it with different theoretical claims and consequences. For some theorists, it is regarded as a manifestation of class struggle,[26] while for other theorists it is a protective system against oppressive government.[27] Some theorists regarded representative democracy as a positive form of democracy while others regarded it as a reflection of passivity. For example, John Stuart Mill regarded voting as part of an educative process, providing an incentive for more active participation.[28] The 'realists' such as Schumpeter, by contrast, viewed democracy as choosing and authorising governments and representatives to carry out their decisions.[29] For some theorists representative democracy would provide equality. Bentham, for example, advocated 'one person, one vote'. Others, such as J.S. Mill, however, who were afraid of the so–called 'power of mediocrity', favoured plural voting for the better educated.

This range of interpretations of representative democracy carries with it a number of problems for representative democracy. For example, the reality of a pluralistic society is that the representatives do not represent all people but at best a majority of the people. This gives rise to the possibility of a majority rule becoming a potential tyranny of the majority. Democracy therefore cannot simply be an unqualified rule of the majority but needs instead to find ways of accommodating the views of the minority. Another problem for representative democracy is the potential for the rulers to become detached from their electors. A number of theories claim that representative democracy, by encouraging passivity from its citizens, will result in leaders who do not respond to the needs and wishes of those they govern. The level of control that the electors have over their representatives is therefore important to democracy. How do the representatives obtain the views of their electors? How can representative democracy ensure that the representatives behave responsibly? It is at this point that another dimension of democracy becomes relevant. The development of the theory of democracy

---

26   See the account of liberal democracy by MacPherson in which he suggests that early liberal democrats accepted class division and built on it: MacPherson (1977), above note 21, ch. 2, esp. p. 24.

27   See eg James Mill's *Essay on Government* (Augustus M. Kelley, Fairfield, 1986).

28   J.S. Mill also advocated more positive activity at local level, but voting for or against the government at least would give to citizens a direct interest in the actions of the government and an incentive to participate actively: this was the interpretation made by MacPherson (1977), above note 21, at p. 51.

29   Schumpeter, above note 21.

in the twentieth century led to advocates of participation. Participatory democracy requires active involvement of citizens in political life. Such participation could take a variety of different forms. Voting is regarded by some as participation but this is a very low level of participation. As MacPherson observes, this confines political activity to voting every few years for a member of parliament and perhaps a little more often for local councillors.[30] Stronger versions of participation include attendance at meetings, taking part in referenda, petitions, marches and campaigning. The important requirement of democratic participation is that it enables the participants to influence each other in making plans, policies or decisions.[31]

Against this claim in favour of participation, it may be argued that not all citizens want to participate, for a variety of reasons: they may feel inexperienced, alienated, uneducated, or simply uninterested. Some evidence suggests that participation is actually relatively low and that people participate more because they are dissatisfied with politics than because they wish to play a part in that political system.[32] Another charge against participation is that in reality it is actually undemocratic because the more active forms of participation are performed by fewer people whereas voting is more widespread and arguably reflects the character of political behaviour more accurately.[33] Representative democracy could also claim to be a more egalitarian form of democracy not only because it generally operates on the basis of 'one person one vote', but also because participation, by contrast, could be argued to empower the strongest members in society who are often wealthier and better educated. Those who do not participate get left behind.

Some of the problems of participation identified in the previous paragraph may be resolved. For example, the claim that people do not want to participate may be overcome actually by participation; the experience of participating itself can transform attitudes. MacPherson argues, for example, that participation brings about a sense of community.[34] In this way some theorists argue that participation at a local level may encourage more participation in national level politics. Pateman, for example, surveys a range of empirical evidence which suggests that participation locally empowers

---

30   MacPherson (1977), above note 21, at p. 52.
31   Pateman, above note 21, at p. 60, takes this definition from J.R.P. French, J. Israel and D. Aas, 'An experiment in participation in a Norwegian factory' (1960) 13 *Human Relations* 3–19.
32   See eg Geraint Parry and George Moyser, 'More Participation, More Democracy?' in David Beetham (ed.), *Defining and Measuring Democracy* (Sage, London, 1994) 44–62 at p. 50.
33   *Ibid* at p. 49.
34   MacPherson (1977), above note 21, at p. 99.

individuals to be effective in national politics.[35] Indeed, democracy may be regarded as having two dimensions: a national level democracy which is manifested by representative democracy and which is strengthened and developed by a local level democracy which is manifested by active popular participation. Thus, it is possible to see representative democracy at the national level by means of voting and party politics. At the local level it is more possible to participate actively. MacPherson suggests a pyramidal system with direct democracy at the base and delegate democracy at the levels above the base. Those elected must be responsible to those below by being subject to re–election.[36] Ultimately, it might be argued that the two forms of democracy are interdependent: effective representative democracy leads to the establishment of machinery and procedures which make participatory democracy possible and participation raises an awareness and an interest in the representative democratic system.

Another of the problems of participatory democracy identified was that generally only the wealthier and better educated are prepared to participate. This problem may be overcome by encouraging participation as a form of education and self empowerment. Empirical evidence suggests that this is possible.[37] More particularly, some theorists regard participation as a form of class politics. This may have both a positive and a negative aspect. From a negative perspective, the poorest in society are the least likely to participate in politics so that participation effectively helps the wealthy and the educated to protect their privileged position. A positive perspective, however, viewing participation as class struggle,[38] looks to the workplace as the appropriate form for participatory democracy.[39] Indeed, Pateman supports the workplace not least because citizens spend much of their lives at work.[40] Practical reasons for using the workplace for launching participation are that such participation will be on a smaller scale so that the effect is easily observed and the issues are not too removed from those affected.[41] The claim is that

---

35   See esp. pp. 46–49. See also: L.W. Milbrath, *Political Participation* (Rand McNally, Chicago, 1965); G.A. Almond and S. Verba, *The Civic Culture* (Little Brown, Boston, 1965).

36   MacPherson (1977), above note 21, at pp. 108–109.

37   See Pateman and references at note 31 above.

38   Bachrach and Botwinick, above note 21, at pp. 30–32; Touraine, above note 21, at p. 111.

39   Bachrach and Botwinick, above note 21, at pp. 30–32.

40   Pateman, above note 21, at p. 49.

41   MacPherson (1977), above note 21, at p. 104.

once progress is achieved by participants at these levels they will be encouraged to act in the wider political sphere.[42]

Overall, the model of democracy that this book will advocate consists of two dimensions: representative democracy at the wider institutional political level and participatory democracy at the narrower local and workplace level. The two dimensions interact by the representative level creating mechanisms which make participation at the narrower level possible and the participative level encouraging greater interest in developing the representative level. In this way outcomes are as important as procedures. Procedures should only be regarded as democratic if they produce democratic outcomes.

3. CONCLUSION

How might this model of democracy be applied at European Community level? The size of the Community suggests that the political and policy–making aspects will entail the representative form of democracy. This form of democracy, according to de Tracy, renders democracy as 'practicable for a long time and over a great extent of territory'.[43] As Dahl claims, representation had the consequence that 'popular government need no longer be confined to small states but could now be extended almost indefinitely to include vast numbers of persons'.[44] As was noted above, Ress considers that representative democracy is the relevant form of democracy for the European Community. The task for the European Community, then, is to work out what form of representation is most appropriate. In order to operate by mandate and instruction of the citizens the institutional structures and decision–making procedures of the Community must be organised so that the views of the citizens can be obtained. The quality of this representative democracy may well depend on the level of opportunity it provides for participation of citizens in European politics. Clearly, not everyone will be able or want to participate actively in the political activities. As has been observed, participatory democratic theory often regards the workplace as a more appropriate forum for participation. Arguably, this provides a role for European company law, since it is, in reality, the structure of companies that determine the level of opportunity for such participation.

This provides a test for the representative democracy and the procedures used to develop the company laws. The European Commission claims that

---

42   *Ibid*, at p. 104.

43   Destutt de Tracy, *A Commentary and Review of Montesquieu's Spirit of Laws* (Philadelphia, 1811) at p. 19, quoted by Dahl (1989), above note 21, at p. 29.

44   Dahl, *ibid*, at pp. 29–30.

the Community's structures are arranged in such a way as to ensure a democratic decision–making process and that its citizens live in a democratic environment. However, institutional structures and procedures are no guarantee of a democratic outcome. If they produce non–democratic laws then they might be regarded as a failure in democratic terms. If, however, the laws arising from representative democratic decisions provide opportunities for democratic participation then the system may, overall, be regarded as democratic.

In order for this outcome to be possible a number of conditions appear to be necessary. Clear and transparent procedures in which citizens know how decisions are taken are necessary but these alone do not ensure that citizens get what they want. More importantly, there should be availability of and access to information. For example, Saward argues that publicity is a key background condition making responsive rule possible and helping citizens to develop informed interests.[45]

This model of democracy will form the basis of an analysis of the European Community's claims to democracy presented in this book through a discussion of the company law harmonisation programme.

---

45   Michael Saward, 'Democratic Theory and Indices of Democratisation' in David Beetham (ed.), *Defining and Measuring Democracy* (Sage, London, 1994) 6–24, at p. 16. See also Pateman, above note 21, at p. 65.

PART ONE

The Company Law Harmonisation Programme

2 The General Framework of the Company Law Harmonisation Programme

1. INTRODUCTION

The company law harmonisation programme began soon after the European Economic Community was formed. The programme has a purposive function so that for the effectiveness of the internal market the harmonisation of company laws would enable all those dealing with companies in the Community to be operating within a broadly similar legal structure with comparable rights and obligations. Generally, the programme aims to encourage free trade and movement across the Community with the overall objective of improving the economies of the European Community and of the Member States. One of the policies behind the programme is the hope for improved transnational co–operation.

The principal aim of the EC Treaty was to create an economic area for the founding six members of the Community capable of guaranteeing the free movement of persons, goods, services and capital. The creation of a common market would necessitate the elimination of disparities between the national laws of the Member States. In this respect the activities of the European Community in the company law field have been important to the creation and development of the single market. The steps taken by the European Community were focused on the 'approximation' of the laws of the Member States in order to facilitate the creation and functioning of the common market[1] and aimed at providing equivalent protection for shareholders and third parties in each Member State, together with facilitating freedom of establishment for companies. This has led to a European Community company law which now influences significantly the national company laws of the Member States.

Fundamental to the philosophy of the internal market and freedom of establishment is the concept of mutual recognition.[2] The EC Treaty provides

---

1   See in this respect Art. 3(h), EC Treaty. For a discussion of the terminology see Ignaz Seidl–Hohenveldern, 'Harmonisation of Legislation in the Common Market and the Heritage of the Common Law' (1962) *JBL* 247–252 and 363–372, esp. pp. 247–8.

2   See G.K. Morse, 'Mutual Recognition of Companies in England and the EEC' (1972) *JBL* 195–205 and Stephan Rammeloo, 'Recognition of Foreign Companies in

for mutual recognition in Article 220, which states that Member States shall so far as necessary:

> enter into negotiations with each other with a view to ensuring for the benefit of their nations: the mutual recognition of firms or companies as defined in Article 58(2), the maintenance of legal personality in the event of transfer of registered office from one country to another, and the possibility of mergers between firms and companies which are subject to different domestic laws.

In furtherance of this provision the original six Member States signed the Convention for the Mutual Recognition of Companies and Legal Persons in 1968. However, this Convention has never entered into force because it was not ratified by the Netherlands,[3] although a supplementary protocol[4] enables the European Court of Justice to make preliminary rulings on the interpretation of the Convention.[5] The Directives themselves have gone some way in furthering the objective of mutual recognition by pursuing the equalisation or the co–ordination of the laws of the Member States and thereby eliminating some of the obstacles to freedom of establishment within the internal market, although it cannot be said that the demands of Article 220 have been met fully.

The harmonisation programme was not defined clearly. The EC Treaty refers equally to 'approximation' of laws as to 'co–ordinating' laws in order to

---

"Incorporation" Countries: A Dutch Perspective' in Jan Wouters and Hildegard Schneider (eds), *Current Issues of Cross–Border Establishment of Companies in the European Union* (Metro, Maastricht, 1995), 47–73 and in the same text, Wulf–Henning Roth, 'Recognition of Foreign Companies in "Siège Réel" Countries: A German Perspective', 29–46.

3   There are three possible reasons for the refusal by the Netherlands to ratify the Convention: the Netherlands was the only country of the six which followed the 'incorporation' philosophy while the others favoured the 'siège réel' theory; the Netherlands was the 'Delaware' country (see below) at the time and saw the Convention as too strict; political barriers meant that the Netherlands would have had to pull out of the Hague Convention of 1966 in order to ratify the 1968 Recognition Convention. I am grateful to Hildegard Schneider and to Stephan Rammeloo for offering these reasons suggested here.

4   Signed on 3 June 1971.

5   For a discussion of the history of the Convention and the concept of mutual recognition see Frank Wooldridge, *Company Law in the United Kingdom and the European Community: Its Harmonisation and Unification* (Athlone Press, London, 1991), Chapter 9.

give 'equivalent' safeguards to the relevant members and third parties.[6] These words do not suggest a complete unification of company laws.[7] The fact that directives are chosen as the primary legal instrument for harmonising the company laws in order to achieve the single market and European Union lends support to this claim. The point of utilising directives is to preserve for the Member States some discretion as to the means for achieving equivalent results.[8] This does not go as far as unification, which would require identical laws and not merely equivalent laws. The apparent lack of will to create identical provisions across Europe in the harmonisation policy is problematic. For example, Schmitthoff suggests that incomplete uniformity of rules could encourage the creation a kind of 'Delaware situation' in which Member States would compete with each other in order to attract business by creating more lax rules.[9] The name comes from the so–called 'race to laxity'[10] in the United States of America in which the state of Delaware took the lead. The purpose of the more liberal laws created by the competing states was not to protect stockholders and third parties but to provide a convenient juridical basis for the creation of companies, and thereby to gain more revenue through taxation and use of services.[11] The harmonisation programme itself grew out of a desire to avoid this 'Delaware effect'. In any event, Schmitthoff's perception that uniformity is necessary for multinational enterprises and effective cross–frontier mergers leads him to suggest that we are likely to have a 'virtual unification of national company laws under the guise of harmonisation'.[12] At the very least there would need to be uniform minimum standards.

---

6   Neither do the Treaties provide a definition of these different terms: Noreen Burrows and Hilary Hiram, 'Legal Articulation of Policy in the European Community', in Terence Daintith (ed.), *Implementing EC Law in the United Kingdom* (John Wiley, Chichester, 1995), Ch. 2.

7   Ficker distinguishes between the two when he says 'Harmonisation, *and beyond this* (my emphasis), unification of law is normally considered as a fruitful undertaking between states interested in facilitating international relations among their citizens'. See Hans Claudius Ficker, 'The EEC Directives on Company Law Harmonisation', in Clive M. Schmitthoff (ed.), *The Harmonisation of European Company Law* (UKNCCL, London, 1973).

8   As per Art. 189, EC Treaty.

9   Clive M. Schmitthoff, 'The Future of the European Company Law Scene' in Schmitthoff, above note 7, pp. 3–27, at p. 9.

10   Per Mr. Justice Brandeis, in *Liggett Co. v Lee* (1933) 288 US 517, at 557–60.

11   For further information see Cary, 'Federalism and Corporate Law: Reflections Upon Delaware' (1974) 83 *Yale LJ* 663, at p. 705.

12   Schmitthoff, above note 9, at p. 8.

Related to this problem is the fact that the adoption of the Directives has, so far, been piecemeal and fragmented, giving rise to accusations of the harmonisation programme being akin to a 'frankenstein model', insofar as it has been pieced together without any real control over what was being created.[13] In this sense Ficker points out that the 'salami tactics' make it difficult to agree to one directive without knowing how other aspects of company regulation will be treated by a later directive.[14]

2.   THE LEGAL BASES OF THE COMPANY LAW PROVISIONS

A number of provisions in the EC Treaty have helped to shape this European Community company law. Article 52 provides for the progressive abolition of restrictions on the freedom of establishment of individuals of a Member State in the territory of another Member State. This right of freedom of establishment extends to companies or firms who, under Article 58, should be treated in the same way as natural persons who are nationals of Member States.[15]

The EC Treaty also contains a number of provisions which grant to the Community institutions extensive law–making powers. These enable the Council to issue directives[16] and these have been adopted as the main legal instrument for the harmonisation of the national company laws. Most of the company law harmonisation programme is based on Article 54.[17] In particular, Article 54(3)(g) of the EC Treaty states that the Commission and the Council shall carry out their duties:

> by co–ordinating to the necessary extent the safeguards which, for the protection of the interests of members and others, are required by Member States of companies or firms within the meaning of the second

---

13   See José Domingo Rodríguez Martínez, 'La Reforma de las Sociedades en el Derecho Comparado' in Various Authors, *Estudios Sobre La Reforma De La Legislación De Sociedades Mercantiles* (Colegio de Registradores de la Propiedad, Madrid, 1990), Tomo 1, 279–302, at pp. 280–1.

14   Ficker, above note 7, at p. 73.

15   Article 58 defines companies or firms as 'companies or firms constituted under civil or commercial law, including co–operative societies, and other legal persons governed by public or private law, save for those which are non–profit making'.

16   Article 100 enables the Council to issue directives: 'for the approximation of such provisions laid down by law, regulation or administrative action in Member States as directly affect the establishment or functioning of the common market'.

17   First, Second, Third, Fourth, Sixth, Seventh, Eighth, Eleventh, Twelfth Directives.

paragraph of Article 58 with a view to making such safeguards equivalent throughout the Community.

This provision is founded upon the view that 'unharmonised national safeguards may make establishment too burdensome or even impossible'.[18] Article 54 also presents some interpretational problems. For example, the term 'co–ordination' could be argued to have a different meaning than the term 'approximation' which is to be found in Article 100. What is meant by 'others'? The European Commission claims that no weight is given to one group over another. Under Article 54(3)(g) 'other parties' basically means creditors but in the 1980s and 90s this term would possibly include consumers, suppliers, employees, environments, and public authorities.

Article 54(3)(g) should be interpreted so that any measure founded on it must serve the purposes of the Treaty, which are laid out generally in Article 2. Article 2 of the EC Treaty states that the overall objective in establishing the EEC was 'establishing a common market and progressively approximating the economic policies of Member States to promote throughout the Community a harmonious development of economic activities, a continuous and balanced expansion, an increase in stability, an accelerated raising of the standard of living and closer relations between the States belonging to it'. The vagueness of this Article means that it does not provide an adequate basis for the company law measures. Perhaps a more focused approach is gained from Article 3. Article 3(h) EC Treaty states that the Community shall aim for 'the approximation of their respective municipal law to the extent necessary for the functioning of the Common Market'. Thus, any measures under Article 3(h) should have a functional purpose with the aim of developing or achieving the Common Market. They should be adopted only where discrepancies between Member States' laws interfere with the functioning of the Common Market.

A number of provisions have been adopted under Article 100 although these are mostly related to securities law, worker participation measures and taxation rather than to mainstream company law. Article 100 empowers the Council to issue directives:

> for the approximation of such provisions laid down by law, regulation or administrative action in Member States as directly affect the establishment or functioning of the common market.

---

18   See Gisbert Wolff, 'The Commission's Programme for Company Law Harmonisation: The Winding Road to a Uniform European Company Law?', in Mads Andenas and Stephen Kenyon–Slade (eds), *EC Financial Market Regulation and Company Law* (Sweet and Maxwell, London, 1993), 19–39 at p. 22.

Article 100 is generally regarded as having significant flexibility, though there are some limitations so that unification of laws should not become an end in itself, but should be directed towards achieving the Treaty's objectives. Article 100A was introduced by the Single European Act to facilitate the internal market and makes possible the adoption of measures by qualified majority voting. Regulations, as well as directives, are possible under this provision. Article 100A is employed as the legal basis of the proposed European Company Statute. This legal base is challenged since it is arguable that the proposal should have been based instead on Article 235.[19]

Article 235 provides:

> if action by the Community should prove necessary to attain, in the course of the operation of the common market, one of the objectives of the Community and this Treaty has not provided the necessary powers, the Council shall, acting unanimously on a proposal from the Commission and after consulting the European Parliament, take the appropriate measures.

This is effectively a safety net provision where other avenues fail. The Council must act unanimously on a proposal from the Commission following consultation with the European Parliament. Article 235 forms the legal basis of the Regulation establishing the European Economic Interest Grouping as a vehicle for transnational collaboration. The original proposal for the European Company Statute was based on this Article but its requirement of unanimity led to the proposal taking a different form of a draft regulation under Article 100A and the worker participation provisions in the form of a draft directive under Article 54.

3.   LEGAL INSTRUMENTS ADOPTED

Article 54(2) requires action by directives. However, some Treaty provisions do not specify the type of instrument required, leaving this to the discretion of the Commission. It has been suggested that the Commission would normally favour the use of regulations because these are directly applicable,[20] but, increasingly, the favoured legislative form has been the

---

19   See House of Lords Select Committee 19th Report, Session 1989–90, *European Company Statute*, HL Paper 71, 10 July 1990, at p. 17, p. 21 and Appendix 3, pp. 25–9.

20   A.J. Easson, 'EEC Directives for the Harmonisation of Laws: Some Problems of Validity, Implementation and Legal Effects' (1981) 1 *YBEL* 1, at p. 3.

directive, which adapts more easily to the different needs and characteristics of the Member States' legal systems. Directives are said to advance integration and at the same time respect the national legal environment.[21] In this way they might be regarded as federalist instruments.[22]

Under Article 189 of the EC Treaty:

> a Directive shall be binding as to the result to be achieved, upon each Member State to which it is addressed, but shall leave to the national authorities the choice of form and methods.

The distinguishing feature of directives is that they are binding on the Member States but only as to the result aimed for, since Member States may choose the form and method of implementing them. Thus, whereas a regulation, regarded as a supranational instrument, lays down the same rules to be applied throughout the Community, the details of the implementing legislation for directives may vary from Member State to Member State, allowing more flexibility.

This distinction can be qualified. First, the fact that directives have been granted direct effect blurs the distinction. Although directives do not automatically have direct effect the European Court considers certain directives to have direct effect regardless of the normal requirements: that they are clear, precise and unconditional. Secondly, some regulations do require further action at national level in order for them to be workable. For example, some regulations allow Member States discretion, such as with the policing measures to be used for enforcing the regulation on home territory. The company law regulation on Economic Interest Groupings provides an appropriate example of the need for implementing legislation. Additionally, the discretion granted to Member States in achieving the objectives of a directive is limited to the form and manner of implementing the directive.[23] The choice of form and method means choice only as to instrument and to content and to procedures for enforcement. Curtin suggests that the discretion is further limited by the 'guidelines' in the directives.[24] Member

---

21 Christopher Timmermans, 'Methods and Tools for Integration' in R. Buxbaum, G. Hertig, A. Hirsch, and K.J. Hopt (eds), *European Business Law* (de Gruyter, Berlin, 1991) 129, at p. 143.

22 *Ibid.*

23 P.E. Morris, 'The Direct Effect of Directives– Some Recent Developments in the European Court' (1989) *JBL* 233–245 and 309–320 at p. 238.

24 For example, as Curtin remarks: 'the text of the Directive may indicate, expressly or implicitly, a particular rule of implementation.' See Deirdre Curtin 'Directives: The Effectiveness of Judicial Protection of Individual Rights' (1990) 27 *CMLR* 709–739,

States might also be obliged to repeal conflicting laws.[25] In any event, once the time limit for a directive's implementation has elapsed it will have direct effect in the Member States.[26] The national courts of a Member State will be obliged to interpret its law in accordance with the directive.[27] Any subsequent law reforms in the Member State will not be allowed to contradict the requirements of the directive.[28]

The contents and characteristics of the company law Directives have been influenced in many ways. Perhaps chief among these influences is the German company law regime. This is especially the case for the earlier directives. The First and Second Directives, in particular, contain the same prescriptive characteristics as the German law. A number of commentators remark on the 'germanicisation of company law'.[29] It seems therefore appropriate to precede the description of the company law Directives with a summary of the German company law. This may help to inform the reader of the general approach taken within the company law programme, especially in its earlier stages.

at p. 715. See also Case 102/79 *Commission v Belgium* [1980] ECR 1473. Further, Capotorti reports that in practice directives give little freedom to Member States: Francesco Capotorti, 'Legal Problems of Directives, Regulations and their Implementation' in Heinrich Siedentopf and Jaques Ziller (eds), *Making European Policies Work: The Implementation of Community Legislation in the Member States*, Volume 1 (Sage, London, 1988) 151–168, at p. 156.

25 A.J. Easson, above note 20, at pp. 29–30.

26 The directive will not have direct effect before the time limit for its implementation has expired: Case 148/78 *Pubblico Ministero v Ratti* [1979] 1629; [1980] 1 CMLR 96.

27 Case C–106/89 *Marleasing SA v La Comercial Internacional de Alimentación SA* [1990] ECR I–4135; [1992] 1 CMLR 395.

28 A.J. Easson highlights the problems of law reform: above note 20, at pp. 43–44.

29 See eg Aurelio Menéndez Menéndez, 'El Anteproyecto de Ley de Reforma Parcial y de Adaptación de la Legislación Mercantil a las Directivas de la CEE En Materia de Sociedades' in Angel Rojo (ed.), *La Reforma de la Ley de Sociedades Anónimas* (Civitas, Madrid, 1987) 13.

4. THE GERMAN COMPANY LAW[30]

In Germany the various corporate forms are governed by different specific laws that have been imposed on a substructure, based on the statutory rules of two codes: the Civil Code (*Bürgerliches Gesetzbuch*, BGB) and the Commercial Code (*Handelsgesetzbuch*, HGB).[31] Both these Codes came into force in 1900. The Civil Code is of universal application and covers – as well as the general provisions in Part I – the law of obligations, the law of property, family law, and the law of succession. The Civil Code contains references to the law relating to artificial legal persons and rules on partnerships. The Commercial Code contains rules governing the commercial register, the accounts, business names, agency, and commercial partnerships.

There are a number of special company law statutes which exist alongside the two Codes. The Public Limited Company, or the stock company, (*Aktiengesellschaft*, AG) is governed by the Aktiengesetz of 1965. The Limited Liability Company (*Gesellschaft mit beschränkter Haftung*, GmbH) is governed by the GmbH Act of 1892. Partnerships are divided into four categories: the Special Limited Partnership (GmbH & Co. KG), the most common form of business organisation through which the general partner is a company with limited liability established by founding two companies. One is a GmbH already incorporated and the newly established GmbH enters into a limited partnership agreement with the limited partners; the General Partnership (*Offene Handelsgesellschaft*, OHG); the Limited Partnership (*Kommanditgesellschaft*, KG); and the Civil Law Partnership (*Gesellschaft bürgerlichen Rechts*, GbR). This last is governed by the Civil Code.

---

30 For more detailed discussions of German Company law published in English see eg: N. Horn, H. Kötz and H.G. Leser, *German Private and Commercial Law: An Introduction* (Oxford University Press, Oxford, 1982); Thomas Meyding, 'Company Law', in G. Dannemann, *An Introduction to German Civil and Commercial Law* (BIICL, London, 1993) pp. 72–82; E.J.Cohn, *Manual of German Law*, Volume II, 2nd ed. (BIICL, London, 1971); G. Vorbrugg, 'Forms of Doing Business' in Droste Killius Triebel, *Business Law Guide to Germany*, 3rd ed. (CCH, Bicester, 1990), pp. 91–127; Detlev F. Vagts, 'Reforming the "Modern" Corporation: Perspectives from the German' [1966] 80 *Harvard Law Review*, 23–89; for a useful discussion on the 1965 reform law see Rainer M. Kohler, 'The New Corporation laws in Germany (1966) and France (1967) and the Trend Towards a Uniform Corporation Law for the Common Market' (1968) 43 *Tulane LR* 58.

31 M.C. Oliver, *The Private Company in Germany* (Macdonald and Evans, Plymouth, 1976), at p. 1.

1870 witnessed the arrival of the commercial register establishing formal requirements for creating the company. After the First World War proposals were made for structural changes. In 1931 reforms were made concerning accounts, the establishment of a requirement of independent auditors, and rules on the acquisition of own shares by companies. In 1937 the first specific law relating to stock companies was introduced and this law gave strong powers to the executive board, ensuring that it could only be removed for good cause. A supervisory board only could appoint or remove the board of directors. The shareholders were able to appoint and remove the supervisory board. Neoliberal philosophies became influential in German business law post 1945 and this led to a search for ways of enabling companies to gather large–scale capital.[32] Thus broader disclosure, more information in annual accounts, restrictions on hidden reserves and more active involvement of shareholders became necessary. In 1965 the new law relating to stock companies was passed and the reforms it brought with it were influenced by foreign company laws, especially the American corporate law.[33] This influence could be seen in aspects of company accounts, financial documents, and disclosure requirements. The 1965 law was intended to promote a wide distribution of shares, including shares to be held by employees.

The concept of the two–tier board of directors originated in 1870, alongside the establishment of the concept of co–determination, and rules governing related companies. Co–determination was first put into practice after the Second World War in the coal, iron and steel industries. In 1951 the Equal Co–determination of Employees in the Coal, Iron and Steel Industries Act was passed. In 1952, under the Labour Management Relations Act, workers in other sectors were allowed to be represented by a third of the supervisory board. Family owned companies and private commercial companies with less than 500 workers would be exempted from these requirements. Economic committees would also comprise worker representatives and they were entitled to be consulted on various economic matters by the executive board. In 1976 a Co–determination Act was introduced for companies with more than 2,000 employees, who were allowed formal parity of labour and capital on the supervisory board.

---

32   See Vagts, above note 30, esp. p. 29.
33   See Kohler, above note 30, esp. p. 80.

A.   The GmbH

The GmbH, or private limited company, was introduced in 1892. It can be formed for any lawful purpose by one or more persons and has legal personality. The GmbH also has a relatively simple legal structure and is therefore a very popular form of business enterprise, especially for small and medium–sized businesses although many large businesses also operate under this form.[34] The company name must derive either from the name of the shareholder or from the purpose of the Company and it must not mislead the public.[35] The company contract is created by a notarial deed[36] which must specify the company name, the company's domicile, its object, its capital sum and the number of capital shares held by each shareholder.[37] Unlike in the UK, where companies normally have two contractual documents – the memorandum and the articles of association – the German company has just one document. The company must be registered in the Commercial Register[38] upon which it will gain legal personality.[39] The Commercial Register is held by the local courts in the area where the company seat is located. There is a minimum share capital requirement for the GmbH. Its shares cannot be traded on the stock exchange. They can only be transferred by notarial act.[40]

One or more managing directors may represent the GmbH to third parties.[41] The managing directors are appointed by the shareholders in general meeting and there is no limit on their power to bind the company with third parties unless there is more than one managing director and they are supposed to act jointly. The GmbH may also act through a *Proktura* or a *Handlungsvollmacht* which is like a power of attorney. There is no doctrine of *ultra vires* in German company law. Shareholders have ultimate authority and are responsible for approving the accounts and for the appointment and removal of the Managing Director, as well as instructing the supervision of the managers.[42] The shareholders also make decisions relating to the distribution of profits and they have authority to alter the articles. Many

---

34   See Droste, Killius Triebel, *Business Law Guide to Germany*, 3rd ed. (CCH, Bicester, 1990), at pp. 404–5.

35   §4(1) GmbHG.

36   §2 GmbHG.

37   §3 GmbHG.

38   §7 GmbHG.

39   §13 GmbHG.

40   §15(3) GmbHG.

41   §35 GmbHG.

42   §45, 46, GmbHG.

GmbHs also have advisory or supervisory boards, for which the rules applicable to the supervisory board of the AG will apply.[43] Those with less than 500 employees may voluntarily have a supervisory board. If there are more than 500 employees this will be a mandatory board. Duties of directors are to the company, and to shareholders, third parties and creditors. The director must use the skill and care of a prudent businessman.[44]

B.   The AG

By setting up a stock company, an AG, it is possible to raise a large amount of capital from a significant number of individuals because the shares are freely negotiable and transferable. Not all AGs are quoted on the stock exchange; some of them remain closely held companies. Nevertheless, the public aspect of an AGs nature means that in order to protect investors and creditors from fraud or incompetence, the rules relating to this form of company are strict. For example, the 1965 law has 410 sections compared with the law relating to the GmbH, which has 85 sections. The 1965 law has more mandatory provisions and is less flexible.

Incorporation of the AG is established by a notarised single contractual document with at least five subscribers.[45] The AG gains legal personality when it is registered on the Commercial Register.[46] The AG has a minimum share capital requirement.[47] Stockholders have a right to information[48] and a duty to pay the face amount of the shares or the higher issue price. At least 25% of this must be paid up with a premium on it.[49] Bearer shares are the most common form of shares, often held in collective deposit by special banks.[50]

A two–tier system of management is mandatory for the AG and if there are more than 2,000 employees half of the supervisory board must be representatives of the employees with a worker director on the managing

---

43   §52 GmbHG.
44   §43(1) GmbHG.
45   §2 AktG.
46   §41 AktG.
47   §7 AktG.
48   §131 AktG.
49   §54 AktG.
50   In 1989 there were approximately 400,000 GmbH compared with 2,500 AGs. See N. Horn, H. Kötz and H.G. Leser, *German Private and Commercial Law: An Introduction* (Oxford University Press, Oxford, 1982) at p. 264.

board.[51] The board of management is generally appointed for the five year maximum. The board of management is responsible for the conduct of the company's business and usually acts jointly or, if allowed under the company's constitution, by majority decision. As already noted, there is no doctrine of *ultra vires* and the scope of the managing board's power of representation on an external level cannot be limited. The role of the supervisory board is to appoint the board of management, to supervise the board of management, and to approve the financial statements and certain transactions expressly reserved. The supervisory board has a minimum of three members[52] with representatives from among the employees and the shareholders. Traditionally, banks also have a representative member on the supervisory boards of companies in which they have shares or to which they provide loans. The shareholders in general meeting elect and remove representatives on the supervisory board, appoint auditors, and make decisions on the distribution of the profits. The voting rights of smaller shareholders are normally exercised by proxy by the banks with which the shares are deposited. Minority shareholders cannot pursue an action on behalf of the company because the derivative action does not exist in German company law.

In summary, the key characteristics of the German company law system that might appear to have had some influence on the European programme are the strong reliance on codification and prescriptive rules, the need to obtain capitalisation for the company from outsiders, bringing with it the need for disclosure and independent auditors so that investors will have confidence in the system. The German system also regards the company from an enterprise perspective and pays regard to the interests of a variety of stake–holders. Particularly noteworthy among the characteristics of the German company law are the dual management structure with an administrative and a supervisory board and the emphasis on co–determination, with worker representatives and creditor representatives as members of the management board. This book will reveal that a number of these aspects are featured in the company law programme, within both adopted and draft legislation.

As the European Community grew in size it is fair to say that the German influence declined. Thus, while the German view is still important it no longer dominates the agenda. The views of other Member States are also influential. Indeed, the successive enlargements of the Community appear to have brought with them changes to the style of the Community directives.

---

51   §§1, 7 *Mitbestimmungsgesetz.*
52   §95, 96 AktG.

From this perspective it is possible to identify within the company law programme four different stages or 'generations' to date.

5.   THE FOUR 'GENERATIONS' OF DIRECTIVES

The development of EC law generally has demonstrated a variety of different forms of directives. Some are precise and detailed whereas others offer options and have minimum standards to be achieved and which may be exceeded by the Member States, known as 'minimalist directives'. Seidentopf, for example, notes that during the period 1976–1979 the provisions of directives were as precise as possible, but in later years there were attempts made by the UK and Germany under a policy of deregulation to reduce the density and precision of Community directives.[53] Other directives offer more extensive discretion and state the general principles adopted by the policy within a particular field, and are known as 'new approach' and 'framework directives'. The drive towards the Single Market has seen a movement towards the more liberal form of directive.[54] This is possibly a consequence of the will to establish the Single Market; a framework directive avoids deadlock situations and complaints of infringement of the sovereignty of Member States. This may be regarded as an attempt to make the directives more attractive, giving to Member States options and extended time limits for implementation.[55] The legal procedures used may also have led to more flexibility.

The company law field is no exception to this general pattern of development. Some commentators have identified in European company law two 'generations' of directives: 'first' and 'second generation' respectively.[56]

---

53   Heinrich Siedentopf, 'The Implementation of Directives in the Member States' in Heinrich Siedentopf and Jaques Ziller (eds), *Making European Policies Work: The Implementation of Community Legislation in the Member States*, Vol. 1 (Sage, London, 1988) 169, at pp. 172–73.

54   See White Paper 1985, *Completing the Internal Market*, COM (85) 310 final.

55   These remarks were made of the second generation directives in the company law field, ie the Fourth and Seventh Directives, which contained many options. See Luis Fernández de la Gándara who notes the change in character of directives: 'Problemas político–jurídicos de la armonización societaria desde la perspecitiva de los ordenamientos nacionales' in Various Authors, *La Reforma del Derecho Español de Sociedades de Capital* (Civitas, Madrid, 1987), 35, at p. 46.

56   See eg Rafael Guasch Martorell, 'La Armonización en el marco del Derecho Europeo de Sociedades: la obligación de resultado exigida por las Directivas societarias a los Estados miembros' (1994) 596 *Revista General de Derecho* 5651.

According to this classification, 'first generation' directives[57] were passed prior to the Community's first enlargement, when Community drafting was heavily influenced by German legal drafting style. These directives tend to be prescriptive, leaving little discretion to national governments. 'Second generation' directives[58] post–date the entry to the EEC in 1973 of Denmark, Ireland and the UK. Although still being precise in their requirements, these directives tend to be more flexible than the 'first generation' directives which preceded them, offering a range of methods of implementation, thus allowing room for national diversity and giving some discretion to Member States. Member States are given a choice, but not total freedom, since they must follow one of the formulae laid out in the directive. The influence of the newer Member States after 1973 is evident in these directives.[59] It is possible to identify a further two generations since the first two. The third identifiable generation of directives[60] corresponds with those directives which were adopted under the co–operation procedure, following, approximately, the entry of Spain, Portugal and Greece. Introducing this generation is the 1985 White Paper *Completing the Internal Market*,[61] which stated an intention to create 'new approach' directives which would be more general and would set out the essential requirements, focusing on what is to be achieved rather than how. The fourth identifiable generation of directives[62] coincides approximately with the accession of Sweden, Finland and Austria and the introduction of the co–decision procedure, as well as the stated intention of the Commission to move towards 'framework' directives.[63] Both the third and fourth possible generations follow the qualified majority procedure. It remains speculative whether the Amsterdam Summit of 1997

---

57   The First and Second Directives. Although the date suggests that the Second Directive should be classified as a 'second generation' directive, its contents have more the characteristics of a 'first generation' directive, hence Guasch Martorell's classification as such, *ibid*, at p. 5664.

58   Third, Fourth, Sixth, Seventh, and Eighth Directives.

59   Notable, is the influence of the UK on the development of the Accounts Directives: see eg Graham Diggle and Christopher Nobes, 'European Rule–Making in Accounting: The Seventh Directive as a Case Study' (1994) 24 *Accounting and Business Research* 313. See also Chapter 6, below.

60   Eleventh and Twelfth Directives.

61   COM (85) 310 final.

62   Draft Thirteenth Directive.

63   European Commission, *Better Law–making – Commission Report to the European Council on the Application of the Subsidiarity and Proportionality Principles, on Simplification and on Consolidation* (Brussels, 21 November 1995).

and the approaching further enlargement of the Community to twenty members will create a fifth generation of directives.

6.   CONCLUSION

Overall, the European Community company law programme is an important aspect of the creation of the single market. The use of directives, based on Article 54, reflects a desire to accommodate the different economic and cultural contexts of the Member States and to balance a variety of interests. This flexibility has become more prominent over the course of time. Initially, the programme, perhaps heavily influenced by the German style of regulation, was rigid and prescriptive. As the programme developed, however, it became increasingly more flexible. This development has passed through four identifiable stages which have coincided with the successive enlargements of the European Community and various procedural changes. The next chapter will provide a description of the company law directives within the four generations.

3 The Company Law Directives

1. INTRODUCTION

The company law harmonisation programme has been broad and is still in progress. Its impact on the national laws across the Community has been significant, giving rise to extensive company law reforms. The previous chapter suggested that the company law directives were developed in four distinct generational stages. This chapter will describe the contents of the company law directives within those four 'generations'. This will highlight the differences between the generations and may provide an indication of the future of the remaining draft directives and any further possible legislation within the company law programme.

2. FIRST GENERATION DIRECTIVES

'First generation' directives are characterised by their detailed and precise provisions, which leave little discretion to the Member States as to their implementation. In this way they tend towards more uniformity and thus have a mandatory character. They also adopt the German characteristic of prescriptive rules. The company law directives that may be identified with the first generation are the First and Second Directives.

A. The First Directive[1]

Adopted in 1968, the First Directive has a broad application, covering public limited liability companies, private limited liability companies, and limited partnerships. The Directive deals with a range of topics, including disclosure of information, validity of obligations entered into by a company, and nullity of the company.

---

1   First Council Directive of 9th March 1968 68/151/EEC on co–ordination of the safeguards which, for the protection of the interests of members and others, are required by Member States of companies within the meaning of the second paragraph of Article 58 of the Treaty, with a view to making such safeguards equivalent throughout the Community [OJ 1968 L 65 14.3.68 p. 8].

(i)   Disclosure

The first section of the Directive provides a system of publicity. Under Article 2 Member States must ensure disclosure of the following: the instruments of constitution of the company, including the company's statutes; any amendments to the instruments with the full text of the new amended document; identity of the officers or company representatives as well as details of their appointment or termination of office; annually, the amount of the subscribed capital; the balance sheet and profit and loss account for each financial year; any transfer of the company's seat, winding up of the company; any declaration of nullity of the company by the courts; the appointment of liquidators, details concerning liquidators and their respective powers if these are different to the powers set out in law or in the company's statutes; and the termination of the liquidation.

Member States are required to establish a Register and the details to be disclosed must be filed or entered in the register.[2] Persons must be able to obtain certified true copies of the documents upon application in writing and for a price not above the administrative costs of providing the copy.[3] The documents must also be publicised in a national gazette.[4]

The letters and order forms of the company must contain information regarding the company's registration including its registration number as well as its name, registered office address and, if it is in liquidation, this also.[5] The Directive requires the provision of penalties for failure to give this information and for failure to disclose the financial position of the company in its balance sheet and profit and loss account.[6] Member States should make clear who is responsible for the disclosure formalities.[7]

(ii)   Validity of Obligations

The Directive contains provisions relating to transactions entered into on behalf of the company, both before the company has acquired legal personality and after the company is fully incorporated. Article 7 provides that if, before the company being formed has acquired legal personality, action has been carried out in its name and the company does not assume the

---

2   Article 3(1) and 3(2).
3   Article 3(3).
4   Article 3(4).
5   Article 4.
6   Article 6.
7   Article 5.

obligations arising from such action, the persons who acted shall, unless otherwise agreed, be jointly and severally liable without limit. Article 9 provides that acts done by the organs of the company shall be binding upon it even if those acts are not within the objects of the company, unless such acts exceed the powers that the law confers or allows to be conferred on those organs. It is possible, under Article 9, for Member States to provide that the company shall not be bound where such acts are outside the objects of the company, if it proves that the third party knew that the act was outside the objects or could not have been unaware of it.

(iii) Nullity of the Company

The Directive provides an exhaustive list of the causes of nullity of the company and it is not possible for Member States to declare a company null for any other cause. The relevant causes are: failure to execute the constitutional documents or that the rules of preventive control or the requisite legal formalities were not complied with; that the objects of the company are unlawful or contrary to public policy; that the instruments do not state the name of the company or the amount of individual subscriptions or total subscribed capital; failure to comply with national provisions regarding minimum paid up capital; the incapacity of all the founder members; that the number of founder members is less than two if this is contrary to the national law.[8] Article 12 sets out the consequences of a declaration of nullity, which entails the company's winding up but does not affect the validity of any commitments entered by or with the company.

B. The Second Directive[9]

The Second Directive was adopted in 1976 and applies only to public companies, stating in its preamble that these are the most important companies economically. The Directive lays down minimum requirements for the formation of the company and the maintenance, increase

---

8   Article 11.
9   Second Council Directive of 13 December 1976 77/91/EEC on co–ordination of safeguards which, for the protection of the interests of members and others, are required by Member States of companies within the meaning of the second paragraph of Article 58 of the Treaty, in respect of the formation of public limited liability companies and the maintenance and alteration of their capital, with a view to making such safeguards equivalent [OJ 1977 L26 31.1.77 p. 1].

and reduction of share capital. There are no separate headings in the directive but the provisions can largely be broken down into categories: disclosure requirements, minimum capital requirements, payment for shares, distribution of profits, loss of capital, maintenance of capital, increase and reduction of capital, redemption of shares.

(i)   Disclosure

The Directive contains specific disclosure requirements to be disclosed in the company's statutes or instrument of incorporation. The disclosure requirements complement those set out in the First Directive in that they are designed to provide shareholders and creditors with information about the company and its capital status. The required list includes: the type and name of the company; its objects; the amount of subscribed and/or authorised share capital; the rules governing the number of and the procedure for appointing the company's representatives; and duration of the company unless this is indefinite.[10] Further information is necessary in either the statutes, the instrument of incorporation or a document published in the Central Register. This includes: the registered office; the nominal value and number (once a year) of shares subscribed, or, if valid under the national law, the number of shares subscribed without the nominal value; any special conditions limiting the transfer of the shares; the different classes of shares; information concerning shares for non–cash consideration; the identity of the persons who sign the statutes or document of incorporation; the costs of formation; any special advantages granted at the time of the company's formation to any person who took part in the formation or in transactions leading up to the grant of such authorisation.[11]

(ii) Minimum Subscribed Share Capital

The capital requirements are perhaps the most important aspect of the Directive. Article 6 of the directive provides that, in order to be incorporated or authorised to commence business, the company shall have a minimum subscribed share capital of at least 25,000 ECU. Further, if a national currency falls in value so that the minimum national amount required falls to below the equivalent of 22,500 ECU then the national statutory minimum should be altered to bring the minimum back up to 25,000 ECU in value.

---

10   Article 2.
11   Article 3.

(iii) Integrity of the Share Capital

The integrity of the company's share capital is provided for by the Directive in several ways. Under Article 7 of the Directive the share capital must be formed only of assets capable of economic assessment, which does not include an undertaking to perform work or to supply services. Article 8 states that shares may not be issued at a price lower than their nominal value or their accountable par. Under Article 9, where shares are issued for consideration they must be paid up at the time the company is incorporated or authorised to commence business at no less than 25% of their nominal value. Non–cash consideration must be transferred in full within five years. Any non–cash consideration shall, as provided by Article 10, generally be the subject of a report by an independent expert.

(iv) Protection of Share Capital

The Directive lays down requirements regarding maintenance and stability of share capital. In this way, under Article 15, shareholders are not generally entitled to distributions from the company when the net assets are or would become lower than the amount of the subscribed capital. In any event, the amount distributed to the shareholders shall not exceed the net profits.[12] There are a number of conditions provided in the Directive in this situation. Should there be a serious loss of subscribed capital by 50%, Article 17 requires that the company call a general meeting to consider a winding up or other measure.

The Directive contains a provision in support of the principle of maintenance of capital. Article 18 states that a company may not generally acquire its own shares, except where this is allowed by the national laws of Member States.[13] However, a number of derogations to this rule are offered by Article 19. In this way, the general meeting must authorise the acquisition and determine the terms and conditions and such acquisition may be only to a maximum of 10% of the company's subscribed capital. The general meeting can be dispensed with where imminent harm would occur if the company did

---

12   Article 15(1)(c).

13   A later directive amended the Second Directive by treating as acquisition of its own shares the subscription, acquisition or holding of its shares by a company in which the company holds a majority of the voting rights or in which it can directly or indirectly exercise a dominant influence: Directive 92/101/EEC, 23 November 1992, [OJ L 347/64, 28.11.92]. See Article 24a, Second Directive.

not acquire the shares or where the company acquires them as part of an arrangement for distribution of the shares to employees.

(v)   Increase and Reduction of Capital

Shareholders are protected in the event of an increase of capital. Under Article 25 of the Directive, such an increase of capital must be approved by the shareholders in general meeting or authorised by the company statutes and the shareholders are given pre–emptive rights under Article 29. Further, by Article 30, a reduction of capital requires an agreement of at least two–thirds majority in general meeting. Article 31 adds that where a reduction of capital affects a particular class of shareholders that reduction shall require a separate vote by that class. Article 34 prohibits the reduction of capital to below the minimum required.

(vi)   Protection of Shareholders

Article 40 of the Directive sets out the majorities necessary for reduction and redemption of capital. Article 42 states that all shareholders who are in the same position shall be treated equally. Article 41 recognises the possibility of worker participation in share capital.

From the above descriptions of the first two company law directives it is clear that, while they differ in their subject matter, they are both linked in a number of ways. Although the Second Directive is much longer than the First Directive, both contain very precise requirements. The Member States have little opportunity to deviate in their own regulations from the specific provisions of the directives. In this way they both match the characteristics which typify the first generation of directives. They are easily distinguishable from the later directives which are more flexible in their approach.

3.   SECOND GENERATION DIRECTIVES

The second generation of directives progressed from the prescriptive character of the first generation to a more flexible approach, though still with some relatively precise objectives and requirements. The different approaches of the Member States and business practices were accommodated by the use of options and alternative formulae, though with an equivalent ultimate goal. Another notable aspect of the second generation directives is that the German influence became less obvious. These directives followed the first enlargement of the European Community, and the entry of other Member States brought a greater diversity of views and opinions which would have to be taken into account. The directives which fall into the second generation category are the Third and Sixth Directives and the Accounts Directives. The Accounts Directives, in particular, are identifiable with this generation whereas the Third and Sixth Directives still lean in many respects towards the first generation.

A. The Third and Sixth Directives

The Third Directive, concerning mergers of public limited liability companies, was first proposed in 1970[14] and was finally agreed in 1978.[15] The Sixth Directive,[16] concerning divisions of public limited liability companies, was agreed in 1982. These Directives can be analysed under a number of headings: their scope; the types of merger or division to be covered; the procedures required to achieve a merger or division; the parties granted protection; legal effects of the merger or division. Generally, the two directives contain the same principles, but some aspects of divisions do not apply to mergers. The description will therefore consider the Directives simultaneously, highlighting the relevant differences.

(i) Scope of the Directives

The Third Directive requires Member States to introduce provisions for facilitating mergers covered by the directive.[17] In this respect the Directive goes beyond co–ordinating existing laws[18] and further than the Sixth Directive, which does not oblige Member States to make the same provisions for divisions but requires that where Member States do have rules on company divisions these at least should be co–ordinated. This apparent inconsistency between the two Directives seems strange in the light of the Preamble to the Sixth Directive which expressly seeks guarantees for parties involved in divisions equivalent to those provided for mergers. However, the difference between the directives is really a pragmatic one. The long term

---

14   OJ C 89, 14.7.1970, p. 20.
15   Directive 78/855/EEC, OJ L 295, 20.10.1978, p. 36.
16   Sixth Council Directive of 17 December 1982, based on Article 54(3)(g) of the Treaty, concerning the division of public limited liability companies (82/891/EEC) OJ L 378, 31.12.82, p. 47.
17   Article 2.
18   As claimed in Article 1(1).

motive behind the Third Directive, to set a basis for a convention on international mergers, would require a much stronger level of co–ordination, and, further, the non–imperative character of the Sixth Directive is influenced by the fact that divisions are much more scarcely implemented in practice, and their tax implications as well as their theoretical distinctions would make it much more difficult to impose them in an obligatory manner.[19] In any event, Member States are given options not to apply the Directives to co–operatives or to companies which have begun a course of winding up. This latter option enables such companies to avoid further costs and adding to the complex winding up procedures in which they will already be involved.[20]

In all types of merger or division envisaged by the Directives the administrative or management bodies of the participating companies must draw up draft terms of the proposed merger or division containing, as a minimum, specified information.[21] This information primarily concerns the

---

19   Adolfo Sequeira Martín, 'La Fusión y La Escisión: Tercera y Sexta Directivas' in E. García de Enterría et al (eds), *Tratado de Derecho Comunitario Europeo*, Vol III (Civitas, Madrid, 1986) 27, at p. 29.

20   Sequeira Martín, *ibid*, at p. 33.

21   Article 5(2) of the Third Directive requires that the draft terms of the merger provide at least the following information: (a) the type, name and registered office of each of the merging companies; (b) the share exchange ratio and the amount of any cash payment; (c) the terms relating to the allotment of shares in the acquiring company; (d) the date from which the holding of such shares entitles the holders to participate in profits and any special conditions affecting that entitlement; (e) the date from which the transactions of the company being acquired shall be treated for accounting purposes as being those of the acquiring company; (f) the rights conferred by the acquiring company on the holders of shares to which special rights are attached and the holders of securities other than shares, or the measures proposed concerning them; (g) any special advantage granted to the experts referred to in Article 10(1) and members of the merging companies' administrative, management, supervisory or controlling bodies. Where the merger involves the acquisition of all the assets and liabilities by a company which holds all their shares and other securities conferring the right to vote at general meetings (as described in Article 24) there will be no need to provide information about the share allocation or exchange since shares are not transferred in that type of merger. In cases of division a number of extra requirements are made which are relevant to the special circumstances of a division. For example, the draft terms of division to be published must include all the information required by Article 5 of the Third Directive and further information relating the description and allocation of the assets and liabilities to be transferred to each of the recipient companies as well as the allocation to the shareholders of the company being divided

effect of the proposed merger or division on shareholdings and the date from which the legal transfer of rights and liabilities becomes effective under the proposed merger or division, as well as accounting for any benefits which might be gained by those who are charged with managing and supervising the operation of the proposal. The draft terms of the merger or division must be published in accordance with Article 3 of the First Directive,[22] ie in the national gazette or bulletin at least one month before the date fixed for the general meeting which is to decide upon the planned merger.[23] This draft plan is intended to be a factual statement of the implications of the merger or division without providing any explanation or justification of the proposed scheme. For this purpose the draft plan must be supplemented by two reports for mergers or divisions by acquisition or by forming a new company. First, a detailed written report from the administrative or management bodies containing the legal and economic grounds for the merger and the share exchange ratio, as well as any special valuation difficulties which have arisen.[24] Secondly, one or more independent experts must provide the shareholders with a written report evaluating the planned merger or division with a statement of whether, in their view, the share exchange ratio is fair and reasonable, at least indicating the method or methods used to arrive at the proposed share exchange ratio and whether such method or methods are adequate, indicating the values arrived at using each such method with an opinion on the relative importance of such methods.[25] Any special valuation difficulties should also be described in the report.[26] In order to arrive at this report the experts are entitled to obtain from the participating companies all relevant information and documents and to carry out all necessary investigations.[27]

Each of the merging or dividing companies should approve the scheme in general meeting with a majority of at least two thirds of the votes attaching to the shares or to the subscribed capital represented, or where at least half of the subscribed capital is represented the law of the Member States may

---

of shares in the recipient companies and the criterion upon which such allocation is based: Article 3.2(h) and (i), Sixth Directive.

22 Directive 68/151/EEC.

23 Article 6, Third Directive; Article 4, Sixth Directive.

24 Article 9, Third Directive; Article 7, Sixth Directive. The Sixth Directive also requires the directors to inform the general meeting of the company being divided as well as the directors of the recipient companies of any material changes in the assets and liabilities since the date of the draft terms of division.

25 Article 10.

26 Article 10.

27 Article 10(3). See also Article 8, Sixth Directive.

prescribe for a simple majority of the relevant votes to be sufficient.[28] The Sixth Directive also provides that where shares from the recipient company are being allocated to the shareholders of the divided companies in proportions not corresponding to their existing rights, Member States may provide that the minority shareholders may exercise the right to have their shares purchased.[29] For the purpose of arriving at their decision the shareholders affected by a merger by acquisition and a merger by a company which holds more than 90% of the shares, are entitled to inspect and obtain copies of certain documents at the registered office at least one month before the date fixed for the general meeting in which the merger will be approved or rejected.[30]

Once completed, the merger or division must be publicised by disclosing it on the file in the central register and by publication in the national gazette in relation to all of the companies participating in the merger or division, though the acquiring company or any recipient company may carry out these publication formalities relating to the company or companies being acquired or divided.[31]

(ii) Parties to be Protected in a Merger or Division

The key objective of the two Directives is the protection of shareholders and others during an asset merger or division. They are based on Article 54(3)(g) EC Treaty, and the preamble of each Directive concentrates particularly on the need for protection of shareholders, employees, creditors, debenture holders and persons having other claims on the merging or dividing companies, as well as third parties. Thus, the directives provide a number of guarantees for these parties. Primarily, each Directive requires that the merging or dividing companies' administrative and managing boards furnish these parties with adequate information to decide whether or not to approve the merger or division. The Directives also aim for certainty in the merger and division processes and in the relations between the interested companies and parties.

Each Directive focuses especially on the shareholders. The protection sought for shareholders through the provision of information empowers them

---

28 Article 7, Third Directive. But see also Article 8 which provides for a possible exception regarding the acquiring company, where certain conditions relating to publicity are satisfied. See also Article 5, Sixth Directive.
29 Article 5(2).
30 Article 11.
31 Article 18, Third Directive; Article 16, Sixth Directive.

to accept or reject the merger or division in an informed way and by majority rule[32] in the general meeting. The Sixth Directive also provides that where shares in the recipient companies are allocated to the shareholders of the company being divided, otherwise than in proportion to their rights in the capital, Member States may provide that the minority shareholders may exercise the right to have their shares purchased.[33] With regard to employees, each directive also makes reference to the Acquired Rights Directive.[34] That Directive provides for the consultation and information of employees as well as the preservation of their contractual rights where there is a transfer of undertakings. Thus, the employees who are transferred to the acquiring or recipient company will be treated in the same way as those employees who work in undertakings which are transferred in other ways.

Member States are given more freedom with regard to protection of creditors as long as they provide them with an adequate system of protection of their interests where their claims pre–date the publication of the draft terms and have not fallen due at the time of such publication.[35] The provisions are rather vague in this respect. For example, it is not clear what is meant by 'adequate safeguards where the financial situation of the merging companies, or the company being divided, makes such protection necessary'. Presumably this refers to schemes between companies whereby one company has not sufficient assets to cover the value of the creditor's potential claim. Presumably also, adequate safeguards means enough to guarantee that the claim will be met either by the companies themselves or by the Member State. This same protection is granted to debenture holders, unless there has been a meeting of the debenture holders, made possible by the national laws, in which the debenture holders agree to forfeit that protection, or an individual debenture holder agrees to forego such protection. Thus, the protection is more limited for debenture holders, although only by their initiative. The Sixth Directive, in addition, provides for joint and several

---

32   To the extent of at least two thirds majority or, if the Member States so provide, a simple majority when at least half of the subscribed capital is represented. A special majority (at least 75%) is necessary if the planned merger entails an alteration of the memorandum and articles of association. A separate vote is necessary for each class of shareholder affected by the proposed merger: Article 7, Third Directive. See also Article 5(1) Sixth Directive.

33   Article 5(2).

34   Council Directive 77/187/EEC of 14 February 1977 concerning the safeguard of employees' rights in the event of transfers of undertakings, businesses or parts of businesses (the 'Acquired Rights Directive') OJ L 61, 5.3.1977, p. 26. See Article 12, Third Directive; Article 11, Sixth Directive.

35   Article 13, Third Directive; Article 12, Sixth Directive.

liability of the recipient companies where a creditor has not obtained satisfaction.[36] This provision presumably aims to prevent the recipient companies from avoiding their obligations by claiming that the other company is liable and thus risking for the creditor that no company admits responsibility.

Both Directives provide that holders of securities other than shares to which special rights are attached should be given equivalent rights in the acquiring or recipient company unless they have approved the merger or division or are entitled to have their securities repurchased by the acquiring company or company being divided.[37] This protection does not give to such holders of securities any right to participate in the merger or division process although their rights are to be considered by the directors when drawing up the draft terms of merger or division,[38] which suggests a possibility of their views being heard in the process. More fundamentally, it is not clear what is meant by securities other than shares to which special rights are attached. It has been argued that this unclear concept has led to some inconsistency, so that Member States have interpreted the category to include a range of rights such as convertible loans, debentures, exchangeable bonds.[39] Share options and separate share warrants might also be included.

B.　The Fourth Directive[40]

The Fourth Directive is the leading Accounts Directive, which also provides a framework for the Seventh Directive relating to consolidated accounts. The Fourth Directive sets out the requirements for the accounts to be drawn up and laid with the Commercial or Companies Registrar by limited liability

---

36　Article 12. There are limits to this joint and several liability laid out in this Article. Thus, for example, it may be limited to the net assets allocated to each of those companies other than the one to which the obligation has been transferred. Indeed, such joint and several liability may be dispensed with if the division operation is subject to the supervision of a judicial authority and a three–fourths majority in value of the creditors or relevant class of creditors has agreed to forego such liability.

37　Article 15, Third Directive; Article 13, Sixth Directive.

38　See Article 5(2)(f), Third Directive; Article 3(2)(f), Sixth Directive.

39　Report to the European Commission by BDO Binder Hamlyn, *Study on Extension of Third and Sixth Company Law Directives* (Office for Official Publications of the European Communities, Luxembourg, 1993) 8, paragraphs 4.4 and 4.5.

40　Fourth Council Directive of 25 July 1978 78/660/EEC based on Article 54(3)(g) of the Treaty on the annual accounts of certain types of companies, OJ 1978 L 222 14.8.78 p. 11.

companies, unlimited companies, partnerships and limited partnerships.[41] By setting out the required formats of the accounts the Fourth Directive aims to achieve comparability and equivalence of financial information. The annual accounts, as a composite unit, comprise the balance sheet, the profit and loss account and the notes to the accounts.[42] They must be drawn up clearly,[43] providing a true and fair view of the financial position of the company,[44] which, as is recognised by the Directive, may, in certain circumstances, necessitate a digression from the application of legal rules or the layout prescribed by the Directive for the balance sheet and the profit and loss accounts.[45] The Directive allows Member States to choose from two possible balance sheet formats[46] and four possible profit and loss accounts formats.[47] The Directive also sets out rules for valuation of assets.[48] Although the general rule is that valuation must be based on historical cost (purchase price or production cost)[49] this method of valuation may be substituted with other possible options: replacement cost, inflation accounting, or revaluation.[50] The amount of the difference between valuation by the alternative used and the purchase price valuation must be entered under 'Liabilities' in the revaluation reserve, which may not be distributed; disclosure should be made in the notes of any changes in the amount of the reserve, together with an indication of the purchase price in the notes.[51] The Directive seeks consistency in both the formats chosen and the method of valuation chosen by Member States so that they should apply the same format and method from year to year.[52] Furthermore, recognising the individuality of companies and Member States the Directive provides for the possibility of departing from the general principles applied as long as there is disclosure and explanation of such departure. The notes must contain a minimum amount of information[53] as must the annual report.[54] Annual

---

41 As amended by Directive 90/605/EEC 8 November 1990, OJ L 317 16/11/1990 p. 60.
42 Article 2(1).
43 Article 2(2).
44 Article 2(3).
45 Article 2(5).
46 Section 3, Articles 8–10.
47 Section 5, Articles 22–26.
48 Section 7, Article 31.
49 Article 32.
50 Article 33.
51 *Ibid*.
52 Articles 3 and 31.
53 Section 8, Articles 43 and 44.
54 Section 9, Article 46.

accounts must be audited by a person authorised by national law to audit accounts.[55] Publication of the accounts, annual report and auditor's report must be duly approved.[56] There are specific exemptions for small and medium sized companies depending on balance sheet total, turnover and number of employees.[57] The Directive provides for a Contact Committee to facilitate harmonised application of the Directive through regular meetings dealing, in particular, with practical problems.[58] The Committee also has the role of advising the European Commission on additions or amendments to the Directive.

C.　The Seventh Directive[59]

The Seventh Directive regulates the consolidated accounts of groups of companies. Member States must make consolidation of accounts compulsory in cases where a parent company has the legal power to control one or more subsidiaries.[60] Where a parent company actually controls one or more subsidiaries through a minority shareholding, Member States are permitted to make consolidation compulsory.[61] The Directive lays down provisions where a parent company may or must be exempted from the obligation to draw up consolidated accounts.[62] Such exemptions will depend on the characteristics of the parent company so that if the parent company is a financial holding company or the group concerned is small the Member State may exempt the parent from drawing up consolidated accounts[63] and if the parent undertaking is itself a subsidiary undertaking heading a sub–group, the Member State must exempt it from drawing up consolidated accounts.[64] If the parent company is also a subsidiary and its parent undertaking is established outside the Community it may be exempted from

---

55　Section 11, Article 51.

56　Section 10, Article 47.

57　See Articles 11 and 27. Amendments came by three later directives which altered the monetary thresholds: 84/569 [1984] OJ L 317/28; 90/604 [1990] OJ L 317/57; 78/660 [1994] OJ L 82/33.

58　Article 52.

59　Seventh Council Directive of 13 June 1983 83/349/EEC based on Article 54(3)(g) of the Treaty on consolidated accounts [OJ 1983 L 193 18.7.83 p. 1].

60　Article 1(1).

61　Article 1(2).

62　Articles 5–9.

63　Articles 5 and 6.

64　Article 7.

drawing up consolidated accounts as long as there are consolidated accounts drawn up by a larger body of undertakings in a manner equivalent to the consolidated accounts which would be drawn up in accordance with the Seventh Directive.[65] For the structure of consolidated accounts and for the valuation rules the Seventh Directive refers to the Fourth Directive.[66] Member States may permit or prescribe proportional consolidation.[67]

D. The Eighth Directive[68]

The Eighth Directive supplements the Fourth and the Seventh Directives and lays down minimum conditions for the approval of auditors and firms of auditors carrying out audits. The requirements relate to competence and independence of auditors, with the objective of company accounts being audited with integrity and independence. Auditors are required to have completed a course of theoretical instruction, to have undergone practical training for at least three years and passed an examination of professional competence of university final examination level.[69] The Directive prescribes the subjects to be studied relevant to the statutory auditing of the annual accounts and reports of companies and firms of which the auditor must have a certain level of knowledge, and part of the qualification examination must be written.[70] The Directive provides for professional bodies to be designated as the approving authorities. A number of exemptions may be applied for individuals with certain types and levels of practical experience and such exemptions may be granted at the discretion of the Member State.[71] As regards the freedom of establishment[72] this is, strictly speaking, left to the directive concerning recognition of higher education diplomas.[73]

---

65   Article 11.
66   See especially Articles 17 and 29.
67   Article 32.
68   Eighth Council Directive of 10 April 1984 84/253/EEC based on Article 54(3)(g) of the Treaty on the approval of persons responsible for carrying out the statutory audits of accounting documents [OJ 1984 L 126 12.5.84 p. 20].
69   Article 4.
70   Articles 5 and 6.
71   Articles 7–11.
72   The preamble to the Eighth Directive expressly states that it does not cover the right of establishment or the freedom to provide services.
73   Council Directive 89/48 of 21 December 1988 on the Recognition of Higher Education Diplomas, OJ 1989– L19/16.

The key characteristic of the Accounts Directives is the range of methods for implementation to be chosen by the Member States.[74] For example, Articles 8 to 10 of the Fourth Directive provide a choice of layouts for the balance sheet and Articles 22 to 26 provide a choice of layouts for the profit and loss account. In the Fourth and the Seventh Directives, options relate to a range of issues including goodwill, valuation bases for tangible fixed assets, discretion in treatment of research and development expenditures and pension liabilities. These options illustrate the more flexible approach to the diverse accounting methods practised in the Member States. This flexibility is a recognition of the need to accommodate the differences between the Member States rather than impose rules which would meet with opposition or encounter practical obstacles to their implementation. This flexibility progressed with the introduction of the third generation of directives.

4.   THIRD GENERATION DIRECTIVES

A characteristic feature of 'third generation' directives is that they are relatively short, containing little detail and offering more discretion to Member States. The 'third generation' directives classified in this book are represented in the company law harmonisation programme by the Eleventh and Twelfth Directives. Both Directives reflect the 'new approach', fostered by the Commission's White Paper, and both were introduced and enacted after the entry into the Community of Spain, Portugal and Greece.

A.   The Eleventh Directive[75]

The Eleventh Directive is a 'disclosure directive'. Effectively, it extends the First, Fourth, Seventh and Eighth Directives to cover also the disclosures to be made in one Member State by branches of companies registered in another Member State. The Directive seeks to end the lack of co–ordination where branches, instead of subsidiaries, are opened abroad. In this way, it also extends disclosure requirements to branches opened within the European Community but whose companies may be situated in countries outside the

---

74   Buxbaum and Hopt, for example, note that Member States are given 41 options and business enterprises are given 35 options: R. Buxbaum and K.J. Hopt, *Legal Harmonisation and the Business Enterprise* (de Gruyter, Berlin, 1988) at p. 235.

75   Eleventh Council Directive of 21 December 1989 89/666/EEC concerning disclosure requirements in respect of branches opened in a Member State by certain types of company governed by the law of another State [OJ 1989 L395 30.12.89 p. 36].

European Community. The branch company also has to give information concerning the company of which it is a branch, such as name and form as well as the identities of those persons appointed to represent the company in dealings with third parties and in legal proceedings, its accounting documents, and details of the winding up of the company. Regarding the branch itself the information required to be disclosed is its name, address, activities, and closure of the branch. Article 11 also points out that the existence of the branch should be noted in the annual report of the company of which it is a branch.[76]

B. The Twelfth Directive

The Twelfth Directive on single–member private limited–liability companies[77] is short in length, containing only nine articles, and, while harmonising national laws at the level of principle, leaves the practical issues to be decided by the Member States. By the time the Twelfth Directive was proposed in 1988 the subject of single member companies had evolved from a question of legislative policy, focusing on whether or not single member companies should be possible, to a matter of legal technicality, focusing on how best to make the concept a practical reality.[78] The draft sought to advance the policy set out in the Community action programme for small and medium–sized enterprises[79] of encouraging and developing small firms and promoting access of individual entrepreneurs to the status of company, which was considered to represent 'the best framework for business development in the internal market'.[80] This would support the 'need to promote the spirit of enterprise'[81] and would also help to achieve employment growth.[82] The Twelfth Directive aims to harmonise the different national provisions.

---

76 For further detail on this Directive see eg Frank Wooldridge, *Company Law in the United Kingdom and the European Community: Its Harmonisation and Unification* (Athlone Press, London, 1991) 95–98; Francis Tansinda, 'EC Eleventh Company Law Directive and overseas companies' (1997) 18 *The Company Lawyer* 98–101.

77 Directive (89/667/EEC) [OJ L 395, 30.12.89, p. 40].

78 See Heliodoro Sánchez Ruz, 'La Sociedad Unipersonal' in Expansión (ed.), *Ley de Sociedades Limitadas*, Special Collection (Recoletos, Madrid, 1995) 65–107, at p. 72.

79 This was adopted by the Council on 3rd November 1986: OJ C 287, 14.11.1986; Bull. EC 10–1986, point 1.3.1; Bull EC 11–1986, point 2.1.22.

80 See Explanatory Memorandum to the initial proposal of the Directive in Bulletin of the European Communities, Supplement 5/88, at p. 16.

81 *Ibid.*

The directive allows a private limited liability company to be formed as a single member company or to become a single member company as a result of its shares coming to be held by a single person.[83] The effect of the directive is to provide a legal instrument through which individual entrepreneurs can enjoy the privilege of limited liability.[84] The directive requires public disclosure of the fact that the company is or has become a single member company.[85] The sole member has the powers of the general meeting[86] and decisions taken by the single member must be recorded in writing,[87] as must contracts between the single member and director and the company.[88] The directive contains a number of issues to be decided by the Member States. For example, Member States may, until national laws relating to groups have been co–ordinated, lay down special provisions with respect to a natural person who is the sole member of several companies or a legal person which is the sole member of a company.[89] Member States may choose whether or not to allow single member public limited liability companies, in which case the provisions of the directive will apply.[90] They may also provide for the alternative of allowing liability for individual entrepreneurs to be limited up to a specified sum for a stated activity.[91]

The Twelfth Directive, by its shortness and discretionary nature reflects the new approach adopted generally in the European Community after 1986. This flexibility became even stronger after the Maastricht negotiations and brought with it a potential fourth generation of directives.

5.   FOURTH GENERATION DIRECTIVES

The 'fourth generation' directives follow the move towards proportionality and subsidiarity in the early 1990s. This requires that Member States retain as much freedom from the cost incurred in implementing new laws.

---

82   In pursuance of the Council Resolution of 22 December 1986 on the action programme on employment growth, OJ C 340, 31.12.1986; Bull EC 12–1986, point 2.1.138.
83   Article 2(1).
84   Preamble to the Directive.
85   Article 3.
86   Article 4(1).
87   Article 4(2).
88   Article 5(1).
89   Article 2(2).
90   Article 6.
91   Article 7.

Effectively, this had the effect of watering down legal measures to almost a statement of objectives, leaving the Member States to choose their own way of giving practical effect to those statements of objectives or principle. Within the company law programme no directive has been adopted since this new policy approach became effective. However, the draft Thirteenth Directive illustrates the potential character of such directives.

A.   The Draft Thirteenth Directive[92]

The UK's hope that a take–over directive would be considered simultaneously with the Third Directive was certainly not realised.[93] Indeed, almost twenty years after the adoption of the Third Directive no take–over directive has been adopted. The latest draft Thirteenth Directive was published in November 1997. The original proposal of 1989 failed to gain agreement among the Member States. The latest draft was drawn up under the principle of subsidiarity and proportionality[94] and therefore has all the features of a new style 'framework directive'. In this way the draft does not contain detailed harmonisation provisions but rather sets out the principles which should be applied by the Member States according to their national systems and their cultural contexts.

Member States are required by the draft to designate an authority or authorities to supervise take–over bids and to ensure that parties comply with the rules made by the Member State under the Directive. The draft Directive also states that it is desirable to encourage voluntary control by self–regulatory bodies in order to avoid administrative or judicial action.

(i)   Contents of the Draft Thirteenth Directive

The draft Directive contains 12 Articles (the 1989 proposal contained 23 articles). Based on Article 54(3)(g) it aims to protect the interests of

---

92   COM (97) 565 final, 10.11.97. See also proposal of 1996: COM (95) 655 final, 7.2.96.

93   This wish was expressed in the Twentieth Report of the House of Lords Select Committee on the European Community on the *Draft Third Directive*, Session 1975–76 (112).

94   As was agreed at the Edinburgh Council Summit 1992. The explanatory Memorandum to the latest draft also states that the aim of the directive 'is to guarantee a minimum level of harmonisation while observing the principle of subsidiarity'.

shareholders when their company is subject to a take–over bid or to a change of control and whose shares are admitted to trading on a regulated market. The draft Directive aims to provide adequate protection across frontiers, which Member States acting independently cannot do. Particular reference is made to protection of shareholders having minority shareholdings after the purchase of the control of their company. Protection, in general, for shareholders is that they be informed of the terms of the bid by means of an offer document.[95] Information may be demanded by the supervisory authority, and the board of the offeree company should be required to make public a document setting out its opinion on the bid with reasons for that opinion.

A number of general principles are set out in Article 5 to be respected by the rules created in each of the Member States including: equivalent treatment of all holders of securities in the same position in the company; sufficient time and information to enable them to reach a properly informed decision; the board to act in the interests of the company as a whole, including employment; false markets not to be created; not to hinder offeree companies in the conduct of their affairs for longer than is reasonable by a bid for their securities. Article 6 lays down minimum information requirements concerning the bid. Member States are required to have rules in place to deal with certain matters such as withdrawal or nullity of the bid, revision of bids, competing bids, and disclosure of the results of bids.

A controversial provision in the draft concerns the mandatory offer. Although this itself is not essential if a Member State provides for a mandatory bid, Article 10 states that it should be made to all shareholders for all or a substantial part of their holdings at a price which meets the objective of protecting them. The term 'substantial part' means at least 70% of the securities, and will not be less, except where duly justified authorisation has been given by a supervisory authority. Thus, it is not necessary to include a mandatory bid but if this is the form of protection offered by the Member State then it should cover all shareholders. One problem is that this could be interpreted as allowing a partial bid, which would necessarily create minority shareholders without offering to them any additional protection.

6.   CONCLUSION

All the directives adopted to date are based on Article 54(3)(g), which seeks to co–ordinate the safeguards for shareholders and third parties. This seems

---

95   The latest proposal adds that appropriate information should also be given to the representatives of the company's employees or, failing that, to the employees directly.

to manifest itself in the requirement of disclosure of information and procedural rules. Some technical and political issues also arise in the directives such as the valuation of non–cash assets, validity of obligations, valuation rules in the accounts, the extension of limited liability, protection in take-overs, and protecting minority shareholders.

The company law directives appear to fall broadly within four categories which have developed within generations through the duration of the programme to date. The earliest measures adopted are detailed and prescriptive but gradually the measures have developed towards a more flexible approach to the extent that virtually all the technical aspects are to be left to the Member States' discretion. To some extent these four broad categories might perhaps be too crude as a description of the development of the company law programme since some directives have characteristics of more than one generation and not all of the directives fall within the dates of their relevant 'generations'. For example, the Second Directive strictly falls into the second generation by the date of its adoption but it bears all the hallmarks of a first generation directive. However, the categorisation into generations of directives does at least indicate the overall direction of the programme, which appears to be progressing towards a bare minimum of centralised regulation, leaving the details and technicalities to be decided by Member States at national law level. It remains to be seen whether the so–called 'fourth generation' will come to fruition or whether, in reality, it will have been altered again by the Amsterdam Treaty negotiations. The latest draft of the Thirteenth Directive, however, appears to be consistent with the pattern identified.

There are also a number of company law developments which do not fit into this broad scheme. In particular, the supranational provisions have characteristics of their own. These will be the focus of the next chapter.

4 Supranational Provisions

1. INTRODUCTION

Most of the company law programme has been concerned with harmonising national laws relating to companies situated within one of the Member States. However, trade is not confined to national boundaries. In different states across Europe and the US economic integration and collaboration between enterprises have developed in a variety of ways since the Second World War, ranging from contractual agreements, to trade associations and joint ventures. At European Community level a policy developed by the late 1960s towards industrial concentration. The Commission regarded co-operation among firms as a means of improving the industrial structure of the Community.[1]

The benefits of collaboration were clear, in particular for smaller enterprises which would be able to pool their resources, thus allocating such resources more efficiently. Small and medium–sized firms are not easily able simply to merge. As Petriccione observes, such firms lack the flexibility to adapt suddenly to a broader horizon and they lack knowledge of potential partners needed for a merger.[2] Yet smaller firms seek collaboration for economic reasons such as economies of scale and more efficient allocation of resources, in particular in relation to non–direct–production activities such as marketing, advertising, and research and development.[3] Therefore, as an alternative to mergers other forms of collaboration were sought.

However, neither the EC programme of harmonisation of national company laws by means of directives nor the conclusion of conventions on private international law issues relevant to company law would overcome all the barriers to trans–European economic co–operation. National laws are unable to close all the gaps in European company law and, not only would

---

1   Petriccione refers in this respect to the Commission's communication [OJ C 75, 29 July 1968 p. 3]: 'The Commission looks with favour on co–operation between small and medium sized firms when it enables them to improve the efficiency of their operation and to strengthen their productivity and competitiveness in an expanded market.' See Raffaele Mauro Petriccione, 'New Legal Forms of Organised Economic Activity at Community Level: Council Regulation on a European Economic Interest Grouping (EEIG)' (1986/2) *Legal Issues of European Integration* 17–44, at p. 31 and p. 20, n. 14.

2   *Ibid*, at p. 21.

3   *Ibid*, at p. 21.

these have difficulty in offering appropriate business structures for dealing across the community, they would also impose constraints on cross–frontier co–operation.[4] Wooldridge suggests that business allies could have used a joint operating subsidiary or a contractual agreement not involving joint and several liability to achieve their objectives,[5] but the level of success of these structures might be doubted. Israel points out, for example, that a joint operating subsidiary would only suit national activities, and choice of law problems would create complications for purely contractual devices.[6] The essential problem is that traditional legal forms of co–operation fail to be flexible enough to accommodate different needs and contract leaves too much uncertainty transnationally.

The European Commission, concentrating on the business and economic issues, offered two possible solutions: the European Economic Interest Grouping and the European Company Statute. Both such entities have been introduced by a Community regulation rather than by a directive. The Regulation on the European Economic Interest Grouping was adopted in 1985[7] but the draft Regulation on the European Company Statute is still under negotiation. Both legal instruments contain provisions relating to the structure of these transnational undertakings.

---

4   Specifically, Israel identifies such constraints as the need to use a company structure. See Severine Israel, 'The EEIG – A Major Step Forward for Community Law' (1988) 9 *Company Lawyer* 14–22, at p. 14.

5   Frank Wooldridge, 'Draft Regulation on the European Economic Interest Grouping (1984) 4 *Company Lawyer* 192–194 and 228–230, at p. 193.

6   Israel, above note 4, at p. 14.

7   Council Regulation (EEC) No 2137/85 of 25 July 1985 on the European Economic Interest Grouping (EEIG) [OJ L 199 31.7.1985, p. 1]. Much has been written on the Regulation, see eg: Israel, above note 4; F. Weiss, 'Le Groupement européen d'intérêt économique. Une nouvelle base légale pour la co–opération entre entreprises' (1986) 27 *EFTA Bulletin*, No. 3, 8–10; Dr Karl Gleichmann, 'Europäische Wirtschäftliche Interesenvereinigung' in (1985) *Zeitschrift für das geamte Handelsrecht und Wirtschaftsrecht*, 635; Raffaele Mauro Petriccione, 'New Legal Forms of Organised Economic Activity at Community Level: Council Regulation on a European Economic Interest Grouping (EEIG)' (1986/2) *Legal Issues of European Integration* 17–44; Marcos Sacristán Represa, 'La agrupación europea de interés económico (Antecedentes y caracterización)' in Alonso Ureba (ed.), *La Reforma del derecho Español de Sociedades de Capital* (Civitas, Madrid, 1987) 811–846; Antonio Pau Pedrón, 'La agrupación europea de interés económico: naturaleza, función y régimen' (1988) 587 *Revista Crítica de Derecho Inmobiliario* 1181–1245; Marta Pons de Vall, 'La Agrupación Europea de Interés Económico' (1991) 2 *Derecho de los Negocios* 5–13.

2. THE EUROPEAN ECONOMIC INTEREST GROUPING (EEIG)

A draft regulation on the EEIG was first submitted by the Commission to the Council in December 1973.[8] An amended proposal, taking into account the opinions of the European Parliament[9] and the Economic and Social Committee,[10] was submitted in 1978[11] and it was finally adopted in July 1985, after several meetings of the Council Working Group.[12] Under the Regulation, business enterprises (ranging from natural persons to companies and firms of both a public and private nature) may co–operate with each other in carrying out business activities across national frontiers. The purpose of the grouping is to facilitate or develop the economic activities of its members and to improve or increase the results of those activities.

The EEIG was based on the French *groupement d'intérêt économique* (GIE).[13] The GIE aimed to promote co–operation and concentration among French enterprises and to make them more competitive on the export markets.[14] The co–operative arrangement was of a contractual nature, giving to the parties advantages of both freedom to shape the resulting common organisation and a single reference point for dealing with third parties.[15] At the same time, some fundamental interests of such third parties and of public policy were to be safeguarded through provisions relating to the management, the joint liability of member firms, tax neutrality etc.[16] The GIE was a compromise between partnership and the protective provisions of company law, and contractual freedom enjoyed by the participating enterprises, which was regarded still as very important. The success of the GIE led to the Commission using it as a basis for the European level economic interest grouping Regulation.

Article 1 provides that the grouping shall be formed by a contract made between the parties and registered. Once formed, the grouping shall have legal capacity, though Member States shall determine whether or not such

---

8   OJ C 14, 15.2.74, p. 30.
9   OJ C 163, 11.7.77, p. 17.
10   OJ C 108, 15.5.75, p. 46.
11   OJ C 103, 28.4.78, p. 4.
12   OJ L 199, 31.7.85, p. 1.
13   Ordonnance No 67 – 821, 23 September 1967, Journal Officiel, 28 September 1967. For commentary see eg: J. Delmas, 'Un cadre juridique nouveau pour la co–opération inter–entreprises: le Groupement d'intérêt économique' (1970) 138 *Revue du Marche Commun* 500–522.
14   Petriccione, above note 7, at p. 30.
15   *Ibid*, at p. 30.
16   *Ibid*, at p. 30.

groupings have legal personality. A grouping must consist of at least two companies, firms, or other legal bodies, which have their central administrations in different Member States, or two natural persons, who carry on their principal activities in different Member States, or a company, firm or other legal body and a natural person of which the first has its central administration in one Member State and the second carries on his principal activity in another Member State.[17] The contract of formation must contain a minimum of specified information including: the name, preceded or followed by the words 'European Economic Interest Grouping' or the initials 'EEIG'; its official address; its objects; the name; business name; legal form; permanent address or registered office; number and place of registration, if any, of each member of the grouping; and the duration of the grouping except where this is indefinite.[18] No minimum capital is required.

Under Article 12, the choice of the grouping's official address must be based on objective elements. The location chosen affects the law applicable to the EEIG as well as the tax position.[19] Article 12 is still relatively flexible, the address coinciding merely with a real, and not necessarily the main, activity of the grouping.[20] The official address may also be transferred from one state to another without affecting the capacity of the grouping.[21] Membership of a grouping is also treated flexibly, but Article 4(4) provides that Member States may, on grounds of public interest, prohibit or restrict participation of certain members. Furthermore, Article 4(1)(b) limits membership to those natural persons who carry on any industrial, commercial, craft or agricultural activity or who provide professional or other services in the Community.

The EEIG must have at least two organs: the members acting collectively, and the manager or managers.[22] It is possible to provide for other organs, such as a supervisory body. The decision–making body constitutes the members acting collectively and they may take the decisions necessary for achieving the grouping's objectives. The manager is the second organ of the EEIG. While, generally, managers should be natural persons within the limits set out in Article 19(1), Article 19(2) grants Member States the option to allow legal persons to be managers represented by one or more natural persons. Generally, the manager binds the grouping as against third

---

17 Article 4(2).

18 Article 5.

19 Palmer's *Company Law* (Sweet and Maxwell, London, 1992) Release 48: 17– viii – 92, p. 16055, para. 16.207.

20 Israel, above note 4, p. 16.

21 Article 13. See also Israel, above note 4, at p. 17.

22 Article 16.

party dealings. Normally, any negotiation will require two signatures in order to bind the grouping but this requirement must be published in the contract,[23] otherwise the third party can rely on one signature.

Article 3 is perhaps the most controversial provision in the Regulation. It provides that:

> The purpose of a grouping shall be to facilitate or develop the economic activities of its members and to improve or increase the results of those activities; its purpose is not to make profits for itself. Its activity shall be related to the economic activities of its members and must not be more than ancillary to those activities.

In short, the grouping exists to facilitate the activities of the participating members, enabling them to improve their profits and competitiveness. The grouping can co–ordinate but not dominate the activities of its members. While it should not be the aim of the grouping to make profits for itself, that does not mean that it may not make any profit at all. Its activities may or may not make a profit but they should be for the ultimate benefit of the members, either in the short term by dividing any incidental profits which do arise from its activities, or longer term as a result of the investment which will eventually enable the members to continue their enterprise more effectively or more easily or more profitably.

Article 3(2) sets out some specific restrictions on the grouping and its activities. For example, it may not exercise a power of management or supervision over its members' own activities or over the activities of another undertaking. It may not directly or indirectly hold shares of any kind in a member undertaking; shares may be held in another undertaking only in so far as it is necessary for the achievement of the grouping's object and if done on its members' behalf. A grouping may not be a member of another grouping. This prevents chains, which may be complex and reduce transparency. However, it is possible for a person or undertaking to be a member of more than one grouping.

If the grouping fails to comply with commitments entered into, the members will have unlimited joint and several liability for the grouping's debts and other liabilities. Third party creditors may only claim from individual members after they have sought payment from the grouping and such payment has not been made within an appropriate period. It is possible for the creditor in a contract to agree not to pursue payment from a particular member or members, though technically they will still be liable jointly and severally with the other members.

---

23   Article 20(2).

Article 40 states that the profits or losses resulting from the activities of the grouping shall be taxable in the hand of its members. The grouping is therefore generally regarded as being 'tax transparent'.[24] Otherwise, national tax laws shall apply to the grouping, subject to double taxation treaties. This means that members of an EEIG may be taxed differently depending on where they and the grouping reside. The Regulation also contains detailed provisions on winding up of the grouping.

Whilst the Regulation for the EEIG was adopted the proposal for the European Company Statute has had little success.

3.   THE EUROPEAN COMPANY

The European Company Statute proposals have had a difficult history and remain unadopted.[25] The idea has existed since before the European Community was established. The creation of a European Company for performing public services and public works was discussed by the Council of Europe in 1951.[26] In 1960, the concept was put forward by Professor Sanders of Rotterdam[27] and then in 1970 the Commission published an official proposal.[28] This proposal was amended in 1975[29] and the negotiations were eventually suspended in 1982. Then in 1985 the White Paper *Completing the Internal Market*[30] expressed the need for a European Company and a fresh proposal was published in 1989.[31] This was divided

---

24   For a useful discussion on tax and the EEIG see Tarlochan Lall, 'Taxation and the European Economic Interest Grouping' (1993) *British Tax Review* 134–159.

25   For accounts of the proposals' history see: Alec Burnside, 'The European Company Re–proposed' (1991) 12 *Company Lawyer* 216–220; Andreas Wehlau, 'The Societas Europea: A Critique of the Commission's 1991 Amended Proposal' (1992) 29 *CML Rev* 473–510.

26   See Dennis Thompson, 'The Project for a Commercial Company of European Type' (1961) *ICLQ* 851.

27   See Burnside, above note 25, at p. 216, his note 3.

28   OJ C 124, 10.10.70, p. 35; *Bulletin of the European Communities*, Supplement 8/70.

29   *Bulletin of the European Communities*, Supplement 4/75.

30   COM (85) 310 final, point 137.

31   OJ C 263, 16.10.89, p. 41; *Bulletin of the European Communities*, Supplement 5/89, drawn up on the basis of COM (89) 268 final. See also Commission *Internal market and industrial co–operation – Statute for the European Company*, Internal Market White Paper, Point 137 (Memorandum from the Commission to the Parliament, the Council, and the two sides of industry) COM (88) 320, final. See also, commentary

into two parts: a draft Regulation, based on Article 100A, to deal with the core company law aspects, and a draft Directive, based on Article 54(3)(g), to deal with the worker participation aspects. Following reactions from Member States and the European Parliament and the Economic and Social Committee to that proposal[32] a new amended proposal was published in 1991[33] and then the latest draft appears to be that of 1996.[34] Negotiations have concentrated on the worker participation issues, preventing the progress of the Regulation. The recent Single Market Action Plan focuses attention on the European Company Statute and efforts are being made to see its advance.[35] Again, recent newspaper reports suggest a further freeze of the negotiations arising from the contrasting views of Germany and the UK on the worker participation issues. This section will provide a summary of the contents of the draft Regulation proposed in 1996.[36]

Article 1 states that, subject to the conditions of the Regulation, companies may be formed throughout the Community in the form of a European public company (Societas Europea, 'SE') with capital divided into shares, limited liability for the shareholders, and legal personality. The SE may be formed by one of a number of means: a merger of two or more public companies, at least two of which are governed by the law of different Member States; formation of a holding company by two or more companies, public and private, at least two of which are governed by the laws of different Member States, or have, for at least two years, a subsidiary company governed by the law of another Member State, or a branch office situated in another Member State; formation of a joint subsidiary company by two or more companies, firms or other legal bodies, at least two of which are governed by the law of a different Member State, or have a subsidiary company governed by or a branch office, for at least two years, in a different Member State; transformation of a public company if it has had a subsidiary governed by or a branch situated in another Member State.[37] A Member

---

on this draft by Janet Dine, 'The European Company Statute' (1990) 11 *Company Lawyer* 208–214.

32   For an example see House of Lords European Communities Select Committee, 19th Report, *The European Company Statute*, Session 1989–90, Paper 71.

33   OJ C 176, 8.7.91, p. 1.

34   See DTI Consultation Paper, *The European Company Statute* (DTI, London, July 1997, Ref: URN 97/786) at Annex B.

35   See Press Release: IP/97/478, Commission adopts Single Market Action Plan for Amsterdam European Council,4.6.97.

36   Although this version does not appear to have been published in the Official Journal, the DTI is working on this version.

37   Article 2.

State may provide that a company the head office of which is not in the Community may participate in the formation of an SE provided that the company is formed under the law of a Member State, has its registered office in that Member State and has a genuine, permanent link with a Member State's economy.[38] The same methods may be used by SEs which have already been established, although a subsidiary of an SE cannot then create another subsidiary in the form of an SE.[39]

The SE shall have a minimum subscribed capital of at least ECU 120,000.[40] Its registered office must be within the territory of the Community[41] and at the place of the company's central administration, and is transferable.[42] The SE must be registered, with its particulars and documents published in accordance with the First Directive,[43] and then notification of its formation must be published in the Official Journal of the European Communities.[44] A possible ruling may be that an SE may not be registered in a Member State which has not transposed into its legislation the Directive on the establishment of Works Councils.[45] Detailed procedures are provided for the different types of formation.[46]

Article 37 provides the basic structure of the SE. The board structure of the SE may be organised according to a one–tier system, as an administrative board, or as a two–tier system with a management board and a supervisory board. The structure – one–tier or two–tier – may be specified by the Member State in which the registered office is located. The SE must also have a general meeting of shareholders. Within the two possible frameworks the draft Regulation stipulates the role of the different boards, and how these boards must exercise their functions.[47] Articles 52–60 set out the competences of the general meeting and the procedures by which its decisions shall be taken. These provisions are much simpler than the earlier

---

38   Article 2(5).

39   Article 3.

40   Article 4.

41   Article 7.

42   Article 8.

43   Article 12.

44   Article 13.

45   See Article 11, Alternative B. See also Directive 94/45/EEC on the establishment of a European Works Council or a procedure in Community–scale undertakings and Community–scale groups of undertakings for the purposes of informing and consulting employees [OJ L 254, 30.9.94, p. 64] discussed in Chapter 10.

46   Title II, Articles 14–36.

47   Articles 37. On the two–tier system see Articles 38–42. On the one–tier system see Articles 43–45. Rules common to both systems are provided in Articles 46–51.

drafts and basically seek to ensure equal treatment of the shareholders. The proposal makes provision for the publication of annual and consolidated accounts the preparation of which will be governed by the law of the Member State in which the registered office is situated.[48] The proposal also contains rules on winding up, liquidation, insolvency, suspension of payments.[49]

The proposed Statute contains a general subsidiary reference to the law of the Member State in which the company has its registered office. Effectively, it creates a set of hierarchies of laws by which in the first set the national law ranks third, following the rules in the Regulation and the company's statutes. Then if no solution is found in the national law, reference is made to the company's statutes again.[50] The proposed European Company Statute remains high on the Single Market Action Programme's agenda although the discussions on the employee participation issues continue to stall its progress.

4. THE DRAFT TENTH DIRECTIVE

The draft Tenth Directive originated as a draft Convention in accordance with Article 220 of the Treaty of Rome.[51] The negotiations for the draft Convention failed because those Member States in whose legislation employee representation or participation was important were concerned that international mergers could be used to circumvent such laws.[52] In 1985 the Commission issued a draft Directive based on Article 54(3)(g) EC Treaty as an alternative to the Convention, with the aim of facilitating a technique to simplify the procedures for creating or restructuring complex economic entities, so that this would promote and encourage co–operation between Community undertakings, allowing them to pool their resources effectively in order to react to the changing market place.[53] The draft capitalised on the achievements of the Third and Sixth Directives which had already been

---

48   Article 61.

49   Title V.

50   Article 9(1).

51   Article 220 EC Treaty stipulates that the Member States shall, in so far as it is necessary, enter into negotiations with each other with a view to securing the possibility of cross–border merger.

52   See EC Bulletin, Supplement 3/85, p. 5. See also HL Select Committee Report, Session 1977–78, 28th Report on the European Communities – International Mergers (159) at pp. 15–16.

53   EC Bulletin, above note 52, at p. 5.

adopted. The Commission stated that this choice would ensure the uniform interpretation of texts on mergers by the Court of Justice, by rendering this particular form of merger as unexceptional and more as part of a range of merger types.[54] Thus, it seems that the Commission was concerned with achieving a coherent merger programme for EC Company Law.

How has the draft Tenth Directive responded to the fears that led to the failure of the earlier draft Convention? Article 1(3) anticipates the problem that a merger could impede employee participation in an undertaking and thus provides to Member States a veto over such mergers. Member States may therefore refuse to apply the Directive to the merger, with the practical effect of preventing achievement of the merger. This provision is intended as a temporary measure pending the adoption of the draft Fifth Directive.[55] This suggested temporary compromise may, as Welch argues, be rather more permanent,[56] since it is unlikely in the near future that the Fifth Directive will be adopted.[57] Arguably, the Works Council Directive would limit the possibility of a cross–border merger damaging established works council provisions in an undertaking because that Directive would still apply to the newly formed merged undertaking. This may therefore limit the need for Member States to apply the veto granted to them in Article 1(3). However, the Works Councils Directive does not apply to all undertakings. Where it does not apply then, unless Member States intervene to prevent the merger, such an operation could destroy steps towards employee participation in some enterprises.

Little progress has so far been made on the proposed Directive. However, one of the obstacles appears now to have been resolved. A taxation directive was adopted in 1990[58] which, together with the adoption of the Works Councils Directive, could provide some encouragement for advancing the Directive. On the other hand, another eight years has passed since the taxation Directive was adopted, with still little advance.

---

54   *Ibid*, at p. 6.

55   First proposed in 1972 (OJ 1972 C131/49). Amended proposal in 1983 (OJ 1983 C240/2) and an unofficial text appeared in 1988, available in DTI Consultation Document 'Amended Proposal for a Fifth Directive on the Harmonisation of Company Law in the European Community', January 1990. The official 1983 text has been further amended in 1991: OJ C 321, 12.12.91.

56   Janet Welch, 'Tenth Draft Directive on Cross–Border Mergers' (1986) 7 *Company Lawyer* 69, at p. 69.

57   See discussion in Chapter 10.

58   Council Directive (90/434/EEC) of 23.7.90 on the common system of taxation applicable to mergers, divisions, transfers of assets and exchanges of shares concerning companies of different Member States [OJ L 225, 20.8.90, p. 1].

5. CONCLUSION

By comparison with attempts to harmonise national provisions, the supranational proposals have generally faced many obstacles. There are a number of possible reasons for these problems. Their transnational aspects perhaps make them more complex and therefore more difficult to establish. This is indicated by the need for Member States to have implemented the Regulation for EEIGs, whereas normally a regulation would be directly applicable without having to be transposed into national law by implementing legislation. Another barrier to the adoption of the other supranational proposals has been the issue of employee participation. This subject will be explored more fully later in the book.

As a general conclusion to the description of the company law harmonisation programme it has largely concentrated on technical and procedural issues relevant to companies. It has not dealt with more obvious issues of corporate governance such as directors' duties. The main focus of the rules has been the protection of shareholders and creditors through procedural safeguards and delivery of information about certain aspects of the company. Generally, the Directives have each dealt with fairly discrete issues, though clearly these overlap in a number of respects. Since the programme was begun, the Directives have gradually become less detailed and precise. Increasingly, Member States are left to decide issues of detail. A problematic aspect of the programme has been the supranational aspect and the main difficulty has centred around the problem of employee participation. This appears in practice to have imposed limits on the effectiveness of the programme.

The next part of this book will consider how the programme has so far been developed at Community level and will be concerned with the legislative procedures and the representative democracy of the European Community and its institutions.

PART TWO

The Development of the Company Law Programme as a Case Study of Representative Democracy in the European Community

5 Representative Democracy and the Institutional Arrangements of the European Community

1. INTRODUCTION

The institutional arrangements of the European Community have implications for the legislation adopted and they affect opportunities for participating in the creation of those legislative provisions. In turn, the level of participation or opportunities for participation may have consequences for the way in which such provisions are received nationally and by the bodies and individuals affected by the legislation. This chapter will consider the European institutional and decision–making context in which the company law harmonisation programme has been developed. Thus, it will outline the relationship between the legislative institutions, the legislative procedures and the role of Member States and interest groups in the decision–making process. The relevance of voting to the legitimacy of the decisions made at European level will also be explored.

Effectively, the European Community is concerned with representative democracy. The institutional arrangements determine the quality of that representative democracy. In turn, the principle of democracy purports to legitimise the structure of the institutions and their decisions and legislative processes.[1] Some commentators argue that democracy may be regarded as a feature of effectiveness at European Community level. For example, Piris claims that, 'in order to be effective, the actions of the institutions must be accepted by the citizens and that, for this to occur, these institutions must be closer to the citizens, lend them an ear, be under their control, in a word, be more democratic'.[2] These democratic aspirations are also formally

---

1   de Búrca, for example, suggests that one of the four themes which can be identified in the proposals for addressing legitimacy problems is the need for greater democracy within the Union: Gráinne de Búrca, 'The Quest for Legitimacy in the European Union' (1996) 59 *MLR* 349 at pp. 349–350.

2   Jean–Claude Piris, 'After Maastricht, are the Community Institutions More Efficacious, More Democratic and More Transparent?' (1994) 19 *ELR* 449, at p. 461. On effectiveness see Francis Snyder, 'The Effectiveness of European Community

recognised at the European level. The fifth recital of the Preamble to the Treaty of European Union states that it is the Union's goal to enhance further the 'democratic and efficient functioning of the institutions so as to enable them better to carry out, within a single institutional framework, the tasks entrusted to them'.

These claims suggest that the institutional arrangements and the level of representative democracy may affect the quality of the laws produced as a result of these arrangements. On the other hand, it could be argued that the content of the laws may not necessarily be affected by a democratic or non–democratic input. Thus, for example, a draconian law could be enacted through democratic procedures or a 'humane' law could be forced through by undemocratic methods. However, the quality of the democratic input could influence the acceptability and practical outcome of the laws created. In this respect, democracy may require both a democratic structure and a democratic outcome.

This chapter is concerned with the democratic claims of the European Community and therefore focuses on the institutional arrangements, the legislative procedures and the participants in the decision–making process. The following chapter will consider how those arrangements operate in practice.

2.   THE INSTITUTIONS

Some would argue that a democratic union requires the political institutions to be structured by a separation of powers, the principle traditionally regarded as the most effective safeguard for democracy with a system of checks and balances.[3] There does exist a system of checks and balances at Community level although this has, in reality, been overridden by the sheer complexity of the institutional arrangements. To an extremely limited level the Commission might be regarded as the Community's executive, with the Council and the European Parliament acting in the role of the legislature and

---

Law: Institutions, Processes, Tools and Techniques' in Terence Daintith (ed.), *Implementing The EC Directives* (Wiley–Chancery, Chichester, 1995) 51–87 at p. 87.

3   George Ress, 'Democratic Decision–Making in the European Union and the Role of the European Parliament' in Deirdre Curtin and Tom Heukels (eds), *Institutional Dynamics of European Integration – Essays in Honour of Henry G. Schermers*, Volume II (Martinus Nijhoff, Dordrecht, Netherlands, 1994) 153–176, at p. 159 and his n. 27. See also Brigitte Boyce, 'The Democratic Deficit of the European Community' (1993) 46 *Parliamentary Affairs* 458–477, at p. 465.

the European Court of Justice and Court of First Instance as the judiciary. However, this would be an over simplistic view[4] of the Community's institutional arrangement and the overlap between the institutions of these theoretical tasks can be quickly observed. For example, the Commission also has legislative tasks as the sole initiator of Community legislation and the Council has various executive functions. Perhaps a more realistic focus for the purpose of democracy would be on a limitation of powers rather than on a separation of the institutions' powers.

The most important legislative institutions are the Commission, the Council of Ministers, and the European Parliament. In principle, the Commission represents the Community while the Council of Ministers represents national state interests, and the European Parliament represents the people.[5] The Commission, under Article 155 EC Treaty, must act to 'ensure the proper functioning and development of the common market' and therefore initiates policy development and integration, while the Council of Ministers must ensure that the objectives set out in the Treaty are attained under Article 145 EC Treaty. In practice, this means that the Council seeks to ensure a rate of progress which is acceptable to the governments of the Member States. The European Parliament was initially a consultative and advisory body but since the Maastricht Treaty it also participates in the decision–making process.[6] The European Court of Justice also influences Community activity by interpreting legislation and by resolving procedural disputes.[7] The Treaty further provides that the institutions will be assisted by various committees, notably, the Committee of Permanent Representatives, the Economic and Social Committee and the Committee of the Regions.[8]

The reality is that interaction between the institutional bodies is complex and involves struggles for power. A problem which has evolved from this relationship has been lack of clarity and transparency of decisions made by the institutions. The Council, in particular, has received criticism for its secretive behaviour and refusal to disclose voting decisions.[9] By contrast,

---

4   Dashwood argues that the whole tendency to equate Community institutions with familiar national institutions is misconceived: Alan Dashwood, 'The Role of the Council in the European Union' in Deirdre Curtin and Tom Heukels, above note 3, 117–134, at p. 117.

5   See generally, Andrew Duff, John Pinder and Roy Pryce (eds), *Maastricht and Beyond: Building the European Union* (Routledge, London, 1994).

6   Article 138(b) EC Treaty.

7   The Court of Auditors is also an institution within Article 4 EC Treaty but is not relevant to this book.

8   Article 4(2) and Article 151(1) EC Treaty.

9   See eg Brigitte Boyce, above note 3, at p. 458 and p. 470.

under Article 5 EC Treaty Member States have a duty to provide information to the Commission. In the case of *Netherlands* v *High Authority*[10] it was stated that 'the Member States are obliged, by virtue of Article 5 of the EEC Treaty, to facilitate the achievement of the Commission's tasks... Thus, it is necessary for Member States to co–operate with the institutions.' On the other hand, Member States themselves might not feel that this co–operation is reciprocated by the institutions in the process of legislating.[11] The status of the committees may also be relevant. Notably, in this respect, the Economic and Social Committee and the Committee of the Regions seek the *de jure* status of an institution.[12] Piris notes, further, that Committee of Permanent Representatives' relationship with other committees is not clearly defined.[13]

However, the struggle for legitimacy has forced the institutions to respond positively to some criticisms. The Commission made specific reference to a declaration made during the negotiations for the Treaty on European Union in which it was stated that the conference 'considers that transparency of the decision–making process strengthens the democratic nature of the institutions and the public's confidence in the administration'.[14] Consequently, the Commission and the Council adopted a declaration that the results of votes would be published.[15] The Council also adopted a Code of Practice on transparency, committing itself when adopting minutes to examine systematically whether to make public documents submitted to it; the decisions taken by it; and the conclusions reached by the Council where

---

10   Case 9/61[1962] ECR 213, at p. 236. See also John Temple–Lang, 'Community Constitutional Law: Article 5, EEC Treaty' (1990) 27 *CMLR* 645–681, at p. 672.

11   Temple–Lang, *ibid.*, at 672.

12   See the Reports to the Reflection Group for the Intergovernmental Conference 1996 of ECOSOC (Brussels, 4 May 1995) and of the Committee of the Regions (Brussels 1995).

13   Piris, above note 2, at p. 458.

14   EC Commission Communication to the Council, Parliament and ECOSOC, *Public Access to the Institutions' Documents*, COM (93) 191 Final.

15   See EC Commission Communication to the Council, Parliament and ECOSOC, *Public Access to the Institutions' Documents*, COM (93) 191 Final, 5 May 1993; and EC Commission Communication to the Council, Parliament and ECOSOC, *Openness in the Community*, COM (93) 258 Final, 2 June 1993. See also Commission Communication, *The Operation of the Community's Internal Market After 1992: Follow–up to the Sutherland Report*, SEC (92) 2277 final, Brussels, 2 December 1992.

they are related to the adoption of a legislative act.[16] However, to say that this is a progression towards transparency or democracy might be rather too optimistic. The Council is still able to withhold details of meetings and still enjoys considerable power without any stringent threat of accountability. As Armstrong points out: 'the ease with which the Council has adopted the Code also reinforces the point that the legal space for the control of the flow of information is within the control of the Council, as yet free from the control of the Community courts wielding a substantive principle of transparency, and free also from a process of public rule–making underpinned by democratic principles of openness, debate and popular participation.'[17] Nevertheless, closer national scrutiny of the Council's activities and the availability of information to national governments do reflect a considerable improvement.[18] However, in this respect, while the Commission can be regarded positively for having introduced green papers as part of the consultation process,[19] still consultation remains limited because the responses to those green papers do not necessarily get transposed into the legislation drafted. Some bodies would prefer to see more white papers as a supplement to the green papers.[20]

In addition to the complex relationship between the institutions, the Community has developed progressively, but in a piecemeal fashion, a number of different legislative procedures. New procedures were adopted in the 1980s and 1990s in order to strengthen the position of the European Parliament. The following section will consider the impact of these procedures on the European Union's institutional relations.

3. LEGISLATIVE PROCEDURES

The legislative process is complex, with at least three possible different procedures depending on which Treaty provision is the basis for the

---

16   Code of Conduct of December 6, 1993, adopted by the Council and the Commission; and Council Decision of 20 December, 1993. See for commentary, Piris, above note 2, at pp. 470–474.

17   K.A. Armstrong, 'Citizenship of the Union? Lessons from *Carvel and the Guardian*' (1996) 59 *MLR* 582, at p. 586.

18   See eg Martin Westlake, 'The European Parliament, The National Parliaments and the 1996 Intergovernmental Conference' (1995) 66 *The Political Quarterly*, 59–73.

19   On the promise to publish green papers see Commission Communication (93/C63/03) *Increased Transparency in the Work of the Commission* [OJ C 63, 5.3.93, p. 8].

20   For a call for more white papers, this view was obtained by Secretary General of UNICE, Brussels, 20 November 1995; see below note 81.

proposed legislation. These three procedures include the consultation procedure, the co–operation procedure and the co–decision procedure.[21] These have evolved in a piecemeal fashion and ascribe to the different institutions varied powers and degrees of power. The company law Directives were adopted under all of these procedures at different stages of the harmonisation programme's development.[22]

The legislative procedures themselves may each have an impact on the democratic balance between the institutions. Theoretically, the co–operation procedure should have increased the power of the Parliament,[23] which was strengthened again by the co–decision procedure. However, doubts have been raised about the effect of the co–operation procedure in this respect.[24] For example, Lenaerts notes that, although the co–operation procedure would be an improvement as regards the input of the Parliament in the legislative process, there was a weakness in the status of the amendments proposed by the Parliament at the second reading not yet accepted by the Commission. He saw this as problematic in terms of democratic legitimacy, since the Parliament, being democratically elected and the Commission not, ought to give to the Parliament an inroad into the monopoly of legislative initiative of the Commission.[25] In any event, the Commission still retains its privileged position in setting the agenda[26] (even though it is careful to consider the likely view of the Parliament at the early stage of preparing a proposal)[27]

---

21   The assent procedure may also be used for a number of areas such as membership of the EU under Article O of the TEU. These procedures are described in detail in most European Community Law texts, see eg T.C. Hartley, *The Foundations of European Community Law*, 3rd ed. (Clarendon Press, Oxford, 1994).

22   See below, note 31.

23   For example, Fitzmaurice cautiously notes that the procedure gave to the Parliament 'important new powers': John Fitzmaurice, 'An Analysis of the European Community's Co–operation Procedure' (1988) XXVI *JCMS* 389, at p. 400.

24   Westlake saw it as an 'antechamber to the co–decision procedure': Martin Westlake, 'The Role of the European Parliament' (paper presented to the Hart Legal Workshop, *Lawmaking in the European Union*, London, July 1996); and Woods and Villiers suggest that it made little impact on the Parliament's negotiating influence on the 'third generation' of company law directives: Lorna Woods and Charlotte Villiers, 'Legislative Process and Democracy: The Development of European Company Law' (paper presented to the Hart Legal Workshop, 1996, *ibid.*).

25   Koen Lenaerts, 'Some Reflections on the Separation of Powers in the European Community' (1991) 28 *CMLR* 11, at pp. 25–6.

26   Lenaerts describes the 'trias politica' in which the Commission has the monopoly of legislative initiative: Lenaerts, *ibid.*, at p. 16.

27   Fitzmaurice, above note 23, at p. 394.

and the Council still has a stronger position in so far at it has the prerogative of affirming the original common position over and above the views of the Parliament. Furthermore, the Commission is still able to refuse a request by Parliament to initiate a proposal.

In terms of the adoption of legislation, the co–decision procedure does appear to have been relatively successful.[28] On the other hand, in terms of balance of power between the institutions it is probably too early to judge conclusively. Nevertheless, the co–decision procedure is restricted in scope, the Council, unlike the Parliament, still has the advantage of being under no time constraints, it is easier for the Council than for the European Parliament to initiate the conciliation procedure, and the Council can also confirm its common position if conciliation fails.[29] This superiority of the Council to the Parliament in the co–decision procedure also violates the principle that the directly elected chamber should dominate the legislative process, thereby further weakening claims to democratic legitimacy. However, the co–decision procedure gives to Parliament a control over the legislative process, in so far as it acquires an absolute right to reject proposed legislation. It can force the Council into constructive negotiations to reach an acceptable result, the final text of a legislative act requires the Parliament's approval, it now deals directly with the Council in the second round, there are no more unilateral changes to a text approved by Parliament, and the procedure may encourage the Council to follow the rules on reconsultation more closely.[30] Ultimately, the problem still remains that the Council has the final say over legislation, leaving the democracy problem still unresolved; a problem exacerbated by the persistently secretive Council. The conclusion which must be drawn from the relative weakness of the European Parliament is that the true view of the public which elects the Parliament directly might not be reflected in the legislation. An alternative argument is that the ministers who constitute the Council's membership are more representative of the public since national general elections are generally taken more seriously than are European elections, thus reflecting more accurately the political will of the electorate.

A major problem with the procedures is that they are complex and multiple. For example, as has been noted above, the Directives in the company law harmonisation programme have not all been adopted under the same procedure. On the contrary, different directives have been introduced

---

28 Sophie Boyron, 'The Co–decision Procedure: Rethinking the Constitutional Fundamentals' (paper presented to the W.G. Hart Legal Workshop 1996).

29 Philip Raworth, 'A Timid Step Forwards: Maastricht and the Democratisation of the European Community' (1994) 19 *ELR* 16, at pp. 23–24.

30 Raworth, *ibid.*, at pp. 20–21.

through different procedures, all possible procedures being used at least once.[31] This complexity could present a hindrance to the quest for democracy and accessibility to the decision–making process; both aspects are relevant to claims for legitimacy.[32] Indeed, Piris notes that although the new co–decision procedure theoretically helps to improve efficiency and democracy the Treaty of European Union increased the complexity of the decision–making procedures by adding new, complicated procedures to the existing procedures. As Piris remarks: 'This neither makes for efficiency nor democracy: the rules of the Treaty are more and more difficult to apply by the institutions and the Community's decision–making system is more and more difficult for citizens to understand.'[33] The complexity of the procedures also serves to diversify the roles of the institutions, thus increasing further the lack of transparency.[34] This has major consequences for the opportunity for access to and participation in the legislative process.

Voting is possibly the most important formal demonstration of democracy. The departure from unanimous voting,[35] and the later changes made under both the Single European Act and the Maastricht Treaty to decision–making procedures have significant implications for the democratic claims of the European Union. Democracy is popularly identified with 'one person, one vote'.[36] This notion of democracy represents the simplest form of equal political effectiveness. The qualified majority voting procedure, which consists of weighted votes between the Member States, would therefore appear to steer away from the view of democracy as entailing a principle of equal effectiveness. However, it might be argued that the different population sizes of the Member States would justify creating weighted votes so that the larger states, representing a greater number of people, ought to have more voting power. On the other hand, it could be argued that the smaller countries need to be protected from the larger countries. The qualified majority voting mechanism, with the requirement of seventy one per cent

---

31   The Directives introduced under the consultation procedure include: First Directive, Second Directive, Third Directive, Fourth Directive, Sixth Directive, Seventh Directive, Eighth Directive. The Directives introduced under the co–operation procedure include: Eleventh Directive, Twelfth Directive. Currently, the draft Thirteenth Directive is being discussed under the co–decision procedure.

32   de Búrca, above note 1, at p. 350.

33   Piris, above note 2, at p. 469.

34   This was a particular complaint of Lenaerts, as regards the Parliament, following the co–decision procedure: see note 25 above.

35   Partly achieved by the Luxembourg Compromise of 1966.

36   James L. Hyland, *Democratic Theory: The Philosophical Foundations* (Manchester University Press, Manchester, 1995) p. 64.

support for a proposal, does achieve a degree of protection for the smaller states in that a coalition only of the larger states would not provide them with sufficient votes. Currently, they would need the support of at least two smaller states for a vote to succeed. Unanimity, which, by definition, implies a power of veto, may ensure consensus but it cannot be said that there is equal political effectiveness if one dissenting voter can effectively outweigh all the other voters.[37] Furthermore, the delays inherent in unanimous voting in a growing Union are also contrary to the democratic ideal, especially if no decision can effectively be reached. The practical effect of qualified or simple majority voting is greater reliance on coalition building by states fearful of isolation.[38] This appears to be the future for Europe since the Amsterdam summit has resulted in an extension of the area where decisions can be taken by a qualified majority and the weighting of Member States in the Council will be readjusted to ensure that the decisions taken by a majority of Member States corresponds at the same time to a sufficient percentage of the Union's population. Further, as compensation for the loss of a commissioner the larger countries will be given more voting power. The success of the planned further enlargement of the Union will also depend on appropriate voting procedures.[39]

4. THE ROLE OF THE MEMBER STATES IN CREATING THE LEGISLATION

Having considered the contribution of the European institutions to the law–making process it is necessary to pay some attention to the role of the Member States in this process. While the opportunity for national parliaments to participate in the creation of secondary EC legislation still remains relatively limited,[40] this does not signify that the Member States

---

37   *Ibid.*, at p. 65.

38   B. Guy Peters, 'Bureaucratic Politics and the Institutions of the European Community' in Alberta M. Sbragia (ed.), *Euro–politics: Institutions and Policy–making in the 'New' European Community* (Washington DC, The Brookings Institution, 1992) 75–122, at pp. 83–4.

39   See Lionel Barber, 'EU Alert Over Plans for New Members', *Financial Times*, 14 July 1997.

40   See eg Philip Norton, 'National Parliaments and the European Union: Where To From Here?', Paper presented to the W.G. Hart Legal Workshop on *Lawmaking in the European Union*, London, 9–11 July 1996. Note, however, the observations of Westlake which suggest a more active role gained for national parliaments: Martin Westlake, 'The European Parliament, The National Parliaments and the 1996

have no influence. On the contrary, acting through the Council of Ministers, national governments have considerable power. Official recognition of the principles of subsidiarity and proportionality also potentially strengthens the position of the Member States against the centralised European Community institutions.[41]

The influence of the Member States on legislative activity is easily observed by the relative positions of the institutions and to what extent they consider the views of the Member States as well as by the work of the national Permanent Representatives in the drafting and discussion of the legislative documents. The fact that one of the key discussions leading to the Amsterdam Treaty concerned the number of seats in the various institutions for the purpose of national representation also suggests that the Member States play an important role.

In this regard, the size of the Commission has long been a matter of concern. It is considered by some as too large, with the result that it is less cohesive and co-ordinated.[42] This has implications for the democratic effectiveness of the Community: on the one hand, the fact that the larger States have two members provides for a greater political pluralism because they can appoint one member each from the government and opposition party. On the other hand, there is a need to protect the interests of the small Member States.[43] The result of the Amsterdam summit discussions is that the Commission will continue to have twenty members even after the enlargement of the Community and that the larger states will each give up

---

Intergovernmental Conference' (1995) 66 *The Political Quarterly*, 59–73, esp. at pp. 67–69.

41   Cf Deborah Z. Cass, 'The Word That Saves Maastricht? The Principle of Subsidiarity and the Division of Powers Within the European Community' (1992) 29 *CMLR* 1107–1136. Siedentopf claims as fact the stronger national influence on the process of Community decision–making: Heinrich Siedentopf, 'The Implementation of Directives in the Member States' in Heinrich Siedentopf and Jaques Ziller (eds), *Making European Policies Work: The Implementation of Community Legislation in the Member States*, Volume 1 (Sage, London, 1988), 169–180, at p. 171.

42   John Fitzmaurice, 'The European Commission', in Andrew Duff, John Pinder and Roy Pryce (eds), *Maastricht and Beyond: Building the European Union* (Routledge, London, 1994) 179–189 at p. 182.

43   *Ibid.*, at 181–2. See also Juliet Lodge, 'EC Policy–making: Institutional Dynamics' in Juliet Lodge (ed.), *The European Community and the Challenge of the Future* (2nd ed.) (Pinter, London, 1993) 1–36, at p. 6, where Lodge demonstrates the tension between the 'Big Four' and the smaller or newer States.

one of their two commissioners. A review will be made after the next, pending, enlargement of the Community to twenty Member States.[44]

Another indication of the importance of the Member States' views is the need for the Commission to gain their co–operation. As an independent institution, the Commission is 'required to be above national loyalties'.[45] This is open to question since the balance of power requires the Commission to seek the co–operation of national governments.[46] The level of influence and effectiveness of national lobbying of the Commission varies among the Member States.[47] Thus, the German administration is observed by the Commission to be the most developed and reads everything produced by the Commission. This may be because Germany, as the Union's biggest contributor of money, drawing most advantage, through exports, from the open market, has a particularly keen interest.

On the other hand, Germany does not lobby the Commission as effectively as the UK. The UK Permanent Representatives are a very active government lobby. As civil servants they receive instructions from the DTI and they stay in Brussels for a long time. The DTI takes its role seriously and this includes negotiating and lobbying with the Commission and other Member States over new legislation and compliance issues, and advice and support for businesses at home.[48] Further evidence of the UK's strong lobbying activity is that DGXV receives lots of letters from British Members of Parliament asking for information on behalf of constituents. Indeed, approximately 80% of the letters to DGXV come from the UK. In other states, however, MPs have greater freedom and independence and are in less contact with their citizens.

As has been noted, the Council of Ministers became stronger as the Commission's strength declined. The Member States through the Council of Ministers act both collectively and individually. Thus, the collective view is represented by the Council but the individual view is expressed in the negotiations leading to Council decisions. Ministers must therefore be able to commit their governments to decisions taken in the Council.[49] To this end

44 See 'Effective Institutions for an Enlarged Europe', http://europa.eu.int/en/agenda/igc-home/intro/chap4/en_2.htm.
45 T.C. Hartley, *The Foundations of European Community Law* (Clarendon Press, Oxford, 1994) (3rd ed.), p. 12. See also Art 157(2) EC.
46 *Ibid.*, at p. 13.
47 The information noted in the next few paragraphs was obtained in a meeting with Apostolous Iakomidis, of DGXV, Brussels, 21 November 1995.
48 Department of Trade and Industry Report on *Trade in Europe*, 1993.
49 Article 146 EC Treaty.

national interests are defended by the ministers, whose behaviour is motivated by national politics.[50]

The institutional balance of power has also been affected by the use of comitology structures. This 'comitology', in which weighted voting is normal,[51] is alleged to have limited Commission powers to the benefit of national governments, which use the expert and consultative committees tactically to assuage domestic political anxieties.[52] This is made possible because many of the policy–making and administration committees appointed by the Commission for the purpose of harmonisation are staffed with Member State representatives.[53]

Additionally, the Committee of Permanent Representatives (COREPER), which prepares the work of the Council of Ministers, operates through a committee structure and has many sub–committees that are composed of national officials. This allows the views of the Member States to be taken into account. The Permanent Representatives have a national and a European identity. They participate in all stages of the Council decision–making process and have many functions, which include providing information to their national government, putting forward national interests and influencing policy.[54] Although no voting takes place in COREPER the Permanent Representatives will indicate to their ministers how to vote in the Council.[55]

From the UK's perspective,[56] the Permanent Representatives are an outpost of Whitehall civil servants whose role is to seek to ensure that UK policies are understood and if possible taken into account. The UK Permanent Representatives welcome the green papers issued by the Commission and enjoy close informal contact with the Commission, often receiving information before the appearance of a green paper. However, once

---

50   B. Guy Peters, 'Bureaucratic Politics and the Institutions of the European Community' in Alberta M. Sbragia (ed.), *Euro–politics: Institutions and Policymaking in the 'New' European Community* (The Brookings Institution, Washington D.C., 1992) 75–122, at p. 79.

51   Lodge, above, note 43 at p. 14.

52   *Ibid.*

53   For an interesting discussion of the use of committees see Wolf Sauter and Ellen Vos, 'Harmonisation Under Community Law: the Comitology Issue' (paper presented to the W.G. Hart Legal Workshop on *Law Making in the European Union*, London, 1996).

54   Fiona Hayes–Renshaw, Christian Lequesne and Pedro Mayor Lopez, 'The Permanent Representatives of the Member States to the European Communities' (1989) 28 *JCMS* 119–127.

55   *Ibid.*

56   These views were obtained from Anthony Murphy, UK Permanent Representative, in Brussels on 23 November 1995.

a proposal reaches COREPER it has become a political matter by that stage, where there will be strong official national pride with countries fighting their own corner. The working groups which precede COREPER generally look at the detail and normally by then the concept is already secure. The Spanish position is a little different, in part because Spain entered the Community later. The Spanish permanent mission in Europe predated Spain's entry into the Community and was established from 1964.[57] The permanent representation was created by royal decree in 1986.[58] In 1987 Spain had a relatively large number of officials, partly because of Spain's late entry which required as many officials as possible to be educated in a short space of time and partly because of the distance between Madrid and Brussels.[59]

The Spanish Permanent Representative did not consider that Spain had been disadvantaged by her late entry and considered that the conceptual and political aspects of the company legislation presented no problem. Spanish doctrine is similar to the German and many of her rules are similar to the French rules. Furthermore, Spain was willing to compromise with the European position. Spain would also remain outside of what it regards as fruitless discussions, such as those relating to the draft Fifth Directive.[60] The real difficulties for Spain are the technical issues concerning implementation of the Directives and adaptation of Spanish law to them.[61]

At a national level, the Spanish ambassador seeks the views of ministers, lawyers, judges, procurators, academics, and business men who would provide their views indirectly through the Ministry of Economy and Finance or the Ministry of Industry.

Not only the Member States at governmental level have an interest in European legislative activities but so too do those individuals and groups affected by the legislation created. The next section will explore the role of interest groups and how they lobby the European institutions.

5.   THE ROLE OF INTEREST GROUPS AND INDIVIDUALS

The political and institutional structure of the European Community means that national governments no longer have a monopoly over policy making. This has become more centralised and lies strictly with the Commission. The

---

57   Hayes–Renshaw, Lequesne and Mayor Lopez, above note 54 at p. 123.

58   Royal Decree No 260/1986, *Boletin Oficial del Estado*, 13.02.1986.

59   Hayes–Renshaw, Lequesne and Mayor Lopez, above note 54, at p. 124.

60   See Chapters 9 and 10.

61   These views were obtained in a meeting with the Spanish Permanent Representative, who preferred not to be named, in Brussels, 24 November 1995.

European Community has developed what Streeck and Schmitter call a 'supranational political management', meaning that the Community and the Commission would, by having a transnational system of organised interest representation, be able to move away from 'parochial entanglements of national politics and intergovernmental non–decision making' and the Commission would be a 'policy arena and executive body'.[62] Although the Community did not entirely succeed in this objective,[63] it cannot be doubted that lobbying and interest groups have an important role in policy–making and in the legislative process. In particular, the Commission and the Parliament are susceptible to lobbying.[64] The Commission relies on the expertise of specialist groups with the result that for more technical matters expert knowledge carries more political weight.[65] Lobbying takes place at both the European and the national level. Certainly, the DTI has sought more involvement in the UK from individual firms.[66]

The extent of the lobbying of European institutions by interest groups is indicated by the statistics. According to the Commission, there are three thousand special interest groups in Brussels, with more than five hundred European and international federations. There are more than two thousand individual firms with direct representation and one hundred consultants.[67] Kohler–Koch suggests that there are 10,000 lobbyists.[68] Since the introduction of qualified majority voting the need for lobbying has increased with the possibility of blocking votes.[69] This seems likely to stay since the decisions made at the Amsterdam Summit in 1997.

The Commission expressed the two forms of dialogue it has had with specialist interest groups: through advisory committees and expert groups which assist the Commission in the exercise of its own competences; and

---

62   Wolfgang Streeck and Philippe C. Schmitter, 'From National Corporatism to Transnational Pluralism: Organised Interests in the Single European Market' (1991) 19 *Politics and Society*, 133–64, esp. at pp. 134–5.

63   *Ibid.*

64   Mazey and Richardson refer to the Parliament as being subject to lobbying 'overload': Sonia Mazey and Jeremy Richardson, 'Pressure Groups and Lobbying in the EC' in Juliet Lodge (ed.), *The European Community and the Challenge of the Future* (2nd ed.) (Pinter, London, 1993) 37–47, at p. 41.

65   Beate Kohler–Koch, 'Changing Patterns of Interest Intermediation in the European Union' (1994) 29 *Government and Opposition* 166–180, at p. 170.

66   Department of Trade and Industry Report on *Trade in Europe*, 1993.

67   European Commission Communication, *An open and structured dialogue between the Commission and special interest groups* (93/C/02) [OJ C 63, 5.3.93 at p. 2].

68   Kohler–Koch, above note 65, at p. 174.

69   This view is confirmed by UNICE, see below, note 81.

through contact with interest groups on an unstructured, *ad hoc* basis. The nature and intensity of these contacts vary.[70] The Commission has also highlighted the problems which have evolved from this unclear lobbying process: sometimes lobbying can be aggressive, with misdemeanours such as lobbyists selling draft and official documents, lobbyists misrepresenting themselves to the public, and confidentiality problems.[71]

Since the legislative agenda is set by the policies formed it is necessary for lobbyists to act early in the process and so they seek a close relationship with the Commission. While there is much routine and special interest groups have a formally recognised role at European level they have no guarantee of influence.[72] Indeed, there appears to be a growing aversion on the part of the Commission to lobbying consultants.[73] Whilst it appears possible for national permanent representatives to establish informal contact with the Commission, it is perceived that the Commission is wary of talking to individuals and companies and sometimes of national groups because of the potential subtexts they might have. The Commission appears to be more willing to talk to European–wide groups such as Union of Industrial and Employers' Confederations of Europe (UNICE).[74]

Despite the evidence that lobbying activity has grown significantly as the European Union has evolved, much of it appears to be of poor quality. Hull observes that presentations are often poor and ineffective.[75] This leads to dissatisfaction by the lobbyists and those they represent.

Within the company law sphere lobbying has played an important role in the harmonisation process. At European level the key lobbyists with whom the institutions have contact are UNICE and the European Trade Unions Congress (ETUC). Of these the most important is perhaps UNICE (at least

---

70 European Commission Communication, above note 67, at p. 2.

71 *Ibid.*, at p. 3.

72 Jo Shaw, 'A Proposal Too Far? Law, Lawyers and Legal Discourse in the Representation of Interests in the European Union', Paper presented to the W.G. Hart Law Workshop, *Lawmaking in the European Union*, London, 9–11 July 1996.

73 Mazey and Richardson, above note 64, at p. 38.

74 Information provided by Anthony Murphy, UK PR in Brussels, 23 November 1995.

75 Robert Hull, 'Lobbying Brussels: A View from Within' in Sonia Mazey and Jeremy Richardson (eds), *Lobbying in the European Community* (Oxford University Press, Oxford, 1993) 82–92. This could lead to problems of accountability since lobbying squeezes citizens out of the law–making process: see Daniela Obradovic, 'Accountability of Interest Groups in the Union Lawmaking Process'. Paper presented to the W.G. Hart Legal Workshop on *Lawmaking in the European Union*, London, 9–11 July 1996.

in the company law field)[76] where around 2000 people are involved in the lobbying process.

UNICE was set up in 1958 and is 'the official voice of European business and industry *vis-à-vis* the EU institutions'.[77] UNICE is composed of 33 central industry and employers' federations from 25 countries and works on a committee–based structure. Most members of UNICE's federations are small and medium–sized enterprises and craft industries. UNICE has a Committee of Permanent Delegates which acts as an information exchange and has a co–ordinating role.[78] Collie provides a description of the organisation of UNICE and gives an account of how UNICE was considered to be 'lack–lustre, under–resourced and hide–bound in its method of operation and ineffective in representing the interests of business'.[79] UNICE has, since those criticisms, undergone internal reforms and is now regarded as better equipped to deal with the dynamics of the institutional context in which it operates.[80]

The manner in which UNICE corresponds with the Commission follows a basic procedure. This tends to be that the Commission first informs UNICE of its policies at an early stage.[81] UNICE is therefore able to react early to this information, which both helps to achieve a more co–operative relationship between the Commission and UNICE and can accelerate the decision making. The second stage in the procedure is for UNICE to prepare an official paper. UNICE is lobbied in the Council by the national representatives in this respect and, in turn, UNICE lobbies in the European Parliament and the Economic and Social Committee, having a close relationship with the employers' group in that Committee. UNICE sees its contact with the Parliament as more important since the introduction of the co–decision procedure which claims to have given to the Parliament a

---

76   According to the Commission member with whom I spoke, the trade unions tend not to be interested in company law matters apart from aspects of worker participation. However, they are informed of what is going on at EC level in company law: views obtained from Apostoulos Iakomidis, Brussels, 20 November 1995.

77   UNICE publicity leaflet, *The Voice of European Business and Industry*.

78   Lynn Collie, 'Business lobbying in the European Community: The Union of Industrial and Employers' Confederations of Europe' in Mazey and Richardson (1993) above note 75, 213–229, at p. 215.

79   *Ibid*, at p. 213.

80   *Ibid*, at p. 214.

81   The earliness or otherwise of this information passed to UNICE can be variable – information supplied by Heinz Kröger, Secretary General of UNICE, Brussels, 20 November 1995. The following account of UNICE's activities is derived from information obtained in that meeting with Mr Kröger.

stronger official voice. The third stage in the lobbying procedure is for UNICE to report back to the national federations regularly.

The diverse membership of UNICE appears in practice not to have led to major conflicts of interest between members. UNICE witnessed many different views from the national federations leading up to the adoption of the Fourth Directive on accounts but was able to reach a compromise. UNICE favours collective action and is sceptical about single companies making contact with the European institutions. Collective action could be better structured.

Some national federations appear to have more of a presence in UNICE than others. UNICE considers, for example, the CBI, the UK's industry confederation, as very active. The UK appears, from UNICE's point of view, to have been involved in the development of most of the company law Directives. On the other hand, Spain, as a latecomer, joined the Community when most of the current Directives were already in place. Two further reasons for Spain's relatively quiet role suggested by UNICE are that company law is not a priority in Spain, probably because the Spanish company law doctrine is largely compatible with the European Community's approach, and Madrid is still geographically relatively distant from Brussels so that experts are sent from Spain to Brussels only for subjects with high priority.

These different levels of involvement in UNICE may alter the balance of influence between the Member States and the interests being represented. This can lead to dissatisfaction. Even in the UK there has been expressed disappointment at the achievements of the CBI. The potential reasons for the CBI's failure to make significant progress in Europe are that it is, in reality, only one of hundreds of lobbyists; that many decisions are not actually taken in Brussels and so attention is focused in the wrong place; and that Britain has a different regulatory and judicial system, making the UK's representation tasks more difficult.[82]

Clearly, lobbying has an important role in policy and lawmaking in the European Union.[83] The field of company law is no exception. Although it can have a positive influence on the legislation produced there are a number of problems that this lobbying activity presents. The voices of some interest groups may be louder simply because they are better organised or resourced

---

82 See Richard Eberlie, 'The Confederation of British Industry and Policy–Making in the European Community' in Mazey and Richardson (1993), above note 75, 201–212.

83 Both UNICE and ETUC were keen to make their interests known at the Amsterdam Summit in 1997: see press releases at the following websites: http://europa.eu.int/en/agenda/igc–home/instdoc/social/unamsten.htm; and http://europa.eu.int/en/agenda/igc–home/instdoc/social/etucamst.htm.

rather than because their case has more merit. The quality of lobbying can be poor and so leads to time wasting for the institutions being lobbied, and the playing field for different interests competing for information, and finally results, may not be very level. The limits of lobbying for democratic purposes are linked to these problems,[84] despite the fact that it could signify action by the people targeted by laws rather than by the politicians alone. On the other hand, lobbying may, in reality, distance those people from the political arena.

6.   CONCLUSION

The above description of the institutional arrangements of the European Community suggests that the Community is far removed from the most basic definition of democracy: government by the people. The size of the Community and the complexity of its membership means that representative democracy is the only realistic possible form of democracy at the policy and law–making level. As more decisions fall into the remit of the centralised Community institutions the quality of the arrangements for representative democracy becomes more important. However, despite claims to be democratic, the evidence suggests that the Community has not achieved this fully. The focus on separation of powers of the institutions seems to be misplaced and more emphasis should fall on the limitation of their powers, at least by ensuring that they are genuinely accountable. The powers of the European Parliament, as the formal representative of the people should also be taken more seriously if the representatives are to be truly responsive to the electors. Steps have been taken in this direction but there is still too much secrecy and the Council still seems to enjoy too much power. The legislative procedures have altered and seek to redress the balance. These changes, together with increased emphasis on majority voting, may be regarded as positive developments. However, the changes have added to the complexity of the Community's institutional arrangements.

Participation is confined to Member States and to lobbying by interest groups. The problem here is that the representatives become further removed from their electorate. There is also little evidence of equality in these processes. In order to assess the quality of the democracy in practical terms

---

84   James L. Hyland, *Democratic Theory: The Philosophical Foundations* (Manchester University Press, Manchester, 1995) 239–240 (noting the use of money to influence political decisions); cf Patrick Dunleavy, *Democratic Bureaucracy and Public Choice: Economic Explanations in Political Science* (Harvester Wheatsheaf, London, 1991) Ch. 3.

it is necessary to consider the practical operation of the arrangements by exploring how they might have impacted on the legislation produced at European Community level. The company law harmonisation programme provides an interesting case study and its development will be the focus of the next chapter.

6 The Company Law Programme as an Illustration of EC Representative Democracy

1. INTRODUCTION

The previous chapter revealed the difficulties in identifying the influences on European Community legislation. The relationships between the institutions, and the role of the Member States and interest groups in shaping the legislation form an arrangement which lacks transparency and which is made more complex by the variety of procedures used.

The company law programme, in which all the available legislative procedures have been used for its development, provides an opportunity to test these criticisms. The first two generations of directives were adopted under the consultation procedure. The third generation followed the co–operation procedure, which purported to improve the position of the Parliament against the other institutions. The draft Thirteenth Directive represents the fourth generation and is currently being negotiated under the co–decision procedure. Throughout the duration of the harmonisation programme the Community has moved gradually towards replacing unanimous voting requirements with more qualified majority voting. This may also affect the negotiations and the eventual substance of the legislation produced at Community level.

This chapter will provide specific examples from the company law programme of how the different procedures have operated in practice. The development of the Accounts Directives will illustrate the consultation procedure. This will be shown by considering the differences between the drafts, the opinions of the Parliament and of the Economic and Social Committee and the versions adopted. The role of the Member States in the negotiations will also be explored. In a similar fashion, the Twelfth Directive will serve as a case study of the co–operation procedure. The draft Thirteenth Directive, which is following the co–decision procedure, is now in its third draft. This chapter will speculate on the prospective final version by considering the differences between the present draft and the earlier drafts as well as exploring the views of the Member States.

2.   FIRST AND SECOND GENERATION DIRECTIVES

As has been noted, the first and second generation directives were created under the consultation procedure. Under that procedure the opinion of the European Parliament was sought, as was, where appropriate, the opinion of the Economic and Social Committee. On the basis of their opinions a report would be prepared for the Council by the Committee of Permanent Representatives. If the Committee of Permanent Representatives endorsed the proposal it would be adopted by the Council. Otherwise, a full debate would occur and the Council would conduct a vote. The Council would not be required to give reasons if it did not adopt the Parliament's opinion. A new Parliamentary opinion would be required only if the amended proposal were not 'substantially identical' to the original proposal.

A.   The First Directive

The compromise sought in the negotiations for the first generation directives resulted in complex and prescriptive provisions, with very little discretion offered to the Member States. For example, comparing the draft of the First Directive[1] proposed by the Commission with its final form, one can see several changes. From the resolutions of the Parliament[2] and of ECOSOC[3] on the draft it is possible to trace from where or by whom the changes originate. It is also possible to identify which suggestions were not adopted. Generally, both Parliament and ECOSOC welcomed the introduction of the Directive. Many of the amendments proposed concern drafting points rather than substantive issues. Parliament was less critical and approximately half of the Parliament's suggestions were accepted.[4] Overall, Parliament did not appear to enjoy a huge influence. Moreover, many changes which appeared in the final version remain unaccounted for.[5] This may suggest a strong influence of the Council and of Member States.

The first enlargement of the Community introduced the views of more Member States into legislative negotiations. Whilst the procedure remained the same the enlargement appeared to affect the character of the legislation, making it more flexible than the first generation directives. This is reflected in the Accounts Directives which are very detailed and contain many optional

---

1   OJ C 27.11.64, p. 3254.
2   OJ C 96, 28.5.66, p. 1519.
3   OJ C 194, 27.11.64, p. 3248.
4   See eg Articles 4(5) and 9(1) and (2).
5   See Articles 2(1) (f), (2), 2(2), 3(5), 6, 11(2)(c)–(l), 12(1) and (2).

provisions for Member States and companies to operate. The next section will consider the development of the Accounts Directives.

B. The Accounts Directives

The Accounts Directives are a result of compromise, accommodating the different accounting traditions of the Member States. In this respect, the UK was invited to participate in the discussions prior to her joining the Community and it will be seen that the UK's model influenced the eventual character of the Accounts Directives.

(i) The Fourth Directive

Institutional Influences
From the history of the Fourth Directive's legislative development it is not entirely clear to what extent the views of the Parliament and the Economic and Social Committee influenced the final, adopted version of the Directive.[6] The Fourth Directive was adopted in 1978[7] following several drafts. The first working draft on which the European Parliament and the Economic and Social Committee gave their opinions appeared in 1972.[8] Some of the European Parliament's suggested amendments were accepted. For example, the Parliament suggested that the notes to the accounts include disclosure of material income and charges. Provisions to this effect were included in the final version of the Directive.[9]

However, some amendments suggested and taken up in the final version of the Directive were also suggested by other bodies. For example, in Article 23 of the final version of the Directive there appears a prescriptive sub–division of the staff expenditure accounts, taking account of state responsibility such as social security, which the Parliament had suggested in its resolution.[10] Yet, this was also suggested by the Economic and Social

---

6   See Lorna Woods and Charlotte Villiers, 'Legislative Process and Democracy: The Development of European Company Law' (paper presented to the W.G. Hart Legal Workshop, *Law Making in the European Union*, London, July 1996).
7   OJ 1978 L 222, 14.8.78, p. 11.
8   OJ 1972 C 7, 28.1.72 p. 10. The Parliament's Resolution appeared at OJ 1972 C 129, 11.12.72, p. 38. The Economic and Social Committee's Opinion appeared at OJ 1973 C 39, 7.6.73, p. 31.
9   Articles 18 and 21.
10 OJ 1972 C 129 at p. 42.

Committee.[11] Indeed, in other matters the views of the Economic and Social Committee appear to have been given more weight than the European Parliament. For example, the Economic and Social Committee proposed in its opinion that accounts be required to give 'as true a view as possible'.[12] This is closer to the final version than the Parliament's preference for a 'faithful image'.[13] The more pragmatic approach of the Economic and Social Committee, accepting the influence of the Anglo–Saxon approach on the negotiations between the Member States, appeared to win favour over the Parliament's perspective by the Commission and the Council.

Member States' Influence

The first draft of the Fourth Directive was published in 1971 under the influence of the German Aktiengesetz 1965.[14] Its prescriptive nature had a creditor–oriented approach and a conservative, tax–based system of law and accounting.[15] The UK, together with Ireland and Denmark, joined the European Community in 1973, and in 1971 the Group d'Etudes had invited representatives from countries intending to join the Community to discuss the proposed accounting legislation. The UK's influence was visible in the subsequent drafts of 1974 and 1978. For example, liabilities and reserves could be rearranged towards a more British approach. The UK's 'going concern' and 'accruals' conventions were also added to the 1974 draft, together with alternatives to historical cost valuation. In 1971 there had been a move from this German concept, possibly to accommodate the Dutch. For example, the 1971 draft allows use of replacement value for fixed assets and stocks.[16] But the 1974 and 1978 drafts allow greater flexibility, with provision for the British *ad hoc* revaluations of individual fixed assets. Further testimony to the influence of the UK is the Anglo–Saxon concept of 'true and fair view' which became the Directive's overriding principle. The German principle was valuation provisions. By 1974 both principles were on equal terms. In the House of Lords Select Committee Fourth Report on the

---

11   OJ 1973 C 39 at p. 36.

12   OJ 1973 C 39 at p. 33.

13   OJ 1972 C 129 at p. 39.

14   Work for the Fourth Directive began in 1965 under the chairmanship of a German accountant, Dr. Elmendorff.

15   Nigel Savage, 'Law and Accounting – The Impact of EEC Directives on Company Law' (1980) 1 *Company Lawyer* 24–29 and 91–94, at p. 28. See also R. Neihus, 'Harmonised EEC Accounting – A German View of the Draft Directive for Uniform Accounting Rules' (1972) 2 *International Journal of Accounting* 102.

16   Article 30.1.

Fourth Directive,[17] it was suggested that the true and fair view principle should override all the other principles. The Department of Trade recognised the problem of defining the concept, arguing that accounts can only be true if they follow an acceptable accounting policy. Witnesses for the UK accountancy profession also expressed the opinion that the draft of the Fourth directive was 'too rigid and dirigiste' and they asked for more options. By 1978 the concept of true and fair view had fully taken precedence. The final version also contained many options.

(ii) The Seventh Directive

Institutional Influences

The European Parliament and the Economic and Social Committee gave opinions on the draft of the Seventh Directive.[18] The Economic and Social Committee's concerns concentrated on international standards. In this respect the Committee observed the work of international organisations on group accounts and urged the Commission to endeavour to ensure 'maximum conformity between international and European standards'.[19] Corresponding with this observation the Committee suggested a positive duty, rather than a negative duty, to adopt consistent methods of consolidation.[20] This suggestion was taken up in the final version of the Directive.[21] The Economic and Social Committee expressed support for uniformity in preference to ambiguous provisions, thus favouring more specific rules for departures from general principles, ie 'only if and in so far as application of this principle is impossible or in all fairness impracticable'.[22] The final version of the Directive is much more lenient, however, and does not appear to have taken up the Committee's view.[23]

The Committee also considered that some definitions were 'rather vague', such as those relating to 'significant influence' and 'dominant influence'. By contrast, the Parliament approved of these concepts. The same concepts

---

17   HL 24, Session 1975–76.

18   The draft directive appeared at OJ 1976 C 121, 2.6.76, p. 3. The Parliament's Resolution appeared at OJ 1978 C 163, 10.7.78, p. 60. The Economic and Social Committee's Opinion appeared at OJ 1977 C 75 26.3.77, p. 5.

19   OJ 1977 C 75, 26.3.77 at p. 6, para. 1.7.

20   OJ 1977 C 75, 26.3.77 at p. 7, commenting on Article 14(1)(a) of the Commission's draft.

21   Article 25.

22   OJ C 75, 26.3.77, p. 5, para. 1.6.

23   Article 29.2 (a).

appear in the final version of the Directive, suggesting that the Commission and the Council preferred the Parliament's view to the view of the Economic and Social Committee. The Committee also worried about problems for smaller groups and requested that the Commission consider these.[24] For example, it expressed the opinion that the requirement of information on net turnover could be prejudicial to small groups as regards competition.[25] The fears of the Committee in this respect also appear to have been ignored by the Commission and the Council.[26]

The emphasis of the European Parliament was also focused on a need for greater clarity[27] but it did not always appear to be as rigid as that of the Economic and Social Committee. In any event, not all the Parliament's suggestions were taken up. For example, its suggestion to omit the words 'clearly and' with regard to the drawing up and presentation of consolidated accounts was not followed.[28] Neither was the Parliament's suggested requirement of information on non–dependent holdings sought by the final Directive.[29] On the other hand, some more substantive changes suggested by the Parliament were taken up. For example, regarding valuation taking into account deferred taxation, the Parliament suggested that the difference arising on consolidation between tax chargeable for the financial year and earlier years should be shown if that will be a material difference. This is added to the final version, though more specifically with regard to a foreseeable actual tax charge that will arise for one of the undertakings in the group.[30] In conclusion, there does not appear to be a clear line taken by the Commission or Council as regards the views of the other institutions. Some of their substantive suggestions are accepted, others are not. Similarly, some of their suggestions of presentation are taken up and others are not.

Member States' Influence
The Seventh Directive originated as a preliminary draft in 1974, based on the German legislation of 1965. The final version of the Seventh Directive contains 51 articles – almost twice the length of the first draft which had only

---

24   See eg its comments on Articles 6.1 (a) and 20.7.

25   OJ 1977 C 75, 26.3.77 at p. 8, para. 2.16.

26   The same requirement appears, though slightly modified, in the final version: Article 34.8.

27   See eg OJ 1978 C 163/60 at paras 13, 15.

28   Article 16 of the final version retains these words.

29   A more relaxed option is given to Member States to permit or require other information – this other information is not specified.

30   Article 29.4.

27 articles.[31] A memorandum on group accounting was delivered by the Elmendorff Committee to the Commission in 1970. The memorandum highlighted the requirement of compliance with the law and uniformity of formats. Under the German influence, the original draft of the Directive contained rigid rules on structure, form and content of the group accounts.

The German influence was subsequently replaced by the Anglo–Saxon influence. By the time the Directive was adopted in 1983 its character had changed significantly. Major changes to the Directive occurred at the stage of Government negotiations where, according to Diggle and Nobes, political pressures, nationalism, lobbying, government tax concerns, and competitiveness prevail.[32] In the UK the House of Lords Select Committee reacted with interest to the draft directive[33] and stated that the definition of 'group' was the most contentious issue. The definition of parent and subsidiary shows a dramatic change from the German notion of the single economic unit[34] towards the Anglo–Saxon, legalistic approach by the time the Seventh Directive had reached its final draft. Thus, reference is made in the Directive to a majority of the voting rights, and the right to appoint or remove a majority of the board, as examples of control necessary to be classed as a parent undertaking. What may be observed by this definition is a compromise between Continental and British definitions.[35] Thus, an undertaking is a parent undertaking if it holds a majority of the voting rights in the undertaking, *or* it is a member of the undertaking and has the right to appoint or remove a majority of its board of directors, *or* it has the right to direct the operating and financial policies of the undertaking, *or* is a member of the undertaking and controls alone, pursuant to an agreement with other

---

31   Articles 42–46 were intended to replace certain provisions in the earlier adopted Fourth Directive, following the adoption of the Seventh Directive on consolidated accounts.

32   Graham Diggle and Christopher Nobes, 'European Rule–Making in Accounting: The Seventh Directive as a Case Study' (1994) 24 *Accounting and Business Research* 319–333, at p. 321.

33   HL 25, Session 1976–77, *Group Accounts*.

34   See AktG §329, 1965, 'if the combine [sic] enterprises of a combine are under the uniform direction of a stock corporation... the board of management of the head association... shall prepare... a consolidated balance sheet etc': translated by R. Mueller and E.G. Galbraith in *The German State Corporation Law* (Knapp, Frankfurt, 1976) and cited by Diggle and Nobes, above note 32, at p. 322.

35   Richard Plender, 'A Tale of Three Directives' (1992) 104 *Accountancy*, August, 72–73.

shareholders or members, a majority of the voting rights in the undertaking.[36]

The original draft of the Seventh Directive did require a true and fair view on a basis equal to the requirement to comply with the provisions of the Directive but this came to be the overriding principle in the final version.[37] Similarly, changes to the concept of goodwill showed a move away from the German approach. Initially, goodwill could not be recognised as a specific asset. However, it became possible later for goodwill to be amortised over a period of up to five years or longer up to its useful economic life.[38] Diggle and Nobes identify at least fourteen aspects in which the final Directive was closer to the Anglo–Saxon tradition than to the German as a result of substitution or adding options.[39]

(iii) The Eighth Directive

Institutional Influences

The first Commission proposal for an Eighth Directive on the approval of persons responsible for carrying out the statutory audits of accounting documents was published in 1975.[40] However, the proposal worked on and considered by the Economic and Social Committee[41] and the European Parliament[42] was published in 1978.[43] The final Directive was adopted in 1984.[44]

The enacted Directive indicates acceptance by the Commission and the Council of a number of the suggestions of both the Parliament and the Economic and Social Committee. For example, the practical difficulties in harmonising the laws of the Member States are recognised in the longer

---

36   *Ibid.*, referring to the then current Companies Bill, Clause 19(2), my emphasis added.
37   Diggle and Nobes, above note 32, at p. 325.
38   Diggle and Nobes, above note 32, at p. 327.
39   These include: definition of parent; legal form of parent company; groups with no parent company; foreign subsidiaries included; dissimilar subsidiaries excluded; permitted exclusions; true and fair view override; uniform policies required; merger accounting allowed; equity method required for associates; joint ventures to be equity accounted or proportionally consolidated; date of goodwill calculation; use of fair values; choice of goodwill treatment. See Diggle and Nobes above note 32, at p. 328.
40   OJ C 317 18.12.1975, p. 6.
41   OJ C 171 9.7.1979, p. 30.
42   OJ C 140 5.6.1979, p. 154.
43   OJ C 112, 13.5.1978, p. 6.
44   OJ L 126, 12.5.1984, p. 20.

timetable given in the final version. The earlier version required the Member States to implement the Directive within eighteen months and to apply it within the following two years. The final version, however, was to be implemented within three and a half years and applicable within the following two years.[45] Here we can see at least a partial recognition of the European Parliament's concerns about the practical difficulties.[46] The European Parliament's suggestion that a Contact Committee be set up to facilitate the harmonised application of the Directive was also taken up in the final version.[47] The Parliament's suggestion that practical training could come after the examination was taken up too.[48] Some of the Economic and Social Committee's suggestions were also observed, such as deletion of the reference to supervised practical training. The Economic and Social Committee also suggested separating the reference to good repute and independence in order to emphasise the importance of independence.[49] This separation appeared in the final Directive.

On the other hand, the reference to independence also illustrates some departures in the final Directive from suggestions made by the Parliament and the Economic and Social Committee. The need for independence of auditors is clear. Article 11 of the earlier draft gave a detailed indication of what independence should mean. This was replaced in the final version by an article requiring steps to be taken which would not compromise or damage independence.[50] Thus, instead of positive rules on independence, the final version adopts a limited approach allowing freedom up to the point that it adversely affects independence. This came despite clear approval of the focus on the independence of auditors by both the Economic and Social Committee and the Parliament. Another departure is evidenced by the Economic and Social Committee's suggestions of including a non–binding appendix and a committee on the subject matters for study[51] which were not taken up in the final version of the Directive. Similarly, although the Economic and Social Committee and the European Parliament also approved a rule in the earlier draft on confidentiality of audit documents, the rule is omitted from the adopted version.

---

45   Article 30.
46   Parliament had recommended two years for implementation by Member States and a further three years for those implementation measures to be applied.
47   Article 29.
48   Final Directive, Article 4.
49   OJ 1979 C 171 9.7.79 at p. 32, para. 2.3.1.
50   Article 24.
51   OJ 1979 C 171, 9.7.79, at p. 32, paras 2.6.1 and 2.6.2.

Member States' Influence

The Eighth Directive shows a willingness by the legislators to leave key decisions to the Member States. The Member States' individual competences in approving appropriate auditors' qualifications are recognised in the final version. In the earlier draft the initiative for approval appeared to lie with members of professional associations who should seek approval from Member States. In the final version the Member States may give the approval, without being requested to do so by the professions. This change in emphasis shows the importance of the Member States' views and the need to achieve compromise between them. Thus, acknowledgement of the differences between Member States and the need to harmonise without creating uniform or rigid central rules is revealed in Article 11 of the final version. Previously there was a need for 'objectively equivalent' qualifications. The final version leaves this decision to the competent authorities of the Member States, which will not require proof of sufficient legal knowledge obtained in another State. Other Articles in the final version that recognise the autonomy of the Member States' authorities include Article 14, referring to their approval of firms of auditors before entry into force of the Directive, the ability of Member States to apply transitional measures in certain situations,[52] and the issue of independence.[53]

In conclusion, the example of the Accounts Directives displays considerable uncertainty about the level of influence enjoyed by the European Parliament and the Economic and Social Committee on the contents and characteristics of European legislation adopted under the consultation procedure. Notably, neither institution challenged the draft Directives in such a way as to alter their basic character or structure. Their suggestions were focused more on matters of detail. While their views were not consistently ignored it seems that their more practical or pragmatic suggestions had the best chance of being taken up. Their suggestions of substance, however, though sometimes followed, generally faced more difficulty in being accepted. This suggests a relatively weak voice for the formal representatives of European citizens in legislative decision–making. Indeed, the consultation process was notorious for its negative effect on the role of the European Parliament, leading to the development of the co–operation procedure and, later, the co–decision procedure, in order to strengthen the Parliament's position against the other legislative institutions.[54]

---

52   Articles 16 and 18.
53   Article 24. The failure to reach a decision on the definition of independence in the Council of Ministers was confirmed in the European Commission's Green Paper, *The Role, Position and Liability of Auditors*, July 1996.
54   Woods and Villiers, above note 6.

By contrast with the views of the Parliament and the Economic and Social Committee, the views of the Member States appear to have been more persuasive in the elaboration of the Accounts Directives. This is hardly surprising given that in order for the legislation to be genuinely effective Member States would have to be willing to implement it. That would require their co-operation. The fact that all of the Accounts Directives grew considerably in length from their earlier drafts, because of the options and more detailed definitions, reflects a need for compromise between the views of the Member States in order to achieve their co-operation. This is also reflected by the fact that the time limits for implementation and application of the Directives were generally extended. What is also evident in the above discussion is the considerable influence that the UK enjoyed once she entered the negotiations. This suggests that the size of the Community and its membership would influence the content of the Directives.

The 'third generation' directives followed a second enlargement of the Community which may also have affected the character of the legislation. Another influence may have been the change of legislative procedure from consultation to co-operation. The next section will follow the progress of the Twelfth Directive as a case study of the third generation directives.

3.   THIRD GENERATION DIRECTIVES

The third generation directives were created under the co-operation procedure which was introduced by the Single European Act 1986.[55] Under this procedure the Commission proposes the legislation and the Parliament is consulted. The Council then adopts a common position under qualified majority voting which is then passed to the Parliament. If the Parliament approves the common position or makes no decision on it, the Council will then formally adopt it. Alternatively, the Parliament may suggest amendments which will require a re-examination of the proposal by the Commission. Further, the Parliament may reject the common position. This will require a unanimous decision by the Council in order to go on to adopt it. Only if the Parliament has support of a Member State will it be able to veto the common position.

The Twelfth Directive provides an illustration of the operation of this procedure.

---

55   OJ 1986 L 169/1; Article 189(c) EC Treaty. See John Fitzmaurice, 'An Analysis of the European Community's Co-operation Procedure' (1988) 26 *JCMS* 389; Richard Corbett, 'Testing the New Procedure: The European Parliament's First Experiences with New 'Single Act' Powers' (1989) 27 *JCMS* 359.

A.   The Twelfth Directive

Following discussions during 1987 within the Commission, between DGXV and a special task force on small and medium–sized enterprises, the Commission submitted to the Council a proposal for a Twelfth Directive on 19 May 1988.[56] The Commission received the opinions of the European Parliament[57] and of the Economic and Social Committee[58] on its initial proposal and sent to the Council an amended proposal[59] incorporating the substance of the changes requested by Parliament. The Council reached a common position in July 1989[60] on which the Parliament gave a second reading,[61] leading to a re–examined proposal in October 1989[62] detailing the Commission's decision on the Parliament's amendments. The Directive was eventually adopted on 21 December 1989.[63] Through this procedure the views of the Member States were obtained as well as the views of economic and industrial bodies such as UNICE, and of the Institute of Chartered Secretaries and Administrators,[64] under European and national consultation procedures on the proposed Directive,[65] the results of which were passed to the Commission.

By the time the Directive was adopted in December 1989 its detailed contents had altered quite significantly from the original proposal. The initial proposal for the Twelfth Directive was quite restrictive, reflecting more the French position, which approached the subject from the view of giving to the individual entrepreneur limited responsibility.[66] The definitive version has a

---

56   COM (88) 101 final – SYN 135, OJ C 173, 2.7.88, p. 10.

57   OJ C 96, 17.4.1989, p. 92.

58   OJ C 318, 12.12.1988, p. 9.

59   OJ C 152, 20.6.1989, p. 10.

60   Council Document 7459/89 of 20.6.1989.

61   EP Document A3–43/89, Minutes of the sitting of 11 October 1989 (Min. 26 II), p. 22.

62   Commission Document, XV/237/89, 22.10.1989.

63   OJ L 395, 30.12.1989, p. 40.

64   See eg Position Paper of The Institute of Chartered Secretaries and Administrators, *Comments on the Consultative Document on the EC Proposal for a Twelfth Company Law Directive Concerning Single–Member Private Limited Liability Companies* (London, 30 September 1988).

65   For example, in the UK the DTI published a Consultative Document on the proposal in 1988.

66   See Frank Wooldridge, 'The Draft Twelfth Directive on Single–Member Companies' (1989) *JBL* 86–90, at p. 89, noting the criticisms of UNICE in its position paper on the draft Directive, 29 September 1988, at p. 3.

broader approach and offers more possibilities, both for Member States and for individual entrepreneurs. The most notable differences between the two texts include: the eventual omission of the requirement of nominative shares;[67] the eventual possibility of Member States laying down special provisions or sanctions where single member companies are created outside the restricted contexts;[68] deletion of the prohibition on legal persons being the single member of another company;[69] the disappearance of the reference to a fixed minimum capital where the single member is a legal person;[70] addition of the identity of the shareholder being disclosed in a register kept by the company but available to the public;[71] deletion of the prohibition on delegation of powers of the general meeting;[72] and the addition of the need to draw up in writing contracts which would not apply to operations concluded under normal conditions.[73] Overall, the final version has a more flexible character than the original proposal although it emphasised more strongly the need for adequate disclosure to third parties dealing with the company. An examination of who initiated these changes and whose views were noted by the Commission may provide an insight into the co–operation procedure and decision–making process and may indicate the influences on the Commission in setting the initial agenda and overseeing the development of the legislation and how it is drafted and progresses at EC level.[74]

The first observation to make is that the definitive version takes account of the Member States' positions more readily than does the first draft. The final version, like the original proposal, expresses the need for a legal instrument making possible limited liability for individuals. The final version contains this point but adds that this is 'without prejudice to the laws of the Member States which, in exceptional circumstances, require that entrepreneur is to be liable for the obligations of his undertaking'. This reflects a compromise between those States which fully recognise the individual entrepreneur's need for limited liability and those States which demand full responsibility for certain aspects of his or her activities. Similarly, Article 7 of each version are basically equivalent, allowing

---

67 The demand for nominative shares appeared in the original proposal's preamble and in Article 2 of that proposal: OJ C 173, 2.7.88, 10–12.

68 Article 2, Final Directive, OJ L 395, 30.12.89, p. 40–42.

69 Compare original proposal, Article 2.3 with final version Article 2.2.

70 This appeared in the original proposal, Article 2.3(b).

71 Article 3, final version.

72 This appeared in the original proposal, Article 4.1.

73 Article 5, final version.

74 I am grateful to DGXV of the European Commission for providing me with access to internal documentation concerning the progress of the Twelfth Directive.

Member States not to apply the Directive where an entrepreneur can set up business with limited liability devoted to a specific activity on condition that safeguards equivalent to those imposed by the Directive are laid down.[75]

It is not always easy to identify who has more influence. For example, a number of interested participants expressed a wish for nominative shares to be dropped. The initial proposal stated that the shares should be nominative. The final version omits reference to nominative shares, suggesting that these are not necessary. The eventual deletion of the reference to nominative shares came relatively late in the proceedings. UNICE pointed out that this would lead to expense for public companies since such shares would need to be registered.[76] At institutional level the Parliament and the Council were at odds over this provision, the Parliament insisting on nominative shares[77] and the Council suggesting that since under the First Directive the identity of shareholders was already clear these shares were unnecessary.[78] The Commission eventually accepted the view of the Council stating that such a requirement would be superfluous.[79]

Article 2.2 of the Directive states: 'Member States may, pending co–ordination of national laws relating to groups, lay down special provisions or sanctions for cases where: (a) a natural person is the sole member of several companies; and (b) a single member company or any other legal person is the sole member of a company.' This is more flexible than the original proposed version which stated that a single–member company whose sole member was a legal person could not be the sole member of another company, the aim being to prevent chains of single member companies. The inclusion of the reference to special provisions and to sanctions in Article 2.2 where single member companies are introduced outside the permitted contexts appears to be a compromise between the views of the Member States, some of which were more strict than others. The final Article 2, which is more flexible, appears to recognise the views of Member States and of industrial bodies who adopted a more practical approach. For example, UNICE suggested that if the Directive were too restrictive entrepreneurs would not opt to set up single member companies but would continue to use artificial devices to have multi–member companies and the ordinary laws relating to private limited

---

75   This accommodates the Portuguese position.

76   UNICE position paper, 29 September 1989.

77   See eg European Parliament, 1989–90 Session, Doc. PE 135.123.

78   See eg Common Position adopted by the Council, 21 June 1989, Commission Document, SEC (89) 1201 final – SYN 135. This position was reached by deliberations between national representatives, but unfortunately the documents containing these details are restrained.

79   See SEC (89) 1201 final – SYN 135, Brussels, 20 July 1989, at p. 5.

companies applying to them which would be more liberal.[80] The Economic and Social Committee also suggested that the problem of chains of single member companies had been exaggerated.[81] Thus, the eventual Article 2 indicated a recognition by the Commission of the commercial realities, giving to Member States the option to decide to what extent legal persons should be sole members of companies.

Article 3 also became more relaxed by the time it was adopted in that it gives to companies the choice of disclosing the fact that the shares have come to be held by one holder and the identity of that shareholder, either in the file or register within the meaning of the First Directive or in a register kept by the company and accessible to the public. The official introduction of this requirement in the amended proposal was explained as taking account of national legislation of some Member States.[82] There had been suggestions by the Federation Bancaire[83] and the Parliament that single membership of the company should be disclosed on the firm's notepaper and letterheads.[84] The Council, however, regarded this as a bureaucratic and expensive requirement[85] and the Commission also adopted this view, thus leaving out that requirement in the final version.

The later Article 4 omits the earlier expressed prohibition on delegation of the powers of the general meeting but adds an obligation to draw up in writing decisions taken by the sole member. The deletion of the prohibition on delegation of the powers of the general meeting was suggested at all levels of discussion. Taking a practical stance, both the Federation Bancaire[86] and UNICE[87] said that such a prohibition would prevent the use of employee or third party proxies which were frequently used by public companies. A number of Member States[88] as well as the Parliament also suggested dropping this prohibition.[89]

A number of points raised by certain delegations or bodies were not taken up. For example, the criticism by UNICE that the Directive was

---

80   UNICE position paper, 29 September 1989.

81   OJ C 318, 12.12.1988, p. 9.

82   COM (89) 193 final, Brussels, 24 May 1989.

83   Federation Bancaire, *Observations on the Proposal for A Twelfth Council Directive on Company Law Concerning Single–Member Private Limited Companies*, 10.10.1988.

84   European Parliament, Doc. A 3–43/89.

85   Common Position, 21 June 1989.

86   See above note 83.

87   See above note 80.

88   Unfortunately, these details are in restrained documents.

89   See European Parliament, Session 1989–90, Doc. PE 135.123.

limited to small and medium–sized enterprises seems to have been ignored since the real focus of attention appears to be such enterprises. However, it is possible, under Article 6, for Member States to apply the Directive to public companies. The suggestion at several levels of harmonisation on the minimum capital requirement was not taken up, nor were a number of requests for the Directive to include penalties for breach of the provisions.[90] Despite the relevance of other company law directives (the Accounts Directives, in particular) these were only referred to in the recitals rather than more directly in the substantive section of the Directive as had been suggested by the Economic and Social Committee.[91]

The final version of the Directive pays close attention to the need for disclosure. For example, Article 3 makes clear the need to record and disclose the identity of the single member, making that information accessible to the public. The focus on disclosure arguably became stronger by the time the final version of the Directive was adopted. In this way, the original version stated that decisions by the sole member should be recorded. This became mandatory with the final version, substituting the word 'should' with 'must'.[92] In the final version, Article 4 includes an extra requirement to draw up those decisions in writing.

The co–operation procedure was intended to give to the Parliament more power among the EC institutions. Yet the development of the Twelfth Directive, from its initial draft to the version which was finally adopted, does not necessarily confirm that theoretical claim. The evidence suggests that the Commission was prepared to take into account the views of the Parliament. However, the Council also retained significant influence on the outcome of the Directive. In its re–examined proposal the Commission appeared to give more weight to the Council's common position.[93] It is also difficult to say to what extent the Member States influenced the development of the Directive and, more specifically, which Member States had most such influence.[94] For example, it is possible to discern a shift from the French, more restrictive recognition of limited liability for single entrepreneurs, towards a more German sway in favour of full recognition of single member companies. Yet that move may simply be a result of the Commission accepting the commercial reality rather than a preference for German opinions. The views

---

90   Details under restraint.

91   OJ C 318, 12.12.1988, p. 9.

92   Compare the original proposal recitals with the recitals of the final version of the Directive.

93   See Commission Communication to the Parliament, SEC (89) 1201 final – SYN 135.

94   Partly this is because the documents containing details of each Member States' views are under restraint.

of industrial and economic representatives are also important. The suggestion by industrial bodies such as UNICE and the Federation Bancaire that the directive be more flexible and less restrictive in its approach was taken up but this may equally have been a result of the Commission's recognition of the many differences in the views presented by all the participants in the legislative process. One problem in establishing this information is the secrecy surrounding meetings of the Council. Many of the Council documents were restricted, thus it is left to speculation the extent to which Member States influenced the legislation. The remaining suspicion is that such influence was weighty.

Despite these uncertainties, it is clear from the above that the co–operation procedure and the participation of Member States and interest groups in the process all had an influence in shaping the Twelfth Directive. The change towards a more flexible Directive compared with earlier legislation indicates that. This flexibility increased with the introduction of 'framework' directives. In the company law programme these coincide with a fourth generation and a new legislative procedure.

4. THE FOURTH GENERATION DIRECTIVES

There have actually been no directives adopted in the company law programme under the 'fourth generation'. However, this generational label has been ascribed to the draft Thirteenth Directive which is being negotiated under the co–decision procedure, with the latest draft having been introduced since the third enlargement of the Community. Although the eventual adoption of the Thirteenth Directive, if it reaches that point, can only be speculated on, a consideration of how the co–decision procedure operates may shed some light on the prospective characteristics of the Directive.

The co–decision procedure was introduced by the Maastricht Treaty.[95] The key feature of this procedure is that it confers a power of veto on the Parliament. Under the procedure, a common position is reached and then if the Parliament decides by absolute majority to reject the proposed legislation the Council may convene a Conciliation Committee, which comprises representatives of the Council and the Parliament and tries to agree a joint text. If the Parliament then rejects the proposal, the proposal falls. Alternatively, the Parliament may suggest amendments and the Council may then adopt the proposal by qualified majority voting. Effectively, this

---

95 Introduced by Article G(11) Treaty of European Union: See Article 189 (b) EC Treaty. See also Sophie Boyron, 'Maastricht and the Co–decision Procedure: A Success Story (1996) 45 *ICLQ* 293.

procedure gives to the Parliament a negative power of veto. It does not offer to the Parliament a positive power and so the strength of its position against that of the Council is still limited.

A.   The Draft Thirteenth Directive

The original proposal of 1989 for a Thirteenth Directive failed to gain agreement among the Member States. The latest draft, published in November 1997,[96] was drawn up under the principle of subsidiarity and proportionality[97] as was the earlier draft of February 1996[98] and therefore has all the features of a new style 'framework directive'. In this way, the latest draft does not contain detailed harmonisation provisions but, instead, sets out the principles which should be applied by the Member States according to their national systems and their cultural contexts. The draft Directive contains 12 Articles whereas the 1989 proposal contained 23 articles.

In some ways the framework directive has been self–defeating. Member States have pushed for independence (not least the UK) and it appears that when they are granted that independence they then see no need for the directives. Thus, for example, in response to the 1996 draft the DTI stated that 'it is not clear what added value the Directive would have in terms of improved regulation or stronger safeguards, nor what co–ordination or harmonisation would be achieved which was not already in train'.[99]

This draft Directive aims to ensure that shareholders of listed companies throughout the Union enjoy equivalent safeguards in the event of the change of control in the company in which they hold shares and provides minimum guidelines for the conduct and transparency of take–over bids. The current draft reflects the characteristics of a 'framework' directive: it sets out general principles, offers considerable discretion to the Member States in achieving those principles and gives precedence to the differences between Member States. The goal is stated but not the means of achieving that goal.

Article 5 provides some very general principles and gives to the Member States discretion within the framework of those principles. Article 9 also gives to Member States discretion and recognises that they may achieve the objectives in different ways. Thus, it states simply that Member States must

---

96   COM(97) 565 final, 10.11.97.

97   As was agreed at the Edinburgh Council Summit 1992.

98   COM(95) 655, final, 7.2.96.

99   DTI Consultative Document, *Proposal for a Thirteenth Directive on Company Law Concerning Take–over Bids*, April 1996, para. 30, p. 9.

have rules governing the conduct of bids covering at least a number of certain issues (which are listed). However, Article 9 does not say *how* those rules should be formulated.

Introducing the 1996 draft the Single Market Commissioner Mario Monti stated: 'This new proposal is a further demonstration of the Commission's pragmatic approach to ensuring respect for subsidiarity, in line with its undertakings to the European Councils in Edinburgh and Essen to revise a number of proposals. It reflects the results of extensive consultations with the Member States. We have responded positively to the Member States' desire for a new approach to co–ordinating rules on take–overs.'[100]

It is difficult to say anything conclusively about this proposed Directive as it is still under negotiation. We can see that with the last two drafts of the proposal the approach seems to illustrate a willingness to deal with Member States' concerns, leaving more discretion to the Member States than in previous directives. Proportionality and subsidiarity as principles have been given considerable weight in the latest two drafts. In this way, Article 4(1) states that Member States shall designate the authority or authorities that will supervise all aspects of the bid.

It is too early to comment on the balance of power between the institutions before the final draft has been adopted. However, it is worth noting that the Commission in its explanatory memorandum to the 1996 draft, claimed that the European Parliament had delivered a 'favourable opinion' to the earlier draft.[101] Yet the discussions in the Council Working Group led to negotiations on that draft being suspended in 1991 'due to serious opposition from certain Member States'.[102] This indicates that the views of the Member States have significant influence and suggests some weakness in the position of the Parliament and of ECOSOC.[103] It must be noted, however, that ECOSOC is meant to be a consultative body, unlike the Parliament, yet we do not see Parliament being treated any differently. However, the co–decision procedure came into force after that breakdown of negotiations, and the latest draft indicates that this has perhaps granted to the Parliament a degree of influence over the legislative outcome. The latest draft reflects the Commission's acceptance of most of the Parliament's 20 suggested amendments, including controversial proposals such as the principle of disclosure to shareholders being extended to employees. However, not all of the Parliament's proposed amendments have been

---

100 See http://europa.eu.int/en/comm/dg15/takequest.html.

101 [1990] OJ C 38/41 19.2.90.

102 COM (95) 655 final.

103 ECOSOC Opinion [1989] OJ C 298/56 27.11.89.

accepted. It remains to be seen how the Parliament's apparently increased influence will impact on the remainder of the process for creating this Directive.

5. CONCLUSION

What can be observed from the above is that the Parliament has continued to struggle to gain enough power to act as a genuine counter–balance to the Council's influence in the law–making process. The first two generations of directives do not indicate a strong position for the Parliament. The observations on what happened in the negotiations leading to the adoption of the Twelfth Directive do not provide convincing evidence that the co–operation procedure improved significantly the Parliament's position. It remains too early to conclude anything about the co–decision procedure although the theoretical arguments for that procedure have been based on the claim that Parliament's position will be strengthened. Some commentators have offered a more optimistic view still[104] and the evidence provided by the latest draft Thirteenth Directive lends some support to that optimism.

Conversely, the Council has a significant degree of influence. Through the Council the governments of the Member States enjoy their influence. The pattern appears to be that Member States' influence is actually growing rather than being levelled with that of the European Parliament or the Commission. The move to framework directives indicates this trend, with increasing matters of substance being left to the discretion of the Member States.

The Community does demonstrate some concern for democracy. This is reflected in the move from unanimous voting to qualified majority voting. However, such democracy is limited since it does not endow the Parliament with more power and the traditional democratic principle of 'one person, one vote' is not reflected in the voting arrangements between the Member States, although account is taken of the different sizes of the Member States. The development of the company law programme also suggests that lobbyists have an important role to play. This has at least two possible outcomes for democratic quality. On the one hand it provides an opportunity and a platform for subjects of the legislation to put forward to the institutions their views. On the other hand it can have the effect of removing citizens further from the decision–making process since those with the loudest voices and most resources are more likely to have influence.

---

104 Boyron, above note 96.

With the introduction of qualified majority voting a question might be raised regarding the view of outvoted Member States and how they implement the directives adopted as well as the current situation where new Member States must take on existing law for which they have not participated in the negotiations and which they have not influenced. It may also be the case that this stage will have an impact on the subsequent implementation of the legislation at national level.

The quality of the representative democracy of the European Community is shown by the development of the company law harmonisation programme to be poor. The different procedures used increase complexity and exacerbate the lack of transparency. Secrecy also creates obstacles to identifying exactly the influences on the legislation, thus making effective participation at local level more difficult to achieve.

Although procedures alone do not demonstrate the achievement of democracy they may have some effect on the eventual substantive outcome by influencing the contents of the legislation as well its form. What has been observed in this chapter is that a combination of more Member States and changes in the legislative and voting procedures appears to have increasingly made the directives more flexible and general. The result is that the directives have developed towards being more statements of principle than technical rules to be applied universally. The extent to which this progression has achieved a 'harmony' of company laws depends on how these directives have been received and implemented by the Member States and on whether they have altered the nature of business and economics positively within the European Community. The next part of this book consider these issues by comparing the British and Spanish implementation measures.

PART THREE

Implementation of the Company Law Programme – a Comparison of the UK and Spain

7 Member States' Experiences: Comparing Two Legal Systems

1. INTRODUCTION

The success of legislation created at European level may be evaluated by observing how it is received and implemented in the different Member States. The eventual practical results and operation of the European legislation will also depend partly on the character of the system into which the legislation is introduced. Across the European Union the Member States have considerably different legal systems and economies. For example, many Member States have a written constitution while other states do not, and some states have more developed industrial economies while others have greater agricultural strengths. These factors may shape or determine the practical effect of European laws when they are eventually implemented at Member State level. This chapter considers the possible influences on the experiences of the UK and Spain of the EC company law harmonisation programme. In particular, the chapter will outline the manner in which each country entered the Community. Then the chapter will describe the relevant characteristics of each Member State's company laws. This will be followed by a description of the UK and Spanish implementation procedures. Finally, the chapter will offer a comparative analysis and will suggest the implications for the company law programme of the similarities and differences between the Member States.

2. THE ENTRY INTO THE EUROPEAN COMMUNITY OF THE UK AND OF SPAIN

Both the UK and Spain had different experiences with their negotiations for entry into the European Community and they entered at different stages of the Community's development. The UK entered in the first enlargement in 1973, together with Denmark and Ireland. Spain entered more or less coincidentally with Portugal and Greece in 1986, when the Single Internal

Market was high on the European agenda.[1] This section will outline separately the progress towards accession of both the UK and Spain.[2]

A.   The UK's Entry

The UK initially had reservations about the EEC, seeing it as overlapping with the work of the Organisation for European Economic Co–operation; as potentially damaging to its Commonwealth relationships; and as having a supranational approach which would create institutions to which the UK would have to submit. The UK therefore did not participate in the negotiations leading to the 1957 Treaty of Rome. Instead, the UK joined the European Free Trade Area (EFTA) in 1960 as an alternative to entering the Community. The purpose of EFTA was to safeguard and increase the European trade of its members and to provide them with a base from which to negotiate with the EEC.[3]

By the beginning of the 1960s the UK's economy was declining against the economies of the other European countries. The EEC countries were making economic and political progress. At the same time, the Commonwealth was in the process of transformation into a loose association.[4] These factors encouraged Macmillan, the then Prime Minister, to seek membership of the EEC. The UK applied for entry in 1961 under Article 237 of the Treaty of Rome when the member countries were concerned with the development of political union in Europe, and were trying to find solutions to the problems arising from the existence of the two economic groupings in Europe.

During the negotiations for the UK's entry, the EEC members were concerned to develop a single market, which involved the abolition of all customs and barriers, harmonisation of economies, and political co–operation. However, the UK was particularly interested in protecting

---

1   As outlined in the European Commission's White Paper *Completing the Internal Market*, COM (85) 310 final.

2   For an interesting narrative on the events leading to the two enlargements of the Community see Frances Nicholson and Roger East, *From the Six to the Twelve: The Enlargement of the European Communities* (Longman, UK, 1987). This section relies heavily on that narrative.

3   HMSO, *Britain in the European Community* (London 1992), p. 4.

4   John Pinder, *European Community: The Building of a Union*, 2nd ed. (Oxford University Press, Oxford, 1995), pp. 53–56.

Commonwealth trade, UK agriculture and the arrangements which could be made for its EFTA partners.[5]

The UK's main concern regarding the Commonwealth was to maintain Commonwealth trade relations. It was considered that to cut trade with the Commonwealth could lead to severe losses and the possible ruin of some of the Commonwealth countries to which Britain had responsibilities.

The British concerns with EFTA arose from the fact that the UK thought the economic division in Europe into two economic groups should be brought to an end. It thus encouraged as many of the EFTA partners as possible to enter the EEC and to maintain association with the remaining EFTA partners.

The negotiations at ministerial level began in November 1961. In 1963 the negotiations broke down, largely because France appeared to be opposed to the membership of the UK on the basis that the entry of the UK and other EFTA members would completely change the nature of the Community. Despite support from all the other members for the UK to join the Community the French opposition led to the eventual breakdown of the negotiations for entry. France's attitude was hardly surprising given the reluctance on the British side to be wholly co–operative. The motives for joining were tactical rather than strategic and at times the British attitude appeared to be contemptuous.[6] As George remarks:

> Britain was pursuing its consistent view of how Europe ought to relate to the rest of the world. There was no conversion to the ideal of European union that was espoused by the leaders of the founder states; there was no attempt to sell the idea of a British membership in anything other than pragmatic terms to the British electorate; there was no abandonment at either official or popular level of a commitment to a strong sense of national identity.[7]

It was not until 1966 that prospects brightened regarding Britain's potential entry into the EEC. In 1964 the Labour government came into power and the leader who succeeded Gaitskell, Harold Wilson, pledged to make a new high level approach to see whether conditions existed for fruitful negotiations on British membership.

The British government applied for membership in May 1967, and during that same month President de Gaulle of France stated that this would

---

5   See HMSO White Paper, 29 November 1961, Cmnd 1565.

6   Stephen George, *An Awkward Partner: Britain in the European Community*, 2nd ed. (Oxford University Press, Oxford, 1994) at p. 39.

7   *Ibid.*, at p. 40.

bring great changes to the community of the Six. Again, he stressed the difference between the Common Market and Britain in November of 1967, pointing to the economic differences and approaches.

In June 1969 a new French government headed by President Pompidou and Jaques Chaban–Delmas replaced that presided over by de Gaulle. This change of government brought with it a different French attitude and progress was made during that summer for a resumption of talks between the EEC and the applicant countries.

The Conservative government, with the Prime Minister, Edward Heath, which had returned to office in June 1970, finally agreed the terms of entry into the EC for the UK.[8] Throughout the 1970 negotiations Britain remained in close touch with her EFTA and Commonwealth partners and remained committed to protecting national sovereignty. These factors influenced the terms of accession agreed upon.

The terms agreed included[9] the progressive abolition of tariffs and the elimination of quotas between the original six Member States and the new Member States; progressive adoption of the common customs tariff; adoption of the Common Agricultural Policy with a progressive movement towards agricultural support levels; provisions on fishing, moving towards price alignments, and allowing Member States to restrict fishing within six miles of their waters (sometimes twelve miles); gradual liberalisation of capital movements; an offer of special trading terms to developing Commonwealth countries in Africa, the Caribbean and the Pacific; the continued importation of Commonwealth sugar and New Zealand dairy produce; tariff and agricultural pricing arrangements to have a seven year transition period, with a longer transition period for Britain's budget contributions. It was also decided that the UK should have an equal place with France and Germany for participation in the institutions.

The Treaty of Accession was signed on 22 January 1972. The European Communities Act 1972 provided for the UK's entry into the EEC on 1 January 1973. There were renegotiations of membership terms in 1974 when Britain had a Labour Government, under which it was agreed to set up a regional fund to correct economic imbalances, and the first Lomé Agreement in 1975 agreed new trade, aid and co–operation links with the Commonwealth and developing countries.

---

8   The approach of the British government and a review of the negotiations were set out in the White Paper of 7 July 1971 (HMSO, Cmnd 4715).

9   See Treaty of Accession, 22 January 1972 (Cmnd 4862).

B. Spain's Entry

Whereas the first enlargement centred on economic issues the second enlargement, which eventually brought into the Community Spain, Portugal and Greece, was predominantly political. Tsoukalis offers at least three reasons for the political emphasis: that politically, it was almost impossible to exclude any European democracy prepared to adopt the *aquis communautaire*; membership of the Community was seen as a factor of stability and as a means of strengthening parliamentary democracy; and political stability would in turn be a prerequisite for economic and military security.[10]

Initially, Spain hesitated between the EEC and EFTA. The EEC became the favoured option because of the long–term political objectives of the Treaty of Rome and its attention to agricultural issues. Spain requested that negotiations be opened with a view to examining the possibility of establishing association with the EEC in 1962. At first, this request was met with silence due to the Community's attitude to the dictatorship of Franco. President de Gaulle had favoured Spain's entry insofar as this would extend the Community's influence southwards. However, farming issues stalled the negotiations which opened in 1967.

In 1970 agreement was reached on a preferential agreement between Spain and the EEC. This agreement was designed to conform with GATT rules that preferential agreements must lead, in time, to a customs union. About 95% of EEC industrial imports from Spain, subject to tariffs, were covered by the agreement and 62% of agricultural imports, while approximately 61% of Spanish imports from the Communities were affected.[11] The agreement was based on reciprocity by both sides. Following the accession of Denmark, Ireland and the UK to the EC in 1973, a temporary protocol covering Spain's trade relations with the three new European Community member states was signed in January 1973. The first enlargement meant that Spain's 1970 agreement needed to be renegotiated since Spain had enjoyed free access to Britain.

In 1975 negotiations on a new agreement broke down following civil unrest in Spain and executions of five men accused of killing policemen and civil guards. The executions were said to violate the rule of law and the rights of defence. The European Parliament had decided to freeze relations in

---

10   Loukas Tsoukalis, *The European Community and its Mediterranean Enlargement* (Allen and Unwin, London, 1981), pp. 144–145.

11   Nicholson and East, above note 2, at p. 214.

September 1975 'until such time as freedom and democracy are established in Spain'.[12]

In December 1978 a multilateral free trade agreement between Spain and the EFTA countries was initialled. Bilateral agreements were also reached, with Spain and all except Iceland and Portugal of the EFTA countries, to facilitate trade in agricultural products.

Meanwhile, after the death of Franco in November 1975 King Juan Carlos committed himself to the 'peaceful establishment of democratic co–existence based on respect for the law as a manifestation of the sovereignty of the people'. The idea of a free trade association had become obsolete and Spain wanted full membership. Support for full membership came from all three major political parties. Spain's first general elections since 1936 took place on June 15, 1977 after which the government of Adolfo Suarez González agreed to submit a formal application for full membership of the European Communities. Spain applied in July 1977, based mainly on political factors, as a source of support in preserving her democratic institutions.[13] The end of international isolation was seen as a reward for restoring democracy.[14] The growing Spanish economy looked towards Europe; the Spanish people regarded Francoism as too primitive and political democracy became the aspiration.[15] Fernando Morán, the then Foreign Minister, saw the completion of the accession agreement as recognition for having re–established democracy.[16]

By 1977 economic, rather than political, issues had become the most important. This caused difficult entry negotiations.[17] In the first place, there was French doubt as to the likelihood of full membership being achieved for Spain or Portugal before the end of 1983, as had been hoped. This was partly because France wished to resolve the problems which had arisen from the 1973 enlargement of the Community, such as the dispute arising from the Community budget reform commitment.

---

12   Nicholson and East, above note 2, at p. 215.

13   Nicholson and East, above note 2, at p. 215.

14   Tsoukalis, above note 10, at p. 122. See also Kevin Featherstone, 'The Mediterranean Challenge: cohesion and external preferences' in Juliet Lodge (ed.), *The European Community and the Challenge of the Future*, 1st ed. (Pinter, London, 1989), 186, at p. 194.

15   Paul Preston and Denis Smyth, *Spain, the EEC and NATO* (Routledge and Kegan Paul, London, 1984), p. 30.

16   Nicholson and East, above, note 2, at p. 228.

17   Paul Heywood, *The Government and Politics of Spain* (Macmillan, London, 1996), p. 270.

The crucial question for the negotiations with Spain concerned agriculture, which was regarded as a threat to the economies of France, Greece, and Italy. Other serious issues regarding the prospective Spanish entry were fisheries, since there was an imbalance between the size of existing fishing fleets and the amount of available fish stocks, with Spain possessing the third largest fleet in the world, and trade barriers for Spain's industrial goods.[18]

The new Socialist government, which took office in December 1983, pledged to seek membership within four years, despite continued French objections to Spain's entry into the Community.

The Accession Treaty was finally signed on 12 June 1985, with Spain entering on 1st January 1986, at the same time as Portugal. The main terms of agreement for Spain's entry included: customs duties to be dismantled in eight stages over a seven year transition period – by 1989 duties being reduced by 50% and by 1993 abolished; quantitative trade restrictions to be abolished from the date of accession, although Spain was given between three and four years to phase out import quotas on certain sensitive products such as tractors, colour TVs and guns; market access for some textile exports was to be subject to a programme of double checking and statistical surveys of existing Member States' imports; for agriculture, a seven year transition period would generally apply for the implementation of the Common Agricultural Policy and for some products this would be 10 years; for most fish the alignment of price differences and dismantling customs duties would be over a seven year period, and Spain and Portugal would have to conform to European Community rules on minimum fish sizes, fishing gear, catch limits and quotas; Spain to receive pre–accession aid for restructuring its fleet. With regard to institutional arrangements, Spain would have eight votes while the UK, France, Germany, Italy were to have 10 votes. These agreed terms showed that there had been relative inequality of bargaining power between Spain and the Community, the end result not being very generous to Spain.

From the above narrative it can be observed that both the UK and Spain had a number of problems in entering the Community. At the time of the UK's entry there were economic issues to be resolved whereas Spain's entry coincided with a stronger European economy when the Community was looking towards 'fusion' through the Single Market.[19] Thus, the UK took a

---

18   For a detailed discussion of these issues see Paul Preston and Denis Smyth, above
       note 15, chapter 2, esp. pp. 4–14.

19   See eg Rafael Guasch Martorell, 'La Armonización en el marco del Derecho Europeo
       de Sociedades: la obligación de resultado exigida por las Directivas societarias a los

defensive position, keen to protect her strong economy when she entered the Community, whereas Spain aspired towards the prosperity of the modern European economy.[20] Britain sought concessions from the Community as part of her entry negotiations, but Spain had to adapt to the Community's prevailing trade conditions.[21] Consequently, unlike Britain, Spain was not seen to be obstructing the Community's development at the time of her entry. Furthermore, unlike Britain, Spain demonstrated no organised opposition to the Community.[22] Rather, for Spain, entry was regarded as a way of consolidating her recently established democratic system.[23]

These observations indicate the potential for a different reception of European laws in the UK and Spain. One might expect, for example, Spain to be more welcoming of European legislation than the UK. On the other hand, the fact that Spain had not taken part in the negotiations for many of the laws introduced at European level because she entered relatively late in 1986 might cause difficulties for integrating those provisions into the existing Spanish legal system. Connected with this point is the potential relevance of the character of each Member State's legal system and company law to the integration of the European provisions into that state. The next section will outline briefly the company laws of each Member State.

3.   COMPANY LAW CHARACTERISTICS

The two Member States have very different company laws. The UK's law is both statute based and contains much case law. The Spanish law is more codified.

Estados miembros' (1994) 596 *Revista General de Derecho* 5651–5677, at pp. 5652–3.

20   Pinder, above note 4, at p. 62.
21   Economic and Social Committee, *The Community's Relations with Spain* (Brussels, June 1979) at p. 63.
22   *Ibid.*, at p. 1.
23   Pinder, above note 4, at p. 62.

A. UK Company Law[24]

UK company law is part of a common law system and is therefore regulated by case law as well as by statute. The development of UK company law has been slow and unwieldy. Little has changed in over a century apart from technical and administrative changes. The conceptual aspects have largely remained the same. In the UK there are three major forms of commercial vehicle: the sole trader, the partnership which is governed by the Partnership Act of 1890, and the limited company,[25] which is largely governed by the Companies Act 1985, as amended by the 1989 Companies Act and supported by delegated legislation and other Acts, including the Insolvency Act 1986, the Financial Services Act 1986 and the Compulsory Disqualification of Directors Act 1986. UK company law distinguishes between public limited liability companies and private limited liability companies. For example, the public limited company is subject to a minimum share capital requirement of £50,000 whereas the private limited company is not, but both types of company are governed mostly by the same rules, under the Companies Act 1985.

The foundation of the modern registered company was arguably laid by the 1844 Joint Stock Companies Act. This gave ready access to incorporation by a process of registration and in this way set up the office of the Registrar of Companies.[26]

The Companies Act 1908 had introduced an exemption for private companies regarding the safeguards necessary for protecting people who invested in public companies. Under the 1908 Act an exempt company had less than 50 members, had no right to transfer shares and was not allowed to invite the public to acquire its shares. The 1948 Companies Act relieved small family or closely held companies of the burden of filing public accounts. The 1967 Act, which was in force when the UK entered the EEC in 1973, and had implemented the recommendations of the Jenkins

---

24 See L.C.B. Gower, *The Principles of Modern Company Law*, 6th ed. (Sweet and Maxwell, London, 1992); W. Horwitz, 'History of the Development of Company Law' (1946) 62 *LQR* 375; David Milman, '1967–1987: A Transformation in Company Law?' (1988) 17 *Anglo–American* 108.

25 The limited liability partnership is a new corporate form being mooted for certain professional firms: see DTI Consultation Paper, *A New Form of Business Association for the Professions*, February 1997, and Comment by Gray (1997) 18 *Company Lawyer* 119.

26 See Gower, above note 24, at p. 38; see also Paddy Ireland, Ian Grigg–Spall and Dave Kelly, 'The Conceptual Foundations of Modern Company Law' in P. Fitzpatrick and A. Hunt, *Critical Legal Studies* (Blackwell, Oxford, 1987) 149.

Committee Report 1962,[27] took away the exemptions granted to those companies from having to file accounts and from the prohibition on loans to directors.

Although public and private limited liability are not treated by separate Acts of Parliament there are still a number of aspects in which they diverge within the company law system.

(i)   The Private Limited Liability Company

The private limited company is (quantitatively at least) the most popular form of business organisation in the UK.[28] It may be formed by one or more persons and it gains legal personality upon registration when the Registrar certifies that the company is incorporated.[29] The certificate of incorporation is considered as conclusive evidence of the existence of the company and that it is duly incorporated.[30] In order to create the company there must be registered two company documents: the memorandum and the articles of association (if any).[31] There is no minimum capital requirement for a private limited company, and shares in the company are not transferable on the open market. Shares may be paid for in cash or in kind,[32] and the nominal capital must be maintained.

The private limited liability company is managed by a board of directors which is theoretically separate from the shareholders although in practice these will often be the same people. It means that as directors they must take the company management decisions and as shareholders they must take decisions in general meeting. Certain decisions may be effected in writing. Shareholders have the authority to appoint and to dismiss the directors, and to take decisions regarding allocation of profits.

(ii)   The Public Limited Liability Company

The public company must be formed by at least two people[33] and, like the private limited liability company, it must register its memorandum and

---

27   Cmnd 1749.

28   See Andrew Hicks, 'Corporate Form: Questioning the Unsung Hero' (1997) *JBL* 306.

29   Companies Act 1985, s. 13(1).

30   Companies Act 1985, s. 13(7).

31   Companies Act 1985, s. 10(1).

32   Companies Act 1985, s. 99(1). See also s. 738.

33   Companies Act 1985, s. 1(1).

articles of association. Perhaps its main distinction from the private limited liability company is that the public company has a minimum capital requirement of £50,000.[34]

Structurally, the public limited liability company has two separate organs: the board of directors and the shareholders in general meeting. The directors have the management duties of the company and they may be supervised by a board of independent directors. They are also supervised by the shareholders in general meeting who have the power to appoint or dismiss the directors by ordinary majority,[35] and who are entitled to receive copies of the annual accounts[36] and who may decide how the company's profits are to be distributed, for example by declaring a dividend.[37]

In summary, features which might distinguish UK company law include: the possibility of buying shelf companies, more private companies than public companies; non–existence of the concept of nullity (the certificate of incorporation is generally regarded as sufficient evidence that the company has been properly formed); a minimum capital requirement for public companies but not for private companies; a single–tier board of directors; and no developed concept of co–determination. When the UK entered the EEC there also existed the concept of *ultra vires* which was affected dramatically by the harmonisation programme almost from the outset. Finally, directors owe their duties to the company rather than to individual shareholders,[38] and they have a duty of skill and care of a standard which is reasonable for a person with that same level of skill and experience.[39]

34　Companies Act 1985, ss 11, 13 and 118(1).
35　Companies Act 1985, s. 303.
36　Companies Act 1985, s. 238(1).
37　Table A, Article 102.
38　See eg *Percival v Wright* [1902] 2 Ch. 421.
39　Re *City Equitable Fire Insurance Co. Ltd* [1923] Ch. 407. The law has developed considerably since this case and today a higher standard of care may well be required: see eg *Dorchester Finance Co. Ltd v Stebbing* [1989] BCLC 498; *Norman v Theodore Goddard* [1991] BCLC 1028; *Re D'Jan of London Ltd* [1993] BCC 646.

B.   Spanish Company Law[40]

In Spain, company law is part of the system of commercial law. The general sources of Commercial Law in Spain are the Commercial Code of 1885, trade customs and the common law.[41] Both the Civil Code of 1884 and the Commercial Code regard the company as a contractual relationship between persons associated with the object of making profit.[42] Spanish law has passed through a development from codification to decodification by the creation of special laws to cover particular areas.[43] Thus the main regulation of companies lies in the Commercial Code of 1885, the *Reglamento del Registro Mercantil*, and, where appropriate, a particular law to cover a specific form of company. There are special laws which regulate public limited liability companies (*sociedad anónima*) and private limited liability companies (*sociedad de responsabilidad limitada*).[44] The *sociedad anónima* is currently regulated by the *Ley de Sociedades Anónimas 1989* (LSA) which replaced the *Ley de Sociedades Anónimas of 1951*. This reform came about for a number of reasons as have been outlined by Broseta Pont.[45] The *sociedad de responsabilidad limitada* is governed by the *Ley de Sociedades de Responsabilidad Limitada 1995* (LSRL) which reformed the 1953 law of the same name. There are also Resolutions and Directions of the Commercial Registrar, which have influential authority on the interpretation of the laws.

---

40   The major company law texts include historical descriptions of the law's development. See eg J. Garrigues, *Tratado de Derecho Mercantil* (Civitas, Madrid, 1947, 1955, 1966); F. Vicent Chuliá, *Compendio Crítico de Derecho Mercantil* (tirant lo blanch, Barcelona, 1990–1); Rodrigo Uría, *Derecho Mercantil*, 21st ed. (Marcial Pons, Madrid, 1994).

41   As stated in Article 2 of the Commercial Code.

42   Article 116, Commercial Code; Article 1,665, Civil Code.

43   See Fernando Sánchez Calero, *Principios de Derecho Mercantil* (Editorial Revista de Derecho Privado, Madrid, 1994), at p. 15.

44   These are the nearest comparisons that can be made but they are not an exact mirror image of their counterparts in the UK.

45   First, the socio–economic climate had changed considerably by the late 1970s from that of the 1940s when the 1951 law was conceived. Secondly, the demands of the large public companies had not been adequately catered for by the 1951 law. Thirdly, and fundamentally, the entry into the EC demanded a profound reform of the earlier law in order to comply with the Directives based on Articles 54(3) and 100 of the EEC Treaty. Fourthly, the 1951 law had a number of lacunae and defects which had been noted in the jurisprudence of the Spanish courts: Manuel Broseta Pont, *Manual de Derecho Mercantil*, 9th ed. (Tecnos, Madrid, 1991) at p. 212.

Spanish company law has a number of other different types of companies: the *sociedad colectiva* is like a partnership with legal personality. However, the members are wholly and jointly responsible for all the company's debts and liabilities. The *sociedad en comandita* is similar to a sleeping partnership, having a co–existence of partners with limited and unlimited liability. The *sociedad en comandita por acciones* is like a limited partnership. All of these companies are granted legal personality if they are registered with the Commercial Registrar. The only company without legal personality is the *sociedad irregular* which exists as a company but which has not complied with all the formalities for obtaining personality.

The most important companies are the *sociedad anónima* and the *sociedad de responsabilidad limitada*. The main features of the laws relating to these companies will be outlined in this chapter.

(i)   The Sociedad de Responsabilidad Limitada (SRL)

All SRLs, which are similar to (but not the same as) private limited liability companies, are deemed to have a mercantile character or commercial nature whatever their objects.[46] They may be formed with a relatively simple structure and they allow flexibility. An SRL is constituted by registering a public deed on the Commercial Register in order to obtain legal personality.[47] No distinction is made between the public contractual document and the company statutes and they are seen as one document.[48]

The SRL has a minimum capital requirement[49] which must be fully paid up at the time the company is constituted and which is divided into equal shares which are accumulable, indivisible and not negotiable.[50] The shares may be paid for with non–cash consideration. The members are free of personal liability for the company's debts.[51] The member must contribute in the manner agreed at the time the company is formed or on an increase of

---

46   Article 3, LSRL 1995.
47   Article 11.1, LSRL 1995.
48   See Fernando Sánchez Calero, *Principios de Derecho Mercantil*, above note 43, p. 251.
49   Currently, 500,000 pesetas (approximately £2,500 sterling): Article 4, LSRL 1995.
50   Article 5, LSRL 1995.
51   Article 1, LSRL 1995. The LSRL 1995 removed the maximum number of 50 shareholders (see the Exposición de Motivos, Section II, paragraph 2) which had been fixed in the earlier law (Article 3, LSRL 1953).

capital. The shareholder must not vote if he has a conflict of interests with the company since the shareholder has a duty of fidelity to the company.[52]

The structure of the SRL is that of a management separate from the shareholders. The duration of the office of the directors shall be for as long as that determined in the contractual document.[53] However, the *Dirección General de los Registradores* is of the opinion that the term of office may be for no longer than five years if a time limit is not stipulated in the company contract.[54]

(ii)   The Sociedad Anónima (SA)

The capital of the SA is divided into shares and the liability of the shareholders is limited to the value of their contribution, without responding personally to the company's debts.[55] The SA gains its legal personality by registering the contractual document on the Commercial Register.[56] The commercial document is a multilateral contract and an agreement of organisation of at least three people.[57]

The name of the company must appear on the contractual document registered in the Commercial Register.[58] SAs enjoy a freedom of choice between a name which reflects the company's nature or something objective which must refer to the activity described in the company's object clause.[59] The company can be formed either all in one step (*fundación simultánea*) or in a series of steps (*fundación en sucesiva*).[60] The *fundación simultánea* occurs by agreement between the members and the *fundación en sucesiva* reflects a company being created by public share subscription. The usual form is the *fundación simultánea* which is the simplest method, since a single agreement between the founders is executed in a contractual document. In Spain there exists the concept of nullity so that registration of the company does not guarantee its validity.

---

52   Article 52, LSRL 1995.
53   Article 60, LSRL 1995.
54   See eg Resolution of 23 April 1991, *Boletín Oficial del Estado* 12 June 1991.
55   Article 1, Ley de Sociedades Anónimas (LSA) 1989.
56   Article 7, LSA 1989.
57   Article 8, LSA 1989.
58   Article 24, Commercial Code.
59   Article 367, Reglamento de Registro Mercantil approved by Royal Decree 1.597 29 December 1989 (RRM 1989).
60   Article 13, LSA 1989.

Since the LSA1989, the SA, during its existence, must have a minimum capital of 10 million pesetas,[61] which can be fully or partially paid up.[62] Prior to 1989 there was no minimum capital requirement for the SA, which made it an especially popular form of business organisation. The capital is stated in the company's statutes and will appear as a liability on the balance sheet. The management organisation of the SA is divided into two organs. The management organ and the shareholders in general meeting. The general meeting is the sovereign organ through which the members act jointly and make decisions such as the appointment and removal of the directors. The directors can be organised in one of five possible ways: as a sole director, as several directors who act individually, as two directors acting jointly, as a board of directors consisting of at least three directors acting jointly, or as a board together with an executive commission.[63] The director has a duty to act as a loyal and diligent business person to a professional standard of behaviour.[64]

The LSRL 1953 law was perceived as a failure because the public company was favoured as more prestigious. The 1953 law was weakened by its assumption that no problems existed for minority shareholders, by the difficulty in transmission of shares and by the considerable disclosure of information requirements. The relative modesty of the LSA 1951 made public companies appear more attractive. The 1951 and 1953 laws aimed to accommodate the two main types of company in a similar way to the German, but the practice was different insofar as more public companies existed in Spain. In Germany 2% were public companies whereas in Spain 74% were public companies even though both countries had similar aims and legal structures.[65]

There are two key differences between the UK and the Spanish company laws: the UK company law is largely regulated by one Act of Parliament which covers all company types and contains exceptions where appropriate to particular types of company. In Spain, however, the public and private companies are governed by separate rules. In the UK the private company has long been more widely used than the public company whereas in Spain it was the reverse before Spain entered the European Community.

---

61   Approximately £50,000 sterling.
62   Article 4, LSA 1989.
63   Article 9.h, RRM 1989.
64   Article 133, LSA 1989.
65   These figures have since changed considerably: see Chapters 8 and 9.

4.   LEGISLATIVE PROCEDURES IN THE UK AND IN SPAIN

The way in which the European directives were received and acted upon is influenced by the manner in which each country's company law has developed and also by the procedure used to implement the European legislation. These also affect the practical outcome of the European law for each Member State and are also relevant to an analysis of the democratic quality of the European harmonisation programme at national level. This section will provide an outline of the procedures used for creating new legislation in the UK and in Spain in the company law field.

A.   The UK

The European company law Directives have been implemented in the UK by one of two principal methods: primary legislation and secondary or delegated legislation in the form of statutory instruments. The Companies Act 1980, for example, gave effect to the Second Directive; the Companies Act 1981 gave effect to the Fourth Directive; and the Companies Act 1989 implemented the Seventh and Eighth Directives; whilst the Eleventh and Twelfth Directives were implemented by means of statutory instrument.[66]

The procedures adopted for each of these methods of implementation involve consultation although this may be variable. Policies leading to Acts of Parliament originate in a number of ways. They may arise from party manifestos, or government policy or out of a need for reform, such as after a European directive has been adopted.[67] When the need for legislation arises it will normally be considered by a commission, such as a Royal Commission or a Parliamentary Select Committee. Often the Law Commission is empowered to discuss issues of law reform. However, interestingly, the Law Commission has not, until recently, been involved with company law reform, which is seen as a 'contentious matter',[68] and it has been suggested that the Law Commission 'has been kept out of company law matters (apart from

---

66   The Eleventh Directive was implemented by the Companies Act (Disclosure of Branches and Bank Accounts) Regulations 1992 (No. 3178) and the Overseas Companies and Credit and Financial Institutions (Branch Disclosure) Regulations 1992 (No. 3179) and the Twelfth Directive was implemented by the Companies Act (Single Member Private Limited Companies) Regulations 1992 (No. 1699).

67   Phil Harris, *An Introduction to Law*, 4th ed. (Butterworths, London, 1993), p. 143.

68   David Miers and Alan Page, *Legislation*, 2nd ed. (Sweet and Maxwell, London, 1990) p. 29.

consolidation) seemingly for political reasons'.[69] The Department of Trade established a company law panel in 1980 to review and report on proposed improvements and developments of company law. Consultation takes place between various interested parties including ministers, civil service departments, non–parliamentary organisations and interest groups.[70] There is an opportunity at this stage to amend proposed measures. Then the proposal goes through the various reading stages before receiving Royal Assent.[71]

Although for delegated legislation the process of outside consultations is usually more complete than for primary legislation,[72] this process still lacks sufficient consultation and has an inadequate balance of power so that some interest groups will have more powers of persuasion than others.[73] However, typically, the DTI, which has the main responsibility for supervising UK company legislation, will publish the regulations in draft for comment from a variety of different groups and individuals, such as the CBI, IOD, experienced business individuals, and academics.

The main criticism of the company law reforms in the UK is that they have been piecemeal and reactive, leaving us with, as Palmer claims, 'a morass of over–technical and sometimes downright contradictory rules and regulations'.[74] Palmer recognises that this problem has arisen partly because of the pace of the EC legislative developments but he suggests a more fundamental problem in the approach of the legislators to the reform of company law.[75] This tends to be a technical approach rather than a conceptual approach, so that the law loses its coherence and becomes unnecessarily complex.[76] The policy–makers fail to discuss the overall aim of the company law legislation.[77] This supports the claim by Ficker that

---

69   See the editorial of *The Company Lawyer*, 'Can the Law Society get Company Law Reform on the Agenda?' (1991) 12 *Company Lawyer* 162. However, see also the Law Commission publication on company law reform: see note 99 below. See also the recent consultation papers on shareholder remedies (nos. 142 and 246).

70   Phil Harris, above note 67, p.144.

71   See generally David Miers and Alan Page, above note 68.

72   Michael Zander, *The Law Making Process*, 3rd ed. (Butterworths, London, 1990), p. 79.

73   Phil Harris, above, note 67, p. 148.

74   Palmer's *Company Law* (Sweet and Maxwell, London, January 1996 insert), pp. 1036–1036/1, para. 1.133.

75   *Ibid.*

76   See Edward Jacobs, 'Conceptual Contrasts – Comparative Approaches to Company Law Reform' (1990) 11 *Company Lawyer* 215, esp. pp. 220–221.

77   Palmer's *Company Law*, above note 74, p. 1036, para. 1.133.

harmonising company law is problematic because one law reform has an effect on other aspects, since company law is an integrated system of rules.[78] Yet, in response to criticism of company law in the UK,[79] the previous government set up working groups to produce discussion papers on discrete areas in need of reform.[80] These are used for public consultation and the DTI brings these together in its own discussion papers. In practice it may be difficult to achieve workable discrete or isolated reforms. This problem appears, finally, to have been recognised and the DTI has recently announced a forthcoming review of company law which promises to be a comprehensive review.[81]

B. Spain

In Spain, the general procedure for creating new laws,[82] in theory, encourages discussion and openness, although, in practice, it is debatable whether such objectives are achieved.[83] Legislative procedure in Spain is regulated principally by the Spanish Constitution 1978.[84] Under these provisions, the government lays an initiative or proposal before the 'Congreso de los Diputados' – one of the two parliamentary chambers.[85] The

---

78　Hans Claudius Ficker, 'The EEC Directives on Company Law Harmonisation', in Clive M. Schmitthoff (ed.), *The Harmonisation of European Company Law* (UKNCCL, London, 1973) at p. 70.

79　See eg Company Law Committee of the Law Society, *Reform of Company Law* (Memorandum, No. 255, July 1991).

80　See DTI Press Notice, P/93/316. There is no indication that the new Labour Government will change this current approach.

81　DTI Press Release, P/98/053.

82　For a more detailed discussion of Spanish legislative procedure see: F. Rubio Llorente, 'El Procedimiento legislativo en España: El Lugar de la Ley Entre las Fuentes del Derecho' (1986) 16 *Revista Española de Derecho Constitucional*, 83; M. Aragón Reyes, 'La Iniciativa Legislativa' (1986) 16 *Revista Española de Derecho Constitucional* 287; and R. Punset, 'La Fase Central del Procedimiento Legislativo, (1985) 14 *Revista Española de Derecho Constitucional* 111.

83　Ignacio de Otto, *Derecho Constitucional – Sistema de Fuentes*, 2nd ed. (Ariel, Barcelona, 1993) p. 106.

84　Articles 87–91.

85　The 'Congreso de los Diputados' is perhaps most comparable with the House of Commons, while the 'Senado' has a role more similar to, but not the same as, the House of Lords. Both chambers are elected and form the Parliament or 'Cortes

governmental proposal consists of a *'proyecto de ley'*[86] accompanied by an *'exposición de motivos'*.[87] This will have been developed from discussions of an *'anteproyecto de ley'*,[88] produced by the relevant section of the 'General Commission of Codification', which will have been considered by the relevant Ministry. The 'Congreso de los Diputados' considers the text of the government's proposal which is then published with a stated time limit for submitting amendments. Any amendments suggested are then debated. If, however, no amendments are suggested or the text is rejected this decision will be passed back to the General Commission of Codification which debates the text. Once approved by the 'Congreso de los Diputados' the text is then passed onto the 'Senado' which follows a similar procedure, and will refer any objections or amendments back to the 'Congreso de los Diputados' to make a decision. In effect the 'Congreso de los Diputados' has much more influence than the 'Senado'.[89] The text emerges from this process to receive royal assent. When the King has formally introduced the law it is published in the Official State Bulletin with a date fixed for its entry into force.

As has been noted, the company law in force when Spain entered the European Community in 1986 dated back to 1951 and 1953. There were already plans for a new law regulating public companies.[90] These were in anticipation of Spain's entry into the European Community, and the objective was to adapt the law to the Community's rules. However, by the time of Spain's accession six company law directives had already been adopted. This would require not simply an adaptation of the Spanish company law but significant reform. On the other hand the reform would not be so fundamental because the areas addressed by the directives did not deal with issues such as company structure or worker participation. Thus the approach was that a complete reform of the whole company law would be pointless as it would have to be changed again once the directives on those areas had been agreed.[91] It was expected then that the draft Fifth Directive would come to fruition.

Generales'. For more information see eg Elena Merino Blanco, *The Spanish Legal System* (Sweet and Maxwell, London, 1996) at pp. 59–66.

86   This is similar to a government bill and is published in the Official State Bulletin.

87   This is similar to an explanatory memorandum.

88   This is similar to a white paper although is not necessarily published on a general level.

89   See eg Rubio Llorente, above note 82, at p. 298.

90   An *Anteproyecto de Ley de Sociedades Anónimas* had been published in 1979.

91   Eduardo Polo Sánchez, 'La Reforma y Adaptación de la Ley de Sociedades Anónimas a las Directivas de la Comunidad Económica Europea' in Various Authors, *Derecho Mercantil de la CEE: Estudios a Homenaje a José Girón Tena* (Civitas, Madrid,

Some important observations can be made specifically about the two most important laws of 1989 and 1995. The 1989 law which sought to adapt and partially reform the existing law relating to public companies was developed within a framework of three different dimensions: the existing laws of 1951 and 1953; the accession of Spain into the European Community in 1986; and the *Anteproyecto* of 1979. The *Anteproyecto* of 1979 was not published generally[92] but was submitted to relevant institutions and professional circles. Despite a relatively narrow audience the *Anteproyecto* received a number of criticisms which influenced its successor in 1987.[93] The Ministry of Justice commissioned a law professor to revise the 1987 text produced by the General Commission of Codification, which led to both formal and substantive improvements.[94] Again, this later *Anteproyecto* of the Ministry of Justice was not published, but it received a number of reactions from bodies such as the Ministry of Industry, the Ministry of Economics and Taxation, the Ministry of Justice, and the National Institute of Industry.[95] The *Anteproyecto* was finally turned into a governmental 'proyecto de ley'[96] and passed onto the Cortes Generales where it experienced more changes again, the Cortes Generales thus adding a fourth dimension to the framework of development of the law of public companies of 1989.[97]

1991) 775, at pp. 778–781. See also Aurelio Menéndez Menéndez, 'El Anteproyecto de Ley de Reforma Parcial y de Adaptación de La Legislación Mercantil a las Directivas de La CEE en Materia de Sociedades' in Angel Rojo, *La Reforma de Ley de Sociedades Anónimas* (Civitas, Madrid, 1987), 13, at p. 16; and José Girón Tena, 'La Reforma proyectada en España de la Sociedad Anónima', in Instituto de Investigaciones Jurídicas, *Homenaje a Jorge Barrera Graf*, tomo 1 (Universidad Nacional Autónomo de Mexico, Mexico, 1989) 613, at p. 618. For a brief commentary on the company law reforms published in English see Gaudencio Esteban, 'The Reform of Company Laws in Spain' (1991) 28 *CMLR* 935–958.

92   Menéndez Menéndez, above note 91, at p. 14.

93   *Ibid.*, p. 15.

94   Emilio Beltrán, 'Hacia un Nuevo Derecho de Sociedades Anónimas' (1988) 30 *Revista de Derecho Bancario y Bursatil* 329, at pp. 332–3.

95   *Ibid.*, at p. 335.

96   Published in *Boletín Oficial de las Cortes Españolas* (Congreso de los Diputados, Tercera Legislatura, Serie A, num, 80–1, 22 April 1987).

97   Eduardo Polo Sánchez, 'La Reforma y Adaptación de la Ley de Sociedades Anónimas a las Directivas de la Comunidad Económica Europea' in Various Authors, *Derecho Mercantil de la CEE: Estudios a Homenaje a José Girón Tena* (Civitas, Madrid, 1991) 775, at p. 788.

The fact that the development of company law in Spain has progressed through these rather disjointed phases, with drafts which are not published on a universal level, makes for a potentially significant lack of coherence. This problem is deepened by the existence of two separate laws relating to public companies and to private companies. In Spain, the law relating to private companies in 1995 had to follow the 1989 law in many respects, thus denying the legislators the opportunity to improve on some of the errors or faults with the earlier law, and also creating an overlap of rules.[98]

The above description of the characteristics of the UK's and Spain's regulation of corporate activity and each state's procedures for legislative reform reveals a number of points of contrast. These may well influence the manner of developing the laws which originate at European level. The final section of this chapter summarises the characteristics which define each Member State and suggests how these might impact on the reception of the European legislation.

5. SOME CHARACTERISTIC DIFFERENCES BETWEEN THE UK AND SPAIN

As has already been observed the European company law programme was, to a large extent, inspired by the German company law system. Germany's company laws are found in the Civil and Commercial Codes as well as in a number of specific regulations. Germany also has a written constitution. With regard to some particular company law rules and principles German law provides for company contractual capacity and directors must also comply with objective standards of care. German company law also provides for two–tier boards of directors, giving an important role to the supervisory board.

Of the UK and Spain, the Member State which appears to have more similarities with the German system is Spain. Thus, like Germany, Spain has a written constitution, follows Civil and Commercial Codes and has company laws relevant to specific company forms. By contrast, the UK system has no written constitution and has no codified laws but, instead, follows a common law development and has universal company laws insofar as one Act of Parliament will generally cover both types of limited company. For both Member States these different approaches have their own problems. Thus, for example, in the UK there have been appeals for separate Acts of

---

98 See Angel Rojo, 'La sociedad de responsabilidad limitada: problemas políticas y de técnicas legislativas' (1994) 603 *Revista General de Derecho* 12876, esp. pp. 12882–12885.

Parliament for regulating public and private limited companies,[99] while in Spain the disjointed nature of the company law provisions has led to criticisms and suggestions for a more unified system of regulation.[100]

The Spanish company law is similar to the German company law in its provision of corporate contractual capacity. The UK, however, resisted progress in this direction and had problems in implementing the First Directive. The *ultra vires* provisions finally disappeared almost completely in 1989. This slow development may arise from the British emphasis on property based laws[101] and an unwillingness to alter this approach. Finally, the Spanish corporate structure appears to have more in common with the German than does that of the UK. The Spanish provisions are more flexible with regard to the organisation of the management board offering a number of possibilities from single to two–tier boards. In the UK the legal provisions make no distinction between tiers of management but in practice large companies may have non–executive directors or at least a remuneration committee which takes certain decisions away from the executive board. There is very little in British law to encourage participation by other groups within the corporation although it is possible for more informal arrangements to be made in this respect and certain specific sectors may have provision for participation by customer committees such as the water industry.

From the above it can be seen that there are some striking differences between the national legal systems and their general approaches to company law. Such differences could present obstacles to the achievement of harmony sought by the European company law programme. The next chapter will consider the national implementation measures and the extent to which such harmony actually has been achieved in company law.

---

99   See DTI, *The Law Applicable to Private Companies – Consultation Document Seeking Views on the Law Commission's Feasibility Study on Reform of Private Companies* (November 1994). For a discussion of this paper see Andrew Hicks, 'Reforming the Law of Private Companies' (1995) 16 *Company Lawyer* 171.

100   See eg Menéndez Menéndez, above note 91, at pp. 18–19.

101   R.R. Drury, 'A Review of the European Community's Company Law Harmonisation Programme' (1992) 24 *Bracton Law Journal* 45–51.

8 Implementation of the Directives in the UK and Spain

1. INTRODUCTION

For both the UK and Spain the European company law programme has led to many important law reforms. For Member States who were part of the European Community at an earlier stage their reforms appeared to be piecemeal in correspondence with the 'salami–tactics' of the Community's programme. At least for Spain, who entered later, many of the necessary reforms were introduced together, resulting in a more comprehensive legislative package. This chapter will consider the implementation measures taken by the UK and Spain.

This chapter highlights one of the difficulties in comparative law.[1] The countries being compared here entered the Community at different dates. As was observed in the previous chapter, the UK entered in 1973 and Spain entered in 1986. The economic, social and political climate of the Community had altered significantly between these dates. Therefore, the reaction by the two Member States to Community measures would possibly be different. Coupled with this difficulty for comparison is the fact that each country experienced major reforms of its company laws at different dates during the last fifty years. When the UK entered the EEC her company law was dominated by the Companies Acts of 1948 and 1967. A consolidation Act was enacted in 1985, with amendments to that Act in 1989. Spain introduced new laws for public companies in 1951 and for private limited companies in 1953. Then, following Spain's entry into the Community, further new reform laws came in 1989 for public companies and in 1995 for private companies.

---

1   For a general discussion on the problems and imperfections of comparison see Else Øyen, 'The Imperfection of Comparisons' in Else Øyen (ed.), *Comparative Methodology: Theory and Practice in International Social Research* (Sage, London, 1990) 1–18.

2. THE FIRST DIRECTIVE

The First Directive was problematic for both the UK and for Spain. The UK had particular problems with the provisions relating to validity of obligations and Spain experienced difficulties with the nullity provisions.

A. Nullity Provisions

Spain had no specific rules on nullity of companies and would normally turn to general principles such as nullity of contract principles. By contrast, Germany's rules on nullity were exhaustive with limited causes for nullity. The First Directive followed Germany's approach as technically more perfect and complete. Thus, Article 11 contains an exhaustive list of the causes of nullity of the company and it is not possible for Member States to declare a company null for any other cause. Article 12 sets out the consequences of a declaration of nullity, which entails the company's winding up but does not affect the validity of any commitments entered by or with the company.

It was only when Spain entered the European Community that she had to address the issue of nullity. The *Marleasing* decision[2] was about non–implementation of the First Directive. In that case Marleasing sought a declaration that the defendant company, which had been incorporated under Spanish law, was null and void for being in breach of the Spanish Civil Code. It was argued that the defendant company had been incorporated solely for the purpose of defrauding the creditors of one of its co–founders and that the founder's contract incorporating the company was vitiated for lack of cause. The defendant relied on the exhaustive nature of Article 11 of the First Directive to exclude the grounds of nullity invoked by the plaintiff. The Court stated that national courts were obliged to interpret national law as far as possible in the light of the wording and purpose of the Directive. Under Article 5 EC Treaty Member States must ensure the fulfilment of community obligations. They have a duty to adopt a *communautaire* interpretation not only of provisions which have been enacted in order to give effect to a specific directive but also provisions predating directives and enacted without reference to Community law. In Spain, Article 34 LSA 1989 provides an exhaustive list stating that nullity shall only arise for the causes listed. As Vicent Chuliá remarks, the Spanish approach follows the

---

2   *Marleasing SA* v *La Comercial Internacional de Alimentación SA* Case 106/89 [1990] ECR 4135 [1992] 1 CMLR 305. There are many commentaries on this case. See eg Nick Maltby, '*Marleasing*: What is All the Fuss About?' (1993) 109 *LQR* 301–311 and his note 1 for further references.

German.[3] Arguably the *Marleasing* decision gave Spain no option but to adopt that approach.

Whereas Spain had problems with the nullity provisions, the UK had no better experience with the validity of obligations provisions of the First Directive.

B. Validity of Obligations Entered Into by a Company

The provisions in the First Directive relating to validity of obligations of the company were a source of huge difficulties for the UK. The provisions represent an attempt to balance two sets of interests in company law: on the one hand seeking to safeguard transactions and to protect those dealing with the company, and on the other hand to protect shareholders against the consequences of misuse or unauthorised use of the company's property by its management.[4] The original Member States were divided. Five States followed the *spécialité statutaire* principle, which closely resembled the Anglo–American *ultra vires* doctrine and the *mandattheorie* approach which corresponds with the principal–agent relationship. Germany, on the other hand, sought legal security and followed the *organtheorie* approach, whereby the acts of the organs are considered to be the acts of the company.[5]

Articles 7 and 9 attempted to balance these two positions. Under these two Articles, the third party's contract with the company is technically protected before and after the company has been incorporated. Where the company has not yet been formed the promoters will generally pick up responsibility,[6] and where the company has been incorporated the company generally remains liable.[7] Article 9 presented most problems. The compromise reached means that Article 9 has been difficult to interpret. Thus, although the company will normally be liable, it is possible for Member States to provide that the company shall not be bound where such acts are outside the objects of the company, if it proves that the third party knew that the act was outside those objects or could not, in view of the

---

3   Francisco Vicent Chuliá, *Introducción Al Derecho Mercantil*, 9th ed. (Tirant lo Blanch, Valencia, 1996) at p. 204.

4   R.R. Drury, 'A Review of the European Community's Company Law Harmonisation Programme' (1992) 24 *Bracton Law Journal* 45–51, at p. 45.

5   See for more detail, Eric Stein, *Harmonisation of European Company Laws: National Reform and Transnational Co-ordination* (Bobbs–Merrill, Indianapolis, 1971) at pp. 282–292.

6   Article 7.

7   Article 9.

circumstances, have been unaware of it. On the other hand, limits on the company's organs under its statutes or from a decision of the competent organs, may never, according to Article 9.2, be relied on as against third parties, even if they have been disclosed. These provisions created, for the UK at least, enormous problems, hardly to the advantage of the third parties they were designed to protect.

The UK provisions for implementing the Directive had a notoriously complex development, with the UK failing to deal adequately with Article 9. The history has been widely documented.[8] A notable factor in the problems of the UK's implementation provisions was the lack of effective consultation. Professor Sealy provides a telling picture in his account of the enactment of the European Communities Act 1972 which indicates the government's reluctance to do more than the bare minimum in order to satisfy the Directive.[9] The unsatisfactory drafting of Section 9 of the 1972 Act led to almost two decades of further problems with the *ultra vires* rule. Needless to say, a similar expression of dissatisfaction with the reforms in the Companies Act 1989 is also provided by Cheffins! Despite consultations, the time for reflection was 'minimal', and 'interested parties were left with little opportunity to scrutinise the legislation and suggest improvements'.[10] These accounts may be explained in part by the UK's disadvantage in not having been involved in the negotiations for the Directive. Secondly, as Cheffins suggests, the problem could be attributed in part to the time pressures in the British law–making process.[11] Thirdly, the minimalist approach of the UK towards implementation may simply reflect her resentment towards the European regulations.

By contrast with the 'half–measures' for implementing the First Directive, the provisions in the Second Directive relating to share capital were responded to by 'over–reaction'.[12] This will now be considered.

---

8   See eg Boyle and Birds' *Company Law* (Jordans, Bristol, 1995), Ch. 4; J.H. Farrar, and D.G. Powles, 'The Effect of Section 9 of the European Communities Act 1972 on English Company Law' (1973) 36 *MLR* 270–277; D.D. Prentice, 'Section 9 of the European Communities Act' (1973) 89 *LQR* 518–544. L. Sealy, 'More Haste, Less Speed' (1989) 10 *Company Lawyer* 210, N.J.M. Grier, 'The Companies Act 1989 – A Curate's Egg' (1995) 16 *Company Lawyer* 3.

9   L.S. Sealy, *Company Law and Commercial Reality* (Sweet and Maxwell, London, 1984) at p. 80.

10   Brian R. Cheffins, *Company Law: Theory, Structure and Operation* (Clarendon Press, Oxford, 1997) at p. 187.

11   *Ibid.*

12   Sealy, above note 9, at pp. 81–2.

3. THE SECOND DIRECTIVE

The rules in the Second Directive on share capital are very complex and detailed. They concern, briefly, requirement of a minimum capital, maintenance of share capital and provisions on reduction and increase of capital.

The requirement of a minimum capital had dramatic consequences in both Spain and the UK. In the UK there had not previously been a statutory objective minimum capital requirement.[13] When the Directive was adopted in 1976, 25,000 ECU corresponded with approximately £16,000. The UK Department of Trade considered that figure to be too low[14] and the minimum was fixed at £50,000 for public companies.[15] The private company, however, remains without a minimum capital requirement and therefore, in this respect, may be a more attractive choice of company type than the public company. Certainly, the private company is much more commonly used than the public company in the UK, but this company type was also more popular before the Second Directive was implemented in the UK.[16]

By contrast, before Spain's entry into the European Community the most common form of company in Spain was the public company, the *sociedad anónima*. This was because there were fewer restrictions on this company type than on the private company, the *sociedad de responsabilidad limitada*. For example, Article 4 of the LSA 1951 imposed a *maximum*[17] capital figure on private companies and limited partnerships of 500,000 pesetas and Article 3 of the LSRL 1953 imposed a limit of 50 members on private

---

13 Morse, however, points out that the 1948 Act, s. 109(1)(a) provided for a subjective amount necessary for a public company's prospectus to be issued with a trading certificate: Geoffrey Morse, 'The Second Directive: raising and maintenance of capital' (1977) 2 *ELR* 126–132, at p. 127.

14 Department of Trade, *Implementation of the Second EEC Directive on Company Law: An Explanatory and Consultative Note* (July 1977), para. 11. See also Clive Schmitthoff, 'The Second EEC Directive on Company Law' (1978) 15 *CMLR* 43–54, at p. 47.

15 Companies Act 1985, s. 118(1).

16 On 31 March 1996, public companies represented 1.1 per cent of those registered: HMSO, *Companies in 1995–96*, Table A2. However, these figures do not necessarily suggest that the introduction of the minimum capital for public companies made private companies any more preferable. In 1975, before the Directive was adopted, the private company was already hugely more popular in the UK: of the 592,243 companies registered in 1975, 576,653 were private companies, Department of Trade, *Companies in 1975* (1976).

17 My emphasis.

limited companies. For the public company no minimum capital was demanded by the LSA 1951. The explanatory memorandum of the LSA 1951 expressed recognition of the fact that many such companies were family businesses with modest trade activities.[18] These provisions made the public company more attractive with the result that they constituted roughly 80% of all companies in Spain in 1987.[19] The *Anteproyecto*, published in 1979, was severely criticised by the business community for its proposed introduction of a minimum capital requirement of 5 million pesetas.[20] However, Article 4 of the LSA 1989, adapting the law to the Community Directives, goes much further than the 1979 proposal and fixes the minimum capital requirement of public companies at 10 million pesetas and for private companies at 500,000 pesetas. Similar to the UK provisions, the minimum capital required for public companies was much higher than that provided in the Directive (approximately three times the Community figure). The purpose behind the Spanish reform was to discourage the formation of a public company when it was possible for a private company to be formed.[21] The public company was to be reserved for companies of a certain economic type. As Rojo and Beltrán suggest, this was a legal criterion for influencing the choice of company forms adopted.[22]

Why should the Spanish law demand a figure three times as large as that demanded by the Directive? Quintana suggests that this had the purpose of providing the company with a more solid economic base, avoiding cross–subsidies and discouraging the use of public companies for small and medium–sized businesses so that, ultimately, the public company would be the form reserved for companies of a certain economic type. The Community provision, however, which was first proposed in 1970 arguably did not aim

---

18   Ignacio Quintana, 'El Capital Social' in Angel Rojo (ed.), *La Reforma de la Ley de Sociedades Anónimas* (Civitas, Madrid, 1987) 105– 122, at p. 107.

19   Figures provided by the Chambers of Commerce: see Quintana, *ibid.*, at p. 108. Otero Lastres also provides the following figures: from 1975 to 1985 of the 189,559 companies registered, 141,156 were public companies and 48,403 were private companies (public 74.5% and private 25.5%). The tendency during 1982–85 was that the percentage of public companies grew and by 1985 this was 78.3% of companies: José Mañuel Otero Lastres, 'La Reforma de la Legislación Sobre Sociedades: Sociedad Anónima y Sociedad de Responsabilidad Limitada' (1987) 2 *La Ley* 1132– 1142, at p. 1135.

20   Quintana, *ibid.*, at p. 107.

21   Angel Rojo and Emilio Beltrán, 'El Capital Social Mínimo: Consideraciones de política y de técnica legislativas' (1988) 187–188 *Revista de Derecho Mercantil* 149– 173.

22   Rojo and Beltrán, *ibid.*, at p. 152.

to create this company law demographic change. Indeed, among the Member States at the time there were minimum capital requirements ranging between 20,000 and 80,000 ECUs. The fact that the Directive requires 25,000 ECUs appears to be harmonising from the lowest figure, suggesting that the aim was, instead, to avoid the demand in certain Member States being much higher than others, which would discourage the setting up of branches or associated companies in those States. This point appears to be confirmed by the fact that the European Commission has not sought to revise the figure since the adoption of the Directive.[23]

The Commission has indicated the possibility of plans to extend the scope of the Second Directive to cover private companies and limited partnerships with shares as well as public companies.[24] The minimum capital requirement, however, is likely to be the greatest barrier to this proposal, with most opposition from the UK.[25]

A. Integrity of Share Capital

If the parties are to be protected at all, the share capital raised must be genuine. This is recognised by the Directive, which contains provisions seeking to ensure that the capital is realisable. Article 7, for example, requires the assets to be capable of economic assessment. Both the UK and Spain have implemented this provision.[26] Not all of the provisions, however, have been responded to equally by the Member States.

Article 10 is a complex provision which requires a valuation report for non–cash payments. The effect of this complexity was to encourage different approaches between the Member States. The laws of the UK and Spain provide an example of these differences. The valuation report required by the UK is regulated by much more complex provisions than those of the Directive, whereas the Spanish legislation is worded more simply. The UK legislation transposes Article 10 in five statutory sections, containing between them 24 subsections. Spain deals with the Article 10 in one clause containing three short paragraphs! It is no surprise, then, that the UK rules

---

23 Quintana, above note 18, at p. 109.

24 See European Commission, *Study on Second Directive's Extension to Other Types of Companies* (Brussels, 1992).

25 Palmer's *Company Law* (Sweet and Maxwell, London, 1992) R.56 May 1995, p. 16029, para. 16.103.

26 For the UK see s. 99, Companies Act 1985. Morse claims that this provision overruled the old common law rule: Morse, above note 13, at p. 129, his note 15. For the Spanish provision see Article 36, LSA 1989.

have been criticised for their complexity both in the courts and in the commentaries.[27]

In the UK, Section 103 of the Companies Act 1985 sets out the general rule requiring a valuation report for non–cash payments and the relevant procedures are prescribed in section 108. Under section 103, the valuer is appointed by the company. This provision is furnished with the addition of section 108(1), which defines such person as one qualified to be appointed or continue to be appointed as auditor of the company. The valuer may, according to section 108(2), delegate the valuation of the consideration or part of it. The report is to be published by filing it with the registrar[28] at the time the company files the return of the allotment of the relevant shares.[29]

While the UK has been criticised for its over–reaction to the Directive, Spain might be accused of lethargy. The Spanish legislator did not take advantage of the exceptions provided by the Directive and some issues are left to be implied. For example, there is no provision directly requiring publication of the report but Article 38.3, LSA 1989 does state that the report shall be annexed to the memorandum and articles of association, implying that it will be published.[30] There are, however a number of remaining questions regarding the Spanish law; in particular, who might be the appropriate expert to conduct the report. Spanish commentators suggest that this person should not be the person who verifies the company's accounts. Further, the legislation states that the valuer should be appointed by the Registrar.[31] This alters the previous drafts of the legislation by which the expert would be appointed by the judge of the company's location. The transfer of this role to the Registrar has been alleged by Rodriguez Adrados to be discordant with the Directive.[32] This may be because the Registrar is not seen to have such a judicial role as the appointment would require. However, the Registrar has an official administrative function and the Directive provides for the possibility of appointment of expert valuers by administrators. Moreover, Spain appears to be more in line with the Directive on this point than the UK, since section 103 Companies Act 1985

27   *Re Ossory Estates Plc* [1988] BCLC 213; Sealy, above note 9, at p. 82.
28   Under section 111(1), Companies Act 1985.
29   Per section 88, Companies Act 1985.
30   Both Quintana and Villaverde offer this interpretation of the provision. See Quintana, above note 18 and Rafael García Villaverde, 'La Reforma del Registro Mercantil' (1990) 2 *La Ley* 1180–1197.
31   See Article 38, LSA 1989.
32   D. Antonio Rodriguez Adrados, 'Constitución y Nulidad de La Sociedad Anónima' in *Anales de la Academia Matritense del Notariado*, Tomo XXX, Volume I (Edersa, Madrid, 1991) 57–118, at p. 84.

allows the appointment to be made by the company, which does not appear to correspond with the terms of Article 10.

B. Protection of Capital

An aspect in which the Directive has not achieved full implementation is that concerning a serious loss of the subscribed capital. Where this occurs Article 17 requires a general meeting of the shareholders to be called, to consider whether the company should be wound up or any other measure taken. Neither the UK nor Spain appear to have implemented this provision fully. In the UK, section 142 of the Companies Act 1985 requires a general meeting to be called 'for the purpose of considering whether any, and if so what, steps should be taken to deal with the situation'. This is more open–ended than the Directive, which suggests winding up the company or that another measure be taken. The Directive seemingly demands a positive response to the situation. The UK provision, however, offers no guarantee of such a response. Yet, if the directors fail to convene an extraordinary general meeting they may be liable to a fine if that failure were with knowledge or wilful permission. Thus, although they face no civil sanction, the directors face potential criminal penalties. In Spain, Article 260 of the LSA 1989 provides that such a serious loss would be a reason for automatic dissolution of the company. The Spanish provision is therefore much stricter on the company than either the UK or the Directive and lays down a clear procedure. A meeting must be called within two months for adopting the dissolution and if this cannot be achieved by the general meeting a shareholder may attempt to obtain a court order for dissolving the company. The Directive's provision falls between those of the two Member States, indicating that little harmonisation has been achieved.

4.   THE THIRD AND SIXTH DIRECTIVES

Both the UK and Spain implemented the Third and Sixth Directives. An initial observation is that the procedural irregularities in the creation of the Sixth Directive resulted in a lukewarm reception among some Member States. For example, in the UK, the House of Lords Select Committee Report noted that the draft was not published in the Official Journal and was not referred separately for an opinion by the European Parliament or the Economic and Social Committee.[33] Both Member States have adopted rules

---

33   H.L. (Session 1979–80) 43rd Report, paras 11–13.

which combine, partly, the two Directives. The UK treats both Directives simultaneously with additions made relevant to the provisions of the Sixth Directive. Spain's approach has been to state first the rules relevant to mergers followed by rules relating specifically to the Sixth Directive.

The UK implemented the Third and Sixth Directives together in the Companies (Mergers and Divisions) Regulations 1987[34] which amended the Companies Act 1985 and added a new Schedule 15A.[35] A new section 427A was inserted into the 1985 Act, which made the provisions of sections 425– 427 applicable to mergers and divisions of public companies. Those sections make available a procedure by which the court has power to order a meeting which can authorise a compromise or arrangement.[36] The Spanish implementation of the Third and Sixth Directives appears in Chapter VIII of the LSA 1989. Prior to the creation of the Directives, Spain already had provisions for merger by acquisition or by creation of a new company. One problem for Spain was that these provisions applied to different types of companies, leaving a problem as regards scope of application of the Directive and the necessary extent of the implementation provisions.[37] As to divisions, Spain had nothing directly regulating these except those provisions dealing with divisions of co–operatives,[38] and some tax provisions.[39] Regarding divisions, the Spanish law provides that the rules will follow those relating to mergers apart from the exceptions contained in the remaining provisions in Chapter VIII.[40] The Spanish provisions cover 'total' and 'partial' divisions, total divisions being those where the company whose assets are divided is then dissolved, and partial divisions being those where the company whose assets are divided remains in existence.[41] The provisions

---

34   SI No. 1991.

35   This subsequently became Schedule 15B and was renumbered as such by the Companies Act 1989, s. 114(2) as from 1 April 1990 (SI 1990/355(C.13), art. 4(a)).

36   S. 425(2) and Schedule 15B, paragraph 1.

37   See the discussion by Adolfo Sequeira Martín, 'La Fusión y La Escisión: Tercera y Sexta Directivas' in E. García de Enterría *et al* (eds), *Tratado de Derecho Comunitario Europeo*, Vol III (Civitas, Madrid, 1986) 27, at pp. 33–35.

38   *Ley General de Co–operativas de 19 de septiembre de 1974.*

39   As contemplated in the law relating to tax regime for mergers: *Ley de 26 de diciembre de 1980 sobre régimen fiscal de las fusiones de empresas* and its *Reglamento* approved on 24 July 1981.

40   LSA 1989, Article 254.

41   LSA 1989, Article 252. For a discussion of total and partial divisions see Vicente Santos, 'La Escisión de Sociedades En El Derecho Comunitario Europeo', in Various Authors, *Derecho Mercantil de La Comunidad Económica Europea: Estudios en Homenaje a José Girón Tena* (Civitas, Madrid, 1991) 959, at pp. 1000–7.

in the Spanish law on divisions reflect those in the Directive although the Spanish law states expressly that a company which continues to exist after a division remains liable for obligations to third parties.[42]

A. Procedures

The UK's section 427A procedure established in Part XIII of the 1985 Act sets out the relevant information which must be granted to the shareholders and creditors, namely the effect of the compromise or arrangement and the material interests of the directors in the operation.[43] Section 427 sets out provisions by which the court may facilitate a reconstruction or amalgamation through the compromise or arrangement by making one of a number of possible orders, including, *inter alia*, the transfer of assets and liabilities, the allotment of shares, the dissolution of the transferor company without it being wound up, and provision for those who dissent from the compromise or arrangement. Section 427A allows these provisions to apply to a reconstruction of any company or companies or amalgamation of two or more companies and shares would be transferred with or without cash payments in circumstances matching those envisaged by the Third and Sixth Directives. In any such situation, the company or any member or creditor of the company can apply to the court for a meeting to be called in order to give effect to the merger or division.

B. Information

In Spain, Articles 233–251 LSA 1989 dealing with mergers concentrate on the provision of information. The draft merger plan must be signed by all the directors, with an explanation where any directors have not signed the plan.[44] The plan must be approved within six months in order for it to take effect.[45] Once created, the directors should refrain from altering the company's assets or share exchange ratio.[46] In conjunction with the Directive, the rules of the registrar provide that the merger plan should be

---

42   LSA 1989, Article 259.
43   S. 426, Companies Act 1985.
44   LSA 1989, Article 234.
45   *Ibid.*
46   *Ibid.*

filed in the central register and published in the National Bulletin.[47] The information to be made available to the shareholders in the Directive, must also be made available under the Spanish law to debenture holders, holders of other special rights and to the employees' representatives.[48] There is no corresponding right granted to creditors. The agreement adopted by the shareholders for the merger must be published in the National Bulletin three times,[49] which is more than is required by the Directive. Further publicity is required in two widely circulated newspapers in the provinces in which the companies are situated.[50] This requirement indicates recognition of regional differences in Spain, which are particularly important commercially. The Spanish law is also specific as to timing of the merger: one month after the last notice of the agreement.[51]

The UK's section 427A provisions are supplemented by Schedule 15B which lays down detailed requirements. Paragraph 2 states that a draft of the proposed terms of the scheme should be drawn up and adopted by the directors and delivered to the registrar of companies and published in the Gazette. The required information in the draft is largely the same as that demanded in Article 5(2) of the Third Directive and Article 3(2) of the Sixth Directive but there are certain differences in the requirements worth noting. In the UK provisions, the draft merger or division plan should include *restrictions* as well as rights attaching to shares or other securities.[52] The Directives require that any payments or advantages to the directors arising from the scheme should be revealed in the draft terms. This is not required under the UK provisions. However, the directors' report should include information required by section 426 of the Act, 'in particular stating any material interests of the directors of the company'. Arguably, this is a stricter provision since the directors must provide this information in the same document in which they are required to justify the scheme on legal and economic grounds. By contrast, the Directives might allow directors to hide behind the draft terms, which give factual information, without necessarily referring to that aspect of the scheme in the directors' report. A further additional requirement under the UK provisions is that the directors' report

---

47   *Reglamento de Registro Mercantil* (Real Decreto, 29 de diciembre de 1989, 1597/1989), Article 193.
48   LSA 1989, Article 238.
49   LSA 1989, Article 242.
50   LSA 1989, Article 242.
51   LSA 1989, Article 243.
52   Companies Act 1985, Schedule 15B, paragraph 2(2)(f). This is not required by the Directives.

must say if a report on the value of non–cash consideration for shares has been made and if it has been delivered to the registrar.[53]

C. Majority Needed

In the UK, paragraph 1 of Schedule 15B requires a three fourths majority of the value of each class of members in any participating pre–existing transferee company present and voting at a meeting to support the reconstruction or amalgamation. This is more stringent than the requirement in the Directives of at least a two thirds majority,[54] although the Directives require that majority for all companies involved in the merger or division, including the transferor company. Spain is also more stringent. The shareholders' consent to the proposed merger should be obtained by at least a majority in favour in the first meeting called, although if less than fifty per cent are represented then the requisite majority will be two thirds.[55] At the second meeting, twenty five per cent of the voting capital should consent.[56]

D. Experts

The provisions relating to experts in the UK and Spain are also different to the Directives' requirements. The UK provisions expressly state the possibility of the expert being an independent auditor.[57] Furthermore, the auditor is allowed under the UK provisions to delegate the valuation report to another person qualified to provide such a report,[58] which is not provided for in either of the Directives. On the other hand, the Directives make provision for the experts appointed to be able to carry out the necessary investigations in order to give their opinion on the fairness and reasonableness of the scheme and the share exchange ratio arrived at. There is no such express provision in Schedule 15[59] but such power might be implied for an

---

53 Paragraph 4(2).
54 Where at least half the subscribed capital is represented, the Member State may only require a simple majority: Article 7, Third Directive; Article 5, Sixth Directive.
55 LSA, Article 103.
56 LSA, Article 103.
57 Paragraph 5(3).
58 Paragraph 5(4).
59 The House of Lords Select Committee took the view that to include the possibility of asking for all relevant information and carry out necessary investigations would be a

assessment as to the reasonableness of the scheme. The Spanish provisions relating to the experts are also more specific than the provisions of the Directive, Spanish law providing that their level of responsibility is guided by that for company auditors.[60]

In summary, both the UK and Spain have rules which are more extensive than the provisions of the Directives and their respective rules are different. For example, the majority of shareholders required for a decision to merge or divide is higher in the UK. The information requirements in the UK extend to restrictions as well as rights corresponding with the shares. In Spain, all directors should sign the draft merger plan and absent signatures should be explained. A wide range of interested parties are entitled to receive information on the merger or division and repeated publications of the agreement are required in Spain.

5.   THE ACCOUNTS DIRECTIVES

A.   Accounting Systems of the Member States

Both the UK and Spain had very different accounting systems when the Directives were introduced. The UK has long–established accountancy and auditing professions; its accounting system operates largely by its own rules and principles, separate from legislation; its approach is flexible and based on more open than rigid concepts, such as the true and fair view principle. As Savage observes:

> The UK is an example of accounting as an independent pragmatic system which relies less on legalistic restraints and prescription and more on professional standards and self–regulation.[61]

The influence of the UK's system on the Accounts Directives has been demonstrated. However, the Directives originated from the continental approach which did not disappear entirely from the contents of the Directives that were finally adopted. Thus, the Directives also had some impact on the UK's system. In this way, the Directives introduced to the UK's accounting regulations a more legalistic approach, not least because they initiated formal

---

heavy and lengthy task: see H.L. (Session 1975–76) Twentieth Report, at p. v, paragraph 7.

60   LSA 1989, Article 236.

61   Nigel Savage in 'Law and Accounting – The Impact of EEC Directives on Company Law' (1980) 1 *Company Lawyer* 24–29 and 91–94, at pp. 24–5.

legislative rules which would accompany the existing self–regulatory provisions. On another level the Directives required a stricter approach to a number of situations although they also introduced a pragmatic aspect to the UK's technical definitions relating to groups. Finally, the aim of the Directives under Article 54(3)(g) to balance the interests of members and third parties, introduced a different perspective for the UK where the auditing profession had previously been preoccupied with shareholder protection.[62]

When the Accounting Directives were being developed and negotiated Spain had not yet joined the European Community. Spain, therefore, had no opportunity to be involved in shaping the Directives. However, after Spain joined and was obliged to implement the Directives, the introduction of legal rules would bring about significant changes to Spain's accounting system for three major reasons: first, it would introduce a legal framework to a practice regarded by some commentators in Spain as a specialised and technical economic science quite separate from law or legal practice.[63] Secondly, it would demand new skills and activities of the Spanish accountancy profession which was still relatively young compared to some of her European counterparts.[64] Thirdly, Spain had traditionally followed a tax–oriented approach. In this respect, the Directives would introduce to Spain new principles and methods of accounting.

In Spain, an extensive and detailed formal law was considered necessary to implement the Fourth and Seventh Directives. The Directives were thus both implemented by the LSA 1989[65] which also made changes to the Commercial Code of 1885.[66] The reforms of the LSA 1989 were amplified by a *Plan General de Contabilidad* which was introduced by Royal Decree 1643 on 20 December 1990 (1990 Plan). The LSA 1989 and the Commercial Code set out the basic principles and the 1990 Plan is a more detailed regulatory instrument. However, the LSA 1989 had a number of problems. It did not contain an explanatory memorandum and was regarded as a mosaic of reforms that modified the earlier law without having been founded on the basis of any general concepts or prior schemes.[67] In addition,

---

62   *Ibid.*, at p. 25.

63   See Francisco Vicent Chuliá, 'Las Cuentas Anuales' in A. Rojo (ed.), *La Reforma de la Ley de Sociedades Anónimas* (Civitas, Madrid, 1987) 225–292, at p. 230; and 'La legislación mercantil en materia contable (en los últimos diez años) (1991) 564 *Revista General de Derecho* 7709–7743, at pp. 7710–7711.

64   José Girón Tena, 'Las Cuentas Anuales de la SA' (1993) 1 *Revista de Derecho de Sociedades* 9–44, at pp. 14–15.

65   See Chapter VII of the LSA 1989, entitled 'De las Cuentas Anuales'.

66   In particular Articles 34–49.

67   Vicent Chuliá (1991), above note 63, at p. 7732.

and perhaps unfortunately, it was not a general reform but a partial reform. The significance of this was that it required special laws to be developed but which were being applied broadly. Thus, for example, the 1990 Plan has a general application without having the authority of a formal law within the hierarchy of norms prescribed by Article 97 of the Spanish Constitution of 1978.[68]

The main changes introduced by the 1989 Law were: accounting principles independent of tax regulations and publication of financial statements by depositing them in the Commercial Registry. A new authoritative accounting agency, the 'Instituto de Contabilidad y Auditoría de Cuentas', was established with responsibility for issuing, developing and publicising the Plan. The new Plan was obligatory, was extended to cover all business persons, including all companies,[69] and had no link to tax regulations. It also imposed obligatory consolidated accounts for companies with one or more dependent subsidiary.

B.   The Fourth and Seventh Directives

The Fourth Directive was implemented in the UK by the Companies Act 1981[70] which introduced a more formal approach to accountancy with more detailed legal rules. This formality would take away some of the flexibility which characterised the UK's system. In this way the Directive introduced into the UK system compulsory lay–outs, although within a framework of options, and statutory valuation rules. The 1981 Act allowed companies to choose from all the formats available in the Directive, though, as the Directive demands, they should stay with that format in later accounts once chosen, thus ensuring some consistency of method. In any event, whichever format was chosen would require extra disclosure, since, traditionally, the profit and loss account was used more as a summary of the financial position of the company. To have any prescribed format at all was a novelty for the UK.[71]

---

68   *Ibid.*, at p. 7733.
69   This seemed to contradict the fact that other entities might also be businesses.
70   This revised Schedule 8 of the 1948 Act.
71   Although Savage tells us that they had been prescribed for building societies and industrial assurance companies: above note 61, at p. 28 referring to the Companies Act 1948, Schedule 8. This was not so new to the German legal system, which concentrated on cost and management accounting rather than on financial statements for shareholders. Thus, in Germany, for internal management purposes uniform formats were developed. The National Socialist notion of government control of the

An aspect of considerable concern in the Fourth Directive arose from the definition of small and medium–sized companies for the purposes of certain exemptions. This has been a subject of continued controversy and change at European level as well as nationally, leading to further directives amending the Fourth and Seventh Directives in this respect in subsequent years.[72] The DTI recently issued a Consultation Document suggesting increased financial ceilings so that more companies would be able to produce simplified accounts.[73]

The UK's more developed accounting practice in the area of group accounts meant that the Seventh Directive would not affect UK law too dramatically. As with the Fourth Directive, the greatest impact of the Seventh Directive is that it altered the UK's regulatory framework from an emphasis on professional standards to greater use of legal rules.[74] The Directive was implemented by the 1989 Companies Act. This introduced new definitions into the 1985 Act. Thus, section 258 contains definitions of parent and subsidiary undertakings. These added to the existing section 736 of the Companies Act 1985 which defined a 'subsidiary' as a company in which another 'holding company' either owns more than half the equity share capital, or is a member and controls the composition of the board of directors; or a company which is a subsidiary of the holding company's subsidiary. The legislation placed 'emphasis on the legal power to control

---

economy led to compulsory adoption of a charter of accounts. Germany also developed uniform financial statements.

72   Directive 90/604/EEC [OJ L317, 16.11.1990, p. 57] amends the Fourth and Seventh Directives as concerns the exemptions for small and medium–sized companies and the publication of accounts in ECUs. This was implemented in the UK by the Companies Act 1985 (Accounts of Small and Medium–Sized Enterprises and Publication of Accounts in ECUs) Regulations 1992 (SI 1992/2452). The Fourth and Seventh Directives were extended by further European Directives to certain partnerships and unlimited companies in 1990 and this extension was implemented by Regulations in the UK in 1993. Directive 90/605 [OJ L 317, 16.11. 1990, p. 60]. Implemented in the UK by The Partnerships and Unlimited Companies (Accounts) Regulations 1993 (SI 1993 No. 1820).

73   Many Government Consultations have been dedicated to this aspect of the Accounts Directives: the Green Paper, *Company Accounting and Disclosure* Cmnd 7654 (1979), responding to the Fourth Directive, debated the issue of company sizes. More recently the DTI issued a Consultation Document suggesting increasing the financial ceilings: *Accounting Simplifications and Tackling Late Payments* (DTI, 1995).

74   Stuart Turley, 'The Impact of the Seventh EEC Directive on UK Group Accounts' (1986) 7 *Company Lawyer* 10 at p. 16.

another company'.[75] The definition of parent and subsidiary undertaking introduced by the Seventh Directive is broader and more flexible. Apart from a few other small changes, the substantive effect of the Seventh Directive on the UK practice was relatively small.

In Spain, the 1989 Law and the 1990 Plan introduced to Spain's company law, the accounting principles referred to in the Fourth Directive, including true and fair view and clarity; revenue and expense matching principle; no offset principle; going concern principle; consistency principle; principle of prudence; accrual basis principle; cost principle; materiality principle. This approach altered the existing principles stated in the Commercial Code which included: clarity and accuracy, truth and responsibility, confidentiality and verification. The reforms abandoned the principle of accuracy. The principle of truth was limited to the directors signing the accounts to show that these were the true accounts and no more.

The Directives which amended the Fourth and Seventh Directives[76] were implemented in Spain by the LSRL 1995 which both extended their application to partnerships and unincorporated associations and increased the threshold for abbreviated accounts, thus allowing more companies to benefit from the exemption to submit the company's accounts for external audit.

C.   The Eighth Directive

The Eighth Directive was implemented in the UK by Part II of the Companies Act 1989, together with a series of statutory instruments, which established a system of supervisory and qualifying bodies to govern eligibility of persons to become auditors as well as the conduct of audit work.[77] These provisions came into force in 1991. In accordance with the Directive, the 1989 Act aimed 'to secure that only persons who are properly supervised and appropriately qualified are appointed as company auditors, and that audits by persons so appointed are carried out properly and with

---

75   *Ibid.*, at p. 11.

76   See note 72 above.

77   Companies Act 1989 (Commencement No. 2) Order 1990, SI 1990 No. 142; Companies Act 1989 (Register of Auditors and Information about Audit Firms) Regulations 1991, SI 1991, No. 1566; Companies Act 1989 (Commencement No. 12 and Transitional Provision) Order 1991, SI 1991 No. 1996; Companies Act 1989 (Eligibility for Appointment as Company Auditor) (Consequential Amendments) Regulations 1991 SI 1991, No. 1997; Companies Act 1985 (Disclosure of Remuneration for Non–Audit Work) Regulations 1991, SI 1991, No. 2128.

integrity and with a proper degree of independence'.[78] The Act empowers the Secretary of State for Trade and Industry to supervise the auditing profession and to approve appropriate supervisory bodies.[79] He or she could delegate his or her powers of approval and other functions under Part II of the Act to a separate statutory body. An auditor must be a member of one of these supervisory bodies and hold an appropriate qualification.[80] Again, the Eighth Directive has required the UK to formalise the qualification rules for auditors. The UK has granted discretion to the supervisory bodies by taking advantage of the options set out in the Directive.

In Spain, the Eighth Directive was implemented by the *Ley de Auditoría de Cuentas* of 1988 (LAC 1988), which was accompanied by a Regulation.[81] The provisions went beyond the requirements of the Directive by regulating not just the qualifications and independence of auditors but also their activities and the administrative control of the profession by the 'Instituto de Contabilidad y Auditoría de Cuentas'. This was developed against a complex background: lack of confidence in the professional bodies of auditors, a divided profession, the extension of their duties from duties to the company and the shareholders to duties to the public interest, and the need for them to join up with other professionals in order to cope with a changing socio–economic climate.[82] The auditors wanted to be regarded as a true profession and their reports regarded as professional, rather than commercial documents, and they sought autonomy and self–regulation. In order to meet the demands of the Eighth Directive against this background the LAC 1988 provides that auditing is about review and verification of the accounts. The LAC 1988 states that an auditor's report may be relied on by third parties. The LAC 1988 and the Regulation regulate the regime of responsibility of auditors and auditors' firms. If harm arises from irregularities in their reports, auditors will be responsible wholly based on civil law. Finally, the LAC 1988 regulates the role and powers of the Instituto de Contabilidad y Auditoría de Cuentas as well as the handling –

---

78   Companies Act 1989, section 24.

79   These bodies are: the Institute of Chartered Accountants of England and Wales; The Institute of Chartered Accountants of Scotland; the Chartered Association of Certified Accountants; the Institute of Chartered Accountants in Ireland and the Association of Authorised Public Accountants.

80   See Companies Act 1989, section 31.

81   The Law No. 19 of 12 July 1988, published in State Official Bulletin on 15 July 1988. This was developed by a Reglamento by Royal decree 1636/1990 of 20 December.

82   Vicent Chuliá (1991), above note 63, at p. 7736.

confidentiality and custody – of audit documents. Thus the LAC 1988 and Regulation have a very broad scope, going beyond that of the Directive.

6.   THE TWELFTH DIRECTIVE

By the beginning of 1995 only six countries had implemented the Twelfth Directive into their national company laws. These Member States were Denmark, Germany, Italy, the Netherlands, Luxembourg, and the UK.[83] Spain implemented the Directive during 1995.[84] The Directive, being flexible and having wide terms, was also likely to be implemented in variable forms. The experiences of the UK and of Spain illustrate this point.

The British government, conscious of cost and the burden on business and administration, gave a lukewarm response to the Commission's proposal. In a consultative document on the proposal published in 1988 the DTI[85] suggested that the problem of requiring two or more members was being exaggerated by the Commission. Indeed, the Institute of Chartered Secretaries and Administrators commented critically on the DTI's 1988 consultative document and urged the government to enter future negotiations 'with a more positive attitude'.[86]

After the Directive was adopted the DTI published a further consultation paper on implementation in November 1991. The DTI sought a balance between achieving the purpose of the Directive and the cost and administrative burden of making changes to the companies legislation. In this way, the DTI recognised the need to encourage enterprise among small firms but at the same time sought to avoid complexity and burdens for small companies by keeping changes and additions to a minimum.[87] Consequently, the Companies (Single Member Private Limited Companies) Regulations

---

83   At first sight this figure seems disappointing but some Member States did not need to alter their laws as these were already compatible with the Directive: this was the case for France, Belgium and Portugal.

84   An action was started by the Commission against Spain for failure to implement the Directive but was later dropped: Case C–94/95 [1994] OJ C 161, p. 9.

85   DTI Consultative Document on the *EC Proposal for a Twelfth Company Law Directive Concerning Single Member Private Limited Companies* (1988).

86   Institute of Chartered Secretaries and Administrators, position paper, *Comments on the Consultative Document on the EC Proposal for a Twelfth Company Law Directive Concerning Single–Member Private Limited Companies*, 30 September 1988, at p. 4, para. 13.

87   DTI Consultation Paper, *Implementation of the Twelfth Company Law Directive*, November 1991, para. 7.

1992[88] were introduced to implement the Directive. These contain a 'sweeper clause' which states that any legislation applying to private limited companies is to be read with such modification as is necessary to take account of the single member company. Thus Regulation 2 ensures that the same provisions which apply to multi–member companies will also apply to single member companies.

In addition to the UK's 'sweeper clause', the Regulations make specific amendments and additions to those existing legislative provisions which would not otherwise be appropriate for single member companies. In this respect amendments were made to the Companies Act 1985 and to the Insolvency Act 1986. These included an additional section 1(3A) to the 1985 Act making it possible to form a single member private company. Section 24 originally provided that if a company carried on business with one member for more than six months that member would become jointly and severally liable with the company for the company's debts contracted during that period. This section was altered to exclude private companies from its application.

Spanish implementation of the Directive occurred late and indeed the Commission threatened to take legal action against Spain for her non–implementation of the Directive.[89] The Spanish position regarding single member companies basically evolved from denial to recognition and tolerance.[90] In the LSA 1951 Spain did recognise the possibility of companies becoming single member companies as a result of their shares coming into the hands of one owner.[91] Consequently, if a company became a single member company this would not lead to immediate dissolution. Despite coinciding with the Twelfth Directive almost to the same date[92] the LSA 1989 did not contain any regulation relating to the single member company.[93] The requirement of plurality for founding the company was maintained except with regard to companies formed by state bodies.[94] The

---

88   SI 1992/1699.

89   See note 84 above.

90   The account of Sánchez Ruz contains three stages: rejection; implied recognition; express recognition: see Heliodoro Sánchez Ruz, 'La Sociedad Unipersonal' in Expansión (ed.), *Ley de Sociedades Limitadas*, Special Collection (Recoletos, Madrid, 1995) 65–107, at pp. 79–84.

91   1951 *Ley de Sociedades Anónimas*, Paragraph VIII, Explanatory Memorandum. This was also followed in the 1953 Law relating to private companies.

92   The Twelfth Directive was adopted on 21 December 1989 and the LSA was introduced by Royal Decree No. 1564 on 22 December 1989.

93   However, Spain had until 1 January 1992 to implement the Directive: Article 8.1.

94   LSA 1989, Article 14.2.

situation was left unclear by the LSA 1989 because, although a company would not be dissolved for its shares coming into the hands of one person, there was no definitive time limit expressed in which the company had to regain more members.

The Spanish reforms appeared in the LSRL 1995 which adopts a broad approach to the concept of single member companies. Thus, the provisions are applicable not only to private companies but also to public companies. The explanatory memorandum to the LSRL 1995 also observes the existence of two radically different conceptions of the single member company. One is that it should be a legal instrument for small and medium–sized enterprises and the other is that it should also be available to public companies, the single member company serving equally well the larger enterprise. Provision is also made for companies which begin as single member companies and companies which come to be held by one shareholder.[95]

A.   Contracts

In the UK a new section 322B was inserted into the 1985 Act stating that contracts between the company and the sole member, who is also a director of the company, must be in writing or set out in a written memorandum or recorded in minutes of a meeting of the directors. The Act also provides that breach of the section leads the director to be subject to a fine, but that such breach of the formalities will not affect validity of the contract. The section does not apply to 'contracts in ordinary course of business'. This is clearer than the wording of the Directive which refers to 'current operations concluded under normal conditions'.[96] However, neither reference can be said to have a totally clear significance. In Spain, under Article 128, LRSL 1995, contracts between the single member and the company must be recorded in writing or be in the form required for legal formality of the contract and must be recorded in a company register. The company's annual report should also make reference to such contracts. In the case of insolvency of the single member or the company, any contracts which have not been formalised will not be protected by limited liability. During a period of two years from the date of the contracts the single member will remain responsible to the company for any benefits lost to the company as a result of those contracts. Article 129 provides that if, after six months of becoming a single member company, that fact has not been publicised in the register, the single member will be fully liable for debts of the company contracted

---

95   LSRL 1995, Article 125.

96   Article 5.2.

during its state of single membership. However, once registered the member does not become liable for later debts.

B. Disclosure of Information

In the UK, the need for disclosure of the fact that the company has only one member was covered by the introduction of section 352A. A statement to this effect is necessary if there is a fall in the number of members to one or an increase in the number of members to two or more. The name and address of the members is also required. Breach of the section leads to a fine. Despite Spain's seemingly liberal attitude to business enterprise and the will to make single member companies widely available, the LSRL 1995 reveals a stringent approach to publicity requirements and goes beyond the requirements of the Directive in protecting third parties against the risks created by the single member company form. In this respect, Article 126 requires a public document to be registered with the identity of the single member where the company is constituted with a single member, or becomes a single member company, or where there is a change in situation or transfer of shares. This is more wide ranging than the demands within the Directive, and further, Article 126 also requires continuous publicity on notepaper and in dealings and announcements.

C. Meetings

In the UK the new section 370A of the 1985 Act provides that one member constitutes a quorum at company meetings and section 382B expresses a duty to provide a written record of any decision which may be taken by the general meeting. Again, breach of the section leads to a fine but does not affect the validity of the decision. In Spain, a number of formalities are necessary for the benefits of limited liability to be enjoyed by the single member. In conformity with the Directive, Article 127 LSRL 1995, states that the single member shall exercise the powers of general meeting and must sign minutes or arrange for the directors to sign them.

Overall, the UK implementation of the Twelfth Directive was minimalist. The DTI expressly stated its intention to keep reforms to a minimum to avoid complexity and cost. The UK also takes a narrow conceptual approach and does not extend the Directive to public companies. Nor does it take up the option in Article 7 of the Directive to allow other types of enterprise to have limited liability. However, the UK has dropped the reference to unlimited liability where the private company becomes a single member company and a second shareholder is not found after 12 months. By contrast, Spain has introduced very precise rules for single member companies. These came after much debate over the concept of a single member company and a radical shift in company law concepts. For Spain, the traditional view was that the formation of the company arises from a contract between two or more persons or at least two centres of interest.[97] The company is regarded as an organisational contract by which the money, assets or work of two or more persons are brought together in order to profit.[98] The notion of a company originating with one member therefore contradicts these principles. Thus, it seemed impossible for one person to form a company. Yet the end result is a Spanish reform which offers extensive legal recognition to the concept of the single member company. The demands made of a single member company in Spain, however, in terms of publicity and its inevitable cost, place potentially severe limits on the success of this business form.[99]

7.   THE REGULATION FOR THE EEIG

A Community Regulation is normally binding in its entirety and directly applicable in all Member States.[100] In practice this means that once a Regulation is created and published, it becomes law in all the Member States without the need for transposition into national law. However, the Regulation for the EEIG required implementation by the Member States because some options were left to Member States and an administrative framework was needed for national registration of the EEIG. The Member States were given four years before the Regulation became effective.

In the UK the DTI consulted before creating the provisions necessary to implement the Regulation.[101] According to Burnside, the DTI's ideas changed as a result of these consultations.[102] Ultimately, the UK

---

97   The general contractual rules relevant here are found in the Civil Code, Articles 1,254, 1,255, 1,257, 1,261.1 and 1,262.

98   Civil Code, Articles 1,665 and 116. See also Commercial Code Articles 125, 145, and 151.

99   See the strong criticisms expressed in Antonio Roncero Sánchez, 'La Sociedad de Capital Unipersonal' in Fernando Rodriguez Artigas and others (eds), *Derecho de Sociedades de Responsabilidad Limitada* (McGraw–Hill, Madrid, 1996) 1123–1186.

100   Article 189, EC Treaty.

101   DTI, *The EC Regulation on the European Economic Interest Grouping – A Consultative Document*, May 1986.

102   Alec Burnside, 'EEIG – Implementation in the UK' (1990) 11 *Company Lawyer*, 64–65.

implementation[103] was minimal, allowing the mandatory provisions of the Regulation to prevail, with amendments and introductions to UK law where necessary. The Regulations also deal with the optional aspects of the Community legislation. For example, Regulation 3 provides that the EEIG has legal personality, thus taking up the possibility provided in the Community Regulation. Additionally, Regulation 5 deals with the identity of the managers of an EEIG. The UK takes up the option of the manager being a legal person who is represented by one or more natural persons. Where the Community Regulation provides that membership ends with the member's death or because he fails to comply with conditions for a valid EEIG the UK Regulations add that he or she ceases to be a member for bankruptcy or sequestration of assets, and, if a partner, for bankruptcy or winding up. In summary, the UK Regulations appear to treat the grouping more as an unregistered company than as a partnership.

Spain already had a national form of economic interest grouping which was dealt with basically as a form of partnership. The implementation[104] of the EEIG Regulation sought to treat the Spanish and the Community grouping structures as parallel, attempting to align the rules to avoid contradiction and to enable the two structures to merge, when necessary, without legal difficulties. The Spanish implementation was a more comprehensive attempt to deal with the EEIG than the UK Regulations. Under the Spanish law the EEIG is granted legal personality.[105] The provisions in the Community Regulation on purpose and restrictions are expressed in the Spanish law as is the statement that profits belong to the members rather than to the EEIG.[106]

Whereas the UK law refers to the existing Business Names Act 1985 and relevant provisions in the Companies Act 1985 on use of names, the Spanish law states specifically that certain names cannot be used and refers also to the *Reglamento del Registro Mercantil* 1989 in this respect.[107] In Spain, emphasis is placed on the role and potential liability of the managers. Thus, whereas the European Regulation states that those who act before the EEIG is registered will be jointly and severally liable without limitation for any liabilities which arise, the Spanish law places such liability on the managers.[108] Specific reference is made in the Spanish law on allocation of

---

103   The European Economic Interest Groupings Regulations 1989 (SI 1989, No. 638).

104   *Ley de 29 Abril 1991*, No. 12/1991, *Agrupaciones de Interés Económico*, Regulation, *Boletín Oficial del Estado*, 30 April 1991.

105   LAIE, Article 1.

106   LAIE, Article 21.

107   LAIE, Articles 6 and 8; RRM, Article 363.

108   LAIE, Article 7.

votes although there is no prohibition on one member holding a majority of the votes. Spanish law sees this as a matter of contractual agreement. The Spanish law provides expressly the relevant reasons for declaring a winding up order. Under the Spanish law it is possible for EEIGs to merge and for them to transform into national groupings and vice versa. This same law deals with tax treatment of the EEIG and the Spanish Grouping, the emphasis being on transparency and avoidance of double taxation.

Both Member States grant the registration tasks to their existing companies or commercial registries. Both States give legal personality to the EEIG. In each State a fine is imposed for non–compliance with the publicity requirements and both States provide for court orders for winding up the EEIG.

8.   CONCLUSION

Despite the progress of harmonisation measures at the European level there still remains considerable scope for differentiation between the Member States by means of safeguard clauses, minimum standards, optional rules, derogations, etc.[109] These are a formal recognition of the needs of the individual Member States and account for variations in the level of integration between some Member States. The same could be said about differences in their implementation records. Some States implement the European provisions at a much slower pace than others, giving way to a dimension of the 'two speed Europe'.[110]

Both the UK and Spain have had to introduce extensive reforms. For the UK these reforms have been strikingly piecemeal. This has become increasingly the case for Spain after her initial major reform which occurred in 1989 and which dealt with six Directives. Since then Spain has introduced further, more discrete reforms. This dispersed and fragmented implementation, which is apparent in both States, suggests that the Directives are being fitted into existing structures rather than instigating fundamental structural changes. Furthermore, neither State's legislative process is perfect. In the UK commentators have noted that many of the reforms have been rushed through without adequate consideration of the details. In Spain, not all drafts of the legislation have been available for

---

109   Renaud Dehousse and Joseph H.H. Weiler, 'The Legal Dimension' in William Wallace (ed.), *The Dynamics of European Integration* (Royal Institute of International Affairs, London, 1990) 242–260 at p. 257.

110   *Ibid.*

comment by interested parties. These problems cast doubt on the quality of representative democracy at national level.

This chapter has highlighted the differences which continue to exist between the company laws of Spain and the UK, even after having implemented the directives. For example, the requirements of some of the directives bring those directives into the middle of two quite different positions, thereby highlighting the differences rather than eradicating them. There are many possible reasons for the differences in approach and implementation of the directives by the Member States. For example, there may be conceptual difficulties in introducing some provisions into an established system. The UK's experience with the impact of the First Directive on the *ultra vires* provides an example of this problem, as does Spain's experience of the Twelfth Directive, which introduced the concept of the single member company. Further problems might arise from different traditions such as in the accounting field. However, despite the differences which have been highlighted, these seem mostly to be at the level of detail while the overall company law framework in each Member State is not so different. This may be a reality of the commercial environment in which companies are generally pursuing similar aims and objectives.

What has also become apparent by the observations made in this chapter is that the directives have not gained more harmonisation as they have developed through their generations. The First and Second Directives, which sought more uniformity, did not achieve that uniformity. Yet the more flexible 'new approach' directives appear not to have achieved any better harmony between the laws. For example, there was, at first, quite significant reluctance to accept the Twelfth Directive. Similarly, the draft Thirteenth Directive, which is more accommodating still, is facing strong opposition by the UK, on whose law it is based. The claim by Du Plessis and Dine, that accommodation does not necessarily lead to harmonisation,[111] seems accurate. Arguably, the most harmonised field is the accounting field where compromises were reached between the different approaches, and options provided, but within a clear framework.

It has been established that the programme sought not uniformity, but co–ordination of national laws. Nevertheless, this chapter has demonstrated that still some very significant differences remain between Member States' laws. The next chapter will consider if, overall, these differences present barriers to the achievement of harmony sought by the company law programme.

---

111   J.J. Du Plessis and J. Dine, 'The Fate of the Draft Fifth Directive on Company Law: Accommodation Instead of Harmonisation' (1977) *JBL* 23–47.

9   Has Harmony Been Achieved?

1.   INTRODUCTION

An evaluation of the company law harmonisation programme requires a return to its objectives. Briefly, it will be recalled that the first objective is freedom of establishment in the territory of another Member State and to co-ordinate and make equivalent where necessary the safeguards needed for protecting the interests of members and others. This co-ordination has a functional purpose of developing and improving the operation of the Common Market. In practice this requires, through the co-ordinating laws, the removal of barriers to cross-border trade and to establishling co-operation between different entrepreneurs and companies across the Community. Has this plan been achieved by the company law programme? The success of the company laws created for these purposes depends on a number of conditions. First, there must be a willingness on the part of Member States to implement them effectively. Secondly, the Member States' interpretations must be similar enough not to make their implementations give rise to new differences, themselves creating further obstacles to cross-border trade or freedom of establishment. Thirdly, obedience by the business actors to the laws is necessary. Fourthly, take up of the opportunities created by the provisions indicates their effectiveness. Finally, the differences which remain between the company laws of the Member States must not themselves maintain obstacles to the effective functioning of the Common Market.

The previous chapter surveyed the implementation measures taken by the UK and Spain for the European laws which have been adopted to date. This chapter will explore the extent to which those laws have been co-ordinated through the implementation measures taken by the Member States and will consider the differences which still remain. The level of take up of procedures and instruments made available by the company law programme will also be considered, before we conclude whether or not the programme has been successful.

2.   THE DEVELOPMENT FROM UNIFORMITY TO FLEXIBILITY

Despite the apparently prescriptive nature of the First and Second Directives and their positive move towards uniformity,[1] they still did not achieve real harmony among the Member States' laws. The later move towards flexibility, however, was not necessarily an improvement. Indeed, Du Plessus and Dine point out that this led to accommodation of Member States' differences rather than to harmonisation.[2] At each stage or 'generation' the directives have been criticised for allowing many differences to continue. For example, the response to the directives that sought uniformity was that, first, some Member States took advantages of the derogations possible in the directives;[3] secondly, Member States adopted different interpretations of the directives' provisions and their objectives;[4] and thirdly, some Member States entered the Community later, therefore having a different response to those Directives. The Accounts Directives, which were more flexible, had many options which were taken up by Member States. Within the Fourth Directive Buxbaum and Hopt counted 41 options for Member States and 35 options for business enterprises.[5] The Spanish and UK implementation measures each took up different options. The Twelfth Directive was even more flexible, leaving much to the discretion of Member States. For example, Article 2 gives to Member States the option to decide to what extent legal persons should be sole members of companies. The draft Thirteenth Directive is a proposed framework directive and thereby presents itself more as a statement of principles than as a regulatory instrument. Doubts have been expressed about the ability to achieve harmony through such a vague measure.[6]

Overall, the move from uniformity to flexibility appears not to have helped achieve better co-ordination. Whilst it appears not to have been the

---

1   This move followed criticism by the Economic and Social Committee of the aim of equivalence: see José Antonio Gómez Segade, 'La Publicidad de las Sociedades de Capital: La Reforma del Derecho Registral Mercantil' in Angel Rojo (ed.), *La Reforma de la Ley de Sociedades Anónimas* (Civitas, Madrid, 1987) 21–46, at p. 26.

2   J.J. Du Plessus and J. Dine, 'The Fate of the Draft Fifth Directive on Company Law: Accommodation instead of Harmonisation' (1997) *JBL* 23–47.

3   Eg the UK took up the derogations offered in Article 19 of the Second Directive.

4   As was witnessed by the minimum capital requirement.

5   R.M. Buxbaum and K.J. Hopt, *Legal Harmonisation and the Business Enterprise* (de Gruyter, New York, 1988) at p. 235.

6   DTI Consultative Document, *Proposal for a Thirteenth Directive on Company Law Concerning Take–over Bids*, April 1996, para. 30, p. 9.

aim to create uniform company laws among the Member States, the differences which the company law programme has allowed to remain are significant. It is appropriate at this point to identify what kinds of differences exist.

3.   RANGE OF COMPANIES AFFECTED

Among the Member States there are differences as to which companies are covered by the provisions of the directives. Within the directives and their application the range of companies covered has been influenced by compromise and by the choices granted to Member States. The result has been that, often, the directives apply only to public companies. In other cases, Member States are able to apply the provisions to both public and private companies or may choose only to apply the provisions to one company type. For example, the Second Directive is a result of compromise. When the Second Directive was under negotiation the Commission argued that the UK private company was not similar to a *sarl*[7] but was more like a public company to such an extent that the Directive should be applied to UK private as well as public companies.[8] The UK opposed this suggestion since most companies were private companies, contrasting with the position on the continent. The Commission later attempted a compromise by seeking application of the Directive to private companies but with the requirement of a lower capital sum. That suggestion was also rejected by the UK. The final version of the Directive did not apply to private companies. The result of this compromise is that, applying only to public companies, the Second Directive leaves untouched the majority of undertakings across Europe. Consequently, little co–ordination or harmony is achieved within the business environment as a whole.

Other directives leave to the discretion of the Member States whether or not to apply the provisions to certain types of companies. For example, Spain's implementation of the Third and Sixth Directives applies to private companies as well as to public companies, whereas the UK's rules only concern public companies. Thus, in Spain both public and private companies

---

7   The French *société à responsabilité limitée*.

8   The logic was unclear, however, because the Second Directive was also to be applied to private companies in Northern Ireland, which were treated more as *sarls* under the First and Fourth Directives. For a discussion of the classification problems see Jane Welch, 'The English Private Company – A Crisis of Classification' (1974) *JBL* 277– 281.

may merge or divide to make either a public or private company.[9] UK law anticipates the participation in a merger of public companies transferring assets to or creating another company which may or may not be a public company. In a division, the companies among which the assets are divided must be public companies or, if created for or in connection with the scheme, may be public companies or otherwise.[10]

The Spanish implementation of the Twelfth Directive makes available the single member company to both public and private companies. In the UK, on the other hand, this business form is only on offer to private companies.[11] Arguably, this could present obstacles to a Spanish entrepreneur who wishes to set up business in the UK but cannot raise the capital.

In both Spain and the UK the majority of companies are private companies. In the UK, private companies represent approximately 99 per cent of those registered.[12] In Spain they represent 94 per cent.[13] The result of these differences of application, therefore, is that only a small part of the business environment is affected by many of the European company law provisions, leaving the possibility of different national rules applying to the majority of business actors.

4.   REGISTRIES

National responses to the directives may also increase the differences rather than reduce them. This appears to have been the case for the commercial registers within the UK and Spain. Both the UK and Spain have long had a Register such as that required by Article 3 of the First Directive. The English Companies Register was introduced in 1844 by the Joint Stock Companies Act[14] and, in Spain, the 'Registro Mercantil' has also existed for more than a

---

9   See Article 233 LSA 1989 and Article 94 LSRL 1995.

10   S. 427A(2).

11   While, technically, public companies could become single member companies, Section 24 Companies Act 1985 would apply, imposing after six months unlimited joint and several liability on the single member and the company for the company's debts and so the benefit of the business form would be lost.

12   HMSO, *Companies in 1995–96*, Table A2.

13   Francisco Vicent Chuliá, *Introducción al Derecho Mercantil* (Tirant lo Blanch, Valencia, 1996) at p. 184.

14   Section 19. In the UK there are regional registries for Scotland and England and Wales, but no central registry.

hundred years.[15] Spain introduced important changes to the law relating to the Register as part of her implementation of the directives.[16] A new *Reglamento del Registro Mercantil* was adopted in December 1989.[17] A Central Register in Madrid was created to provide a bank of information on companies filed in the regional registries and to administer the domiciliary aspects of companies in the different regions. The Registrar was also given new competences, including the legal authorisation of documents,[18] the appointment of independent experts for the valuation of non–cash payments for shares,[19] appointment of auditors,[20] and administering the deposit and publicity of the annual accounts.[21]

Despite the fact that the First Directive requires a central register in each Member State there are no provisions in the Directive on the role of the registrar. Consequently, the powers and duties given to the registrar may differ between the Member States. This is true of the UK and Spain. The Spanish registrar appears to have a much more extensive role than the English and Welsh or Scottish registrars. This may be partly because the Spanish registrar is a general commercial registrar whereas those in the UK deal only with companies, but it may also arise as a result of Spain's positive response to the directives.

5. MINIMUM CAPITAL

Some variations may arise from the different interpretations of the directives' provisions. For example, the significance of the minimum capital requirement in the Second Directive led to some surprising results.

---

15 See Aurelio Menéndez Menéndez, 'La Primera Directiva de La Comunidad Económica Europea en Materia de Sociedades y El Registro Mercantil Español', in Various Authors, *Derecho Mercantil de la CEE – Estudios en Homenaje a José Girón Tena* (Civitas, Madrid, 1991), 703–727, at p. 705.

16 See eg Gómez Segade, above note 1, 21–46; Rafael García Villaverde, 'La Reforma del Registro Mercantil' (1990) 2 *La Ley* 1180–1197; Menéndez Menéndez, above note 15; Francisco Mesa Martín, 'Aproximación al Registro Mercantil' (1994) 621 *Revista Crítica de Derecho Inmobiliario*, 561–603.

17 Introduced by Royal Decree, No. 1597 29 December 1989, *Boletín Oficial del Estado*, 30 December 1989.

18 See Article 16.2 Commercial Code, and Articles 2 and 293, *Reglamento del Registro Mecantil* (RRM).

19 See Articles 302 to 313, RRM.

20 Articles 314 to 338 RRM.

21 *Ibid.*

Ultimately, harmonisation appears not to have been achieved among the Member States owing to their different interpretations of the purpose of the minimum capital requirement. Current minimum capital requirement figures across the Community are:

		pesetas	£ (approx)
Directive	25,000ECU	3,644,875	18,000
Germany	100,000DM	7,100,000	35,000
Belgium	1,250,000FB	4,218,750	21,000
Spain	10,000,000P	10,000,000	50,000
France	1,500,000F	31,500,000	150,000
UK	50,000St.	10,450,000	50,000
Italy	200,000,000L	19,600,000	100,000
Netherlands	35,000G	2,177,000	11,000
Portugal	5,000,000E	4,475,000	22,000

Source: Ignacio Quintana, 'El Capital Social' in Angel Rojo (ed.), *La Reforma de la Ley de Sociedades Anónimas* (Civitas, Madrid, 1987) 105–122, at p. 109.

These figures show that there remain striking differences in the legal requirements of the Member States. Such differences could make some Member States more attractive locations than others for setting up business. The Spanish interpretation of the minimum capital requirement was that it could deter the use of public companies. In Spain, in particular, the most popular company type was the public company. The key factor for this preference appears to have been the inadequacies of the law relating to private companies by contrast with the law relating to the public company, which was more flexible and accommodating.[22] Spain saw the minimum capital requirement as a mechanism for altering the company demography. By imposing a high capital requirement figure for public companies it succeeded in altering the pattern so that more private companies would be created instead.

6.   DISCLOSURE OF INFORMATION

The Directives are notable for their very strict disclosure provisions. In particular, the First and Second Directives lay down the disclosure requirements as a minimum. In this respect, the Member States had no option

---

22   See Chapter 8.

to omit rules requiring the same documents and contents. Both the UK and Spain implemented the majority of the requirements in the five Articles relating to disclosure in the First Directive. As was demonstrated in the chapter of the introductory book to this *European Business Law Library* series, these Articles generated a lot of new law in the Member States.[23] The UK law relevant to the disclosure provisions spans almost all of the Companies Act 1985. The Spanish provisions for public companies alone are contained in at least three legal sources[24] and such reforms are not confined to small sections of these laws.

Despite the clarity of the disclosure provisions in the directives generally, the Member States' requirements still differ. The UK appears to adopt a more lenient approach than Spain. For example, the implementation provisions for the Third Directive in the UK are not as strict as in Spain with regard to publicity requirements, although Spain appears also to be more stringent than is required by the directives. Spain's strict procedure may give the company an opportunity to cool off before making a final decision as to merger or fusion and possibly offers stronger protection to third parties who might wish to oppose the general meeting's decision.

Regarding the Twelfth Directive, the requirements of publicity are more extensive in Spain, too. Spain requires disclosure of the single member status on the notepaper and in company notices etc whereas this does not appear to be required in UK law. These differences could deter a UK entrepreneur from establishing a business in Spain where the costs of running the business could be increased by the practical and bureaucratic legal requirements he or she would face.

7. EXTENSIVE NATURE OF SPANISH REFORMS

The Member State which appears to have altered its company law most appears to be Spain. For example, while both Member States' laws go beyond the requirements of the Third and Sixth Directives, the rules on mergers and divisions in Spain are also more extensive than the UK's provisions. One reason for Spain's broader approach in this respect may arise from laws which existed prior to the implementation of the directives. For example, in Spain, companies other than public companies were able to participate in a merger or division. The fact that Spain had experienced these

---

23 Charlotte Villiers, 'Harmonisation of Company Laws in Europe – With an Introduction to Some Comparative Issues' in Geraint Howells (ed.), *European Business Law* (Dartmouth, Aldershot, 1996), Ch. 7, 165–191.

24 LSA 1989, RRM 1989, Código de Comercio 1885, as amended.

forms of merger to a greater extent than the UK may also indicate a greater awareness in Spain of the need to protect a broader range of interested parties.

Regarding the Twelfth Directive, it would not be an exaggeration to say that the UK appeared resentful of another European imposition, seeing little practical need for a law to deal with single member companies. The result, as has been observed, was a slender set of Regulations, containing a sweeper clause and alterations to a few existing statutory provisions. By contrast, although for Spain the idea of a single member company was a conceptual revolution in terms of traditional Spanish company law, and despite Spain's delay in implementing the Twelfth Directive, when the reform did arrive it was more positive, with a special section in the LRSL 1995 fully devoted to the single member company.

This more extensive implementation of the company law directives by Spain may be for a number of reasons. The fact that Spain came late to the Community may mean that the directives would have affected her legal system more dramatically since she had no opportunity to participate in the negotiations and influence the directives from her legal system's perspective. By contrast, the UK took part in the negotiations for the Accounts Directives and clearly influenced their content and perspective, with the result that she had less work to do in order to implement the directives. It was a case of formalising what was mostly already being done in practice. For Spain, however, implementation meant, perhaps, a modernisation of her accounting system, and in any event, at least a more formal structure and a new perspective away from the emphasis on taxation.

Another possible reason for Spain's generally more extensive implementation provisions may lie in the fact that she conducted a more complete reform all at once. In the UK on the other hand, reforms have been piecemeal, which might have encouraged a wish only to tinker with rather than to disturb the whole structure of the company law. This may have led to more minimalist implementation provisions.

8.   COST, EFFICIENCY AND FLEXIBILITY

The UK's minimalist approach to implementation may also be explained by her concerns about costs and her deregulatory approach to corporate activity. For example, with regard to the Third and Sixth Directives which require expert reports on proposed mergers and divisions, Spain provides for experts to make all necessary investigations when making their reports, but in the UK this provision was omitted. The House of Lords Select Committee

Report provides some explanation of the UK's omission, since it considered that such a provision would be 'a heavy and lengthy task'.[25]

The UK's deregulatory and cost–conscious approach may also explain the UK legislators' greater use of the options available in the directives. For example, regarding the layout of the balance sheet and the profit and loss account the UK gives to companies a choice, whereas the Spanish law has opted for one of the alternatives in each case without giving to individual companies any choice. Thus, in UK law, there are two possible formats: capital and reserves.[26] By contrast, Spanish law seems to prescribe the layout corresponding to Article 9 of the Fourth Directive only.[27] In UK law there are four possible formats for the profit and loss account, adopting all the alternatives laid out in the Directive at Articles 22–26.[28] Spain adopts the format prescribed in Article 24 of the Directive and the company is given no choice. According to Sánchez Calero, such legalistic schemes help to promote clarity and transparency.[29] This need for clarity also led the legislators to be more detailed in the drafting of the legal schemes. Thus, Articles 175 to 180 LSA 1989 refer extensively to the necessary items to go into the accounts documents and even state the order in which the items should appear. It is only possible to depart from the format in order to achieve a faithful view and this must be stated in the notes. The result of these differences may ultimately be that it is difficult to make genuine comparisons of accounts figures from one Member State to another because they are using different presentational and valuation formats.

9. BALANCING OF INTERESTS: ARTICLE 54(3)(g)

A key objective of the Directives is found in Article 54(3)(g) which, in part, requires a balance of interests. This seems to be more possible in some countries than in others. Spanish law recognises the interests of parties other than those of the shareholders more readily than UK law. For example, in response to the Third and Sixth Directives, the UK provides that the information requirements should benefit the shareholders,[30] but no other

---

25 HL Select Commitee Report, Session 1975–76 (112) Twentieth Report, p. v, paragraph 7.

26 Companies Act 1985, s. 225.

27 LSA 1989, Articles 175–183 and Commercial Code Article 35.

28 Companies Act 1985, Schedule 4, Part 1, Para. 8, Companies Act 1985, section 226.

29 Fernando Sánchez Calero, *Instituciones de Derecho Mercantil*, 16th ed. (Civitas, Madrid, 1992), at p. 276.

30 Article 11, Third Directive; Article 9, Sixth Directive.

parties are directly given this right, although creditors should be given the opportunity to see the draft terms in time to examine them before the date of the meeting of members.[31] In Spain, however, all parties mentioned in the Directives, except creditors, are given the right to inspect the documents.[32] Creditors are at least given the opportunity within six months to oppose a merger or division, which does not appear to be the case in the UK.[33] In the UK the courts decide, when making an order to approve a scheme, if the members' or creditors' interests would or would not be prejudiced.[34]

10.   TAKE–UP OF COMMUNITY PROVISIONS

The level of activity vis–à–vis the type of mergers and divisions covered by the Third and Sixth Directives has been relatively low in the EC. Spain was seen to make more use of the Directives, but in the UK only 17 orders were made by the court by 1993.[35] There are a number of possible explanations for this low take–up of the asset merger and division processes. Wooldridge suggests that the cumbersome procedures would encourage resort to other types of merger, such as take–over bids.[36] Burnside, observing that the Directives inspired 'next to no use', indicated that using the courts would produce delay and expense and thus would not appeal to commercial interests.[37] Regarding Italy and France, it was observed by Binder Hamlyn in their EC Commission Report that divisions were not common because of tax implications.[38] Another problem created by the Directives is that the information requirements strike against the need for confidentiality in situations where a future merger or division is not even guaranteed. Despite the low take–up and the criticisms that the Third and Sixth Directives

---

31   Companies Act 1985, Schedule 15B, paragraph 3(e).

32   LSA, Article 238.

33   Their consent may be required by the court on the application of the company or any creditor or member of it to order a meeting of the creditors or class of creditors or of the members or any class of members: S. 425(1) Companies Act 1985.

34   Companies Act 1985, Schedule 15B, paragraph 11(4)(d).

35   See Binder Hamlyn Report: *Study on Extension of Scope of the Third and Sixth Company Law Directives* (EC, 1993).

36   Frank Wooldridge, *Company Law in the United Kingdom and the European Community: Its Harmonisation and Unification* (Athlone Press, London, 1991), at p. 38.

37   Alec Burnside, 'Overcoming Barriers to European M&A' (1992) 13 *Company Lawyer* 19–25, at p. 24.

38   Binder Hamlyn, above note 35.

inspire, the European Commission is considering extending the provisions of the Directives to cover private companies as well.[39] This may answer the problem of the Directives' limited scope of application but in practice it will probably make little difference to the extent to which they are used.

Another area of low take–up of the company law provisions is that of the Economic Interest Groupings. A survey carried out by the Commission[40] showed that in 1991 322 EEIGs had been formed. In the UK, only 23 EEIGs have been established, although it is possible that UK–based firms are also members of EEIGs registered abroad. These figures do not suggest that the EEIG will have enormous significance.

This low take–up of some of the European provisions may lie in their failure to meet the needs of businesses in the Community. It could be that the laws are dealing with the wrong issues or that they ignore the most important issues. For example, the Twelfth Directive covers only a narrow aspect of company law: recognition of single membership of a company and granting of limited liability to the sole member. It leaves alone matters such as lifting the veil of incorporation, the qualifications of persons to be directors and liquidation. Economics and taxation issues are also ignored by the Directive.

11. REASONS FOR CONTINUING DIFFERENCES

A number of possible reasons exist for the difficulties for the programme. Some of the differences between the Member States may be cultural. For example, the DTI questioned the need for a Thirteenth Directive, arguing that barriers to take–overs were largely cultural and structural rather than a result of different processes among Member States for take–over bids.[41] In Spain, for example, the 'Bolsa' is much smaller than the London Stock Exchange

---

39 In fact the reason is not so much that they are applied widely but that some Member States have extended their rules to cover private companies. Thus, it is arguably an issue of equivalence of legal rules rather than of commercial practice that the Commission aspires to. See Binder Hamlyn Report, above note 35.

40 European Commission, *EEIG–Emergence of a New Form of European Co–operation: Review of Three Years Experience* (Brussels, 1993).

41 See DTI Press Release 90/235, *Barriers to Takeovers: Responses to Consultation*, 26 April 1990. In this document barriers identified included: accounting problems, unequal voting rights, proxy voting procedures, poison pill tactics, obstacles to the appointment and dismissal of directors by majority shareholders, lack of powers to acquire a residual minority of shares, restrictions on the transfer of shares, and problems in identifying shareholders where bearer shares are used.

and many more companies are family run or supported by heavy financial group blocks.[42]

Other cultural differences also exist, which present potential barriers for harmonisation. For example, across Europe there have traditionally been two major systems in accounting. The 'continental' systems tend to follow a macro–economic approach whilst the 'Anglo–Saxon' systems pursue a micro–economic approach, resulting in different perceptions of the objectives of corporate business organisation and accounting.[43] Macro–economic systems concentrate on information that will assist national economic planning.[44] For example, they emphasise the promotion of more reliable national economic and fiscal policies, informing the public of the true distribution of wealth, providing data for the study of market trends, and helping to achieve a more equitable taxation system. In this way, uniform rules tend to be imposed from above, with general accounting principles used as a tool for the general economic planning of the state. The micro–economic approach, by contrast, concentrates on information which assists private investors. Thus, financial reports are regarded as relevant to shareholders, investment analysts, the City, creditors and lenders, other companies, employees, the government and official bodies and the general public.[45] The existence in the UK of an active, open capital market upon which companies may seek to borrow funds, or to issue new equity share capital, influences the provision of financial information for the benefit of the investors. This contrasts with France, where the French capital market equivalent, the Paris Bourse, 'remains no more than a marginal source of finance'.[46] Such

---

42   Whereas there are about two million companies registered on the London Stock Exchange the Spanish Bolsa has a list of about three hundred companies, making the number of companies susceptible to public offer much smaller, see eg Javier García de Enterría, 'El Control del Poder Societario en la Gran Empresa y la Función Disciplinar de las OPAs' (1992) 47 *Revista de Derecho Bancario y Bursátil* 665; Alberto Javier Tapia–Hermida and Juan Sánchez–Calero Guilarte, 'La Adaptación del Derecho Español del Mercado de Valores al Derecho Comunitario' (1991) 46 *Revista de Derecho Bancario y Bursátil* 967; Benito Arruñada 'Crítica a la Regulación de OPAs' (1992) 203/4 *Revista de Derecho Mercantil* 29.

43   Desmond McComb, 'International Accounting Standards and the EEC Harmonisation Program: A Conflict of Disparate Objectives' (1979) *International Journal of Accounting* 35–46 at pp. 42–43.

44   Desmond McComb (1979), above note 43, at pp. 43–44 describing the objectives of the French Plan Compatible, within the macro–economic stream.

45   *Ibid.*, citing a report by the Inflation Accounting Committee, *Inflation Accounting* (HMSO, London, 1975).

46   *Ibid.*, at p. 40.

different approaches may well arrive at different answers when measuring the same event.[47]

These political and cultural differences mean that some states are more bureaucratic and others more informal. For example, different Member States have different methods of raising capital. So, for example, in Germany, where bank loans signify more creditor protection, this will lead to more legal regulation, resulting in a more conservative approach to accounting and financial disclosure. By contrast, Britain's emphasis on capital markets calls for greater shareholder protection, leading to concentration on different aspects of financial information. In the UK there is a greater need for fair presentation because a large number of listed companies receive investments from third parties. Other relevant national differences include population size and degree of industrialisation. Thus, even though both the UK and Ireland are identified as *laissez faire* states with less formality, they are both different from each other because Ireland has much smaller companies and a smaller economy than the UK. This leads to a different orientation of interests in the two States.[48]

These national differences are significant and deep–rooted. Different requirements will arise from different environments and institutions. For example, administrative hierarchies will lead to more specified and standardised flows of information whereas market settings will look for information integrity. As McComb argues, it is necessary to question whether national differences are 'fossilised survivors or spontaneously evolving responses to local information demands and needs'.[49] Alternatively, it might be legitimate to ask if the differences are environmentally determined.[50] According to McComb, if the differences are environmentally determined then it is likely that they will self–destruct in the common market.[51]

Alongside the cultural and political differences between Member States, the range of interested parties is potentially quite vast and these interested parties can be both 'proponents and antagonists of harmonisation'.[52] In the area of accounts, for example, Nobes identifies the following: investors,

---

47   *Ibid.*, at p. 44.

48   *Ibid.*, at p. 38.

49   Desmond McComb, 'Accounting' in Richard M. Buxbaum, Gerard Hertig, Alain Hirsch, Klaus J. Hopt (eds), *European Business Law – Legal and Economic Analyses on Integration and Harmonisation* (de Gruyter, Berlin, New York, 1991) Ch. 7, 267–305, at p. 270.

50   *Ibid.*, at p. 271.

51   *Ibid.*

52   *Ibid.*, at p. 269.

investment analysts, stock exchanges, creditor grantors, multinational companies, multinational firms of accountants, governments, international quasi–governmental bodies, national accounting bodies, and trade unions.[53] One problem with such a multiplicity of interested parties is that they each have only their own interests under consideration. Indeed, all these parties with diverse interests would look for different kinds of information. This could make harmonisation very difficult. However, despite these differences, there will be a degree of common information sought by most institutions and environments. For example, most states have tax requirements which will seek similar information. As Hopwood states, 'it is the patterns of real underlying differences that nevertheless provide both the rationale for harmonisation and, importantly, in the present context, the constraints upon it'.[54]

Commercial activity now takes place on a global scale. The EU is thus forced by events to take a more outward–looking approach. In this way, globalisation has also affected the potential to achieve harmonisation in European law. Indeed, in the accounting environment the International Accounting Standards Committee (IASC) and the EU appear to have different objectives. For example, McComb notes that the intention behind the Fourth Directive is the harmonisation of the content, presentation and publication of the annual accounts of limited companies and of the valuation methods used in preparing these accounts. This seems to coincide with the broad objectives of the IASC but when one looks more closely there are important differences: the Directive calls for both a true and fair view and a mandatory layout but the IASC would argue that a true and fair view does not necessitate a mandatory layout; EC law follows a more prescriptive approach, seeing legal compliance as an end in itself, whereas the IASC is more flexible.[55]

As was noted above, the objectives of the European harmonisation programme include: removal of barriers to the establishment of a single market, creation of a unified business environment, creation of a Community capital market, technological progress in the Community, a need to recognise social and regional aspects of industrial development. On the other hand, the factors which gave impetus to the formation of the IASC include increasing

53　Christopher Nobes, *Accounting Harmonisation in Europe: Process, Progress and Prospects* (Financial Times Business Information, London, 1992) at pp. 68–72.

54　A. Hopwood, 'Harmonisation of Accounting Standards within the EC: A Perspective for the Future', in European Commission, *The Future of Harmonisation of Accounting Standards within the European Communities* (Conference Proceedings, European Commission, Brussels, 17–18 January 1990) at p. 58.

55　*Ibid.*, at p. 46.

internationalism in business, growth of international capital markets, emerging international stance of the accountancy profession. Is it appropriate for the European Union to maintain its own macro–economic perspective when the trend seems to be directing itself towards globalisation? The problem is that strict rules create less flexibility and result in a slower response to changing circumstances. It is not possible to meet dynamic problems with static responses. The macro–economic approach at European level has, in practice, protectionist tendencies at international level: Europe protecting Europe's economy. The IASC is perhaps more pragmatic and to an extent more individualistic, but this allows more flexibility and leaves room to adapt. Ironically, Emenyonu and Gray, citing Price Waterhouse surveys, suggest that more harmonisation has been achieved since the existence of the IASC.[56] Despite their differences, the European Commission prefers the IASC's standards to the alternative Generally Accepted Accounting Principles produced by the United States because the European Community has an opportunity to participate in creating the standards created by the IASC.[57]

12. CONCLUSION

A number of national differences have been identified between the UK and Spain despite the fact that each Member State has implemented the harmonising Directives. There are several possible explanations for these differences. Spain appears to have been a more willing partner than the UK. This might stem from her efforts to join the Community in the first place. Unlike the UK, Spain had to give concessions to join. That may have endowed her with an attitude that she would make an effort to ensure returns

---

56   Emmanuel Emenyonu and Sidney J. Gray, 'EC Accounting Harmonisation: An Empirical Study of Measurement Practices in France, Germany and the UK' (1992) *Accounting and Business Research* 49–58, at p. 50. The surveys focus on regulations rather than on actual practice.

57   European Commission, Communication Document, *Accounting Harmonisation: A New Strategy Vis–à–Vis International Harmonisation*, COM (95) 508 final, Brussels, 14. 11. 1995. This is especially important currently as the IASC is in the process of elaborating a new set of standards which are due to be presented to the International Organisation of Securities Commissions in 1997. For developments at the international level see: Bruce Picking, 'A course for the dash to harmony', *Financial Times*, 29 August 1996; Christopher Nobes, 'The standard setters', *Financial Times*, 10 October 1996; Jim Kelly, Beijing Beckons, *Financial Times*, 5 June 1997; Jim Kelly, 'World accounting wins more converts', *Financial Times*, 9 June 1997.

for her investment in Community membership. The UK's negotiations for entry into the Community, by contrast, involved the UK imposing demands on the Community. This may have encouraged in the UK an attitude of superiority that ultimately leads to her resenting demands imposed on her by the Community.

Another possible reason for the differences may be that Spanish company law was more similar to the laws of the original Member States so that the European instigated reforms would be easier to implement in Spain than in the UK. The Spanish reform in 1989 was also more wide–ranging, allowing for greater coherence in her implementation of the European provisions. Furthermore, her laws deal separately with the different company types so that implementation would not complicate other areas of her company laws. In the UK, however, where all companies are dealt with in the same legislation, the implementation measures would require more exemption provisions to cover those company types not to be covered, hence requiring more complex reforms, and thereby encouraging a reluctance to introduce such reforms. Interpretational differences provide a further explanation for the different implementation measures, leading to different conceptual approaches and different legal definitions of such concepts.

Overall, some important differences remain. The low take–up level of certain provisions also suggests that the programme has not achieved fully what it set out to do. Many of the Directives have a limited application and deal with a narrow range of issues. Connected with this problem is the fact that some proposed directives failed even to be adopted. These are concerned with fundamental issues such as company structure and employee participation. The next part of this book will consider the implications of these issues and will suggest an argument by which these issues may be addressed.

PART FOUR

Towards Participatory Democracy in Company Law?

10 A Labour Law Detour

1. INTRODUCTION

The previous chapter highlighted the continuing differences between the company laws of the Member States. Although the company law programme has been extensive and has led to many reforms in the company laws of the Member States, the remaining differences in the national company laws are strong enough to expose the company law programme to the charge that it has failed to achieve harmony. Other problems are that the laws are also very complex and there appears to be increasing hostility to the reforms initiated in Brussels. It might be argued that these problems are a reflection of the poor quality of representative democracy at European level. The failure of European 'representatives'[1] to respond to their electors may have resulted in provisions which deal with irrelevant subjects and which ignore issues of real concern. The distance between representatives and their electors may cause them not to understand the business cultures and practices of the Member States so that the laws created may be difficult to apply within the different contexts. Simply leaving this to be dealt with by options and derogations encourages differences between the national laws and practices to continue. Another indication of the poor representative democracy is the uneven balance of power between the institutions. The European Parliament is regarded as the official representative of the citizens of the Community; but its continued marginalised position offers little incentive for citizens to become involved in Community activities. The move towards greater flexibility in the European legislation appears to have reinforced the strength of influence of the Member States with the effect that the legislation leaves nearly all the technical details to the Member States but with no less hostility to the European law reforms. Indeed, the flexible approach has possibly served to encourage Member States positively to oppose the reforms. This seems to be the case for the draft Thirteenth Directive, despite the generosity of its provisions in terms of discretion for Member States.

In the introduction to this book it was suggested that participation was a possible route to improved representative democracy; more particularly, workplace participation. Indeed, many theorists have identified participatory democracy with the workplace. For example, Pateman argues that workplace participation, if democratic, may act as an educative process and bring about

---

1   Those with responsibility for the legislative and policy decisions.

more interest in national politics.[2] Similarly, MacPherson claims that workplace democracy is a form of empowerment at a wider level. In particular, he argues that 'those who have proved their competence in the one kind of participation, and gained confidence that they can be effective, will be less put off by the forces which have kept them politically apathetic, more able to reason at a greater political distance from results, and more able to see the importance of decisions at several removes from their most immediate concerns'.[3] Arguments in favour of workplace democracy are relevant to company law since companies themselves are the most common employers and they therefore provide a major opportunity for widespread workplace participation and democracy. Yet, despite the efforts by the company law harmonisation programme to address the issue of employee participation, the proposals offered have fallen on stony ground.

Company law attempts to introduce employee participation have generally met with hostility from Member States and industrialists, as well as from trade unionists. A number of directives have been proposed under the company law programme relating to this subject. The draft Fifth Directive has been the most controversial. Other proposals include the Vredeling Directive and the draft Directive which accompanies the proposed European Company Statute. None of these proposals have been adopted. By contrast, directives under the labour law programme concerned with a very limited form of employee participation have at least been adopted. These include the Collective Redundancies Directive,[4] the Acquired Rights Directive[5] and, most recently, the European Works Councils Directive,[6] the latter being most closely related to the company law proposals. This chapter will outline the measures in support of employee participation in both the company and

---

2 Carole Pateman, *Participation and Democratic Theory* (Cambridge University Press, Cambridge, 1970) esp. at pp. 42–43.

3 C.B. MacPherson, *The Life and Times of Liberal Democracy* (Oxford University Press, Oxford, 1977) at p. 104.

4 Directive 75/127/EEC of 17 February 1975 on the protection of workers' representatives in the event of collective redundancies [OJ L 48, 22.2.75]; revised by Directive 92/56/EEC of 24 June 1992 [OJ L 245, 26.8.92].

5 Directive 77/187/EEC of 14 February 1977 on the approximation of the laws of the Member States relating to the safeguarding of employees' rights in the event of transfers of undertakings, business or parts of businesses [OJ L 61, 5.3.77].

6 Directive 94/45/EEC on the establishment of a European Works Council or a procedure in Community–scale undertakings and Community–scale groups of undertakings for the purposes of informing and consulting employees [OJ L 254, 30.9.94, p. 64].

labour law spheres and will consider the possible reasons for the failure of the company law programme to achieve those aims.

2. THE COMPANY LAW PROPOSALS

A. Draft Fifth Directive

There have been several drafts of the proposed Fifth Company Law Directive.[7] The most controversial provisions of this proposed Directive relate to corporate structure and industrial democracy. The proposed Directive also deals with directors' civil liability, minority shareholder protection, voting at the general meeting, and the adoption and auditing of accounts, but these aspects have been somewhat ignored as a result of the focus of attention on the structure and democracy provisions. The Directive has German origins, its idea being based on the German concept of co–determination which came into existence in 1952 and remained an integral part of the structure of German business organisation.[8]

The first draft appeared in 1972. It proposed a very different corporate structure to what the new Member States at that time were used to. The UK, for example, did not have a two–tier structure, which the draft advocated. These different national approaches led to opposition to the proposal. Despite such opposition, the Commission remained committed during the 1970s to introducing industrial democracy in some form to European company law. In 1975 the Commission produced a Green Paper in which it provided justifications for and set out the alternative forms of employee participation.[9] The Commission argued that there was increasing recognition of the 'democratic imperative' together with a need to address the imbalance of power in the corporate relationship between managers and workers: there were those with power to make decisions and those who carry them out.

---

7   First proposed in 1972 (OJ 1972 C131/49). Amended proposal in 1983 (OJ 1983 C240/2) and an unofficial text appeared in 1988: available in DTI Consultation Document *Amended Proposal for a Fifth Directive on the Harmonisation of Company Law in the European Community*, January 1990. The official 1983 text has been further amended in 1991 [OJ C 321, 12.12.1991].

8   For a description of the background to the draft Fifth Directive see Thomas P. Conlon, 'Industrial Democracy and EEC Company Law: A Review of the Draft 5th Directive' (1975) 24 *ICLQ* 348 and Janet Dine 'Implications for the United Kingdom of the EC Fifth Directive' (1989) 38 *ICLQ* 547.

9   European Commission *Employee Participation and Company Structure in the EC*, Supplement Bulletin 8/75.

These two sets of interests would need to be reconciled. The Commission identified as alternative approaches to participation: negotiation of collective agreements; representative institutions which are informed, consulted and approve certain measures; membership of and active participation in the company's decision–making bodies; and share participation. Responding to the criticisms of the earlier draft Directive, the Commission concluded that the main task was to construct a framework providing for the objectives to be reached in a way that leaves discretion to the Member States as to the precise models which they may adopt.

In 1983 a new proposal was presented.[10] Whereas the 1972 draft had provided for a two–tier system of management and supervisory boards for all public limited liability companies, the 1983 draft allowed the alternative of a single–tier board, as well as participation through consultative councils or collective agreements. Thus, companies with 1,000 or more employees could adopt one of a number of different alternatives: a two–tier structure of management and supervisory boards, the employees electing between one third and one half of the supervisory board and the shareholders exercising the balance; a two–tier structure of management and supervisory boards with shareholders and employee representatives having the right to veto nominations for the supervisory board on the ground that the nominee is not capable of carrying out the duties of a supervisory board member and where the board co–opts its own members; a unitary board of directors with employees electing between one third and one half of the non–executive directors; a consultative council elected by all employees, together with a two–tier or a unitary board; or collective agreements with a guarantee of employee participation together with non–executive directors or a consultative council.

The 1988 'unofficial'[11] text is broadly similar to that proposed in 1983. It provides four options: appointment of a proportion of members of the supervisory organ or administrative organ by employees or their representatives; co–option of candidates onto the supervisory organ or administrative organ with employee representatives having a right to propose or object to candidates; representation through a works council; collective agreements with provision for employee participation or representation.

Although the 'unofficial' draft was created in 1988 and has been consulted on by the DTI in the UK, the 1983 draft does not appear to be

---

10   A useful analysis of this draft is provided by Jane Welch in 'The Fifth Draft Directive – A False Dawn?' (1983) 8 *ELR* 83.

11   See note 7 above.

entirely obsolete.[12] It is therefore unclear what will be the outcome. What is clear is that the provisions are likely to be watered down even further. The Commission has stated recently that the worker participation provisions could be deleted from the draft Directive, being replaced by reference to the Works Council Directive.[13]

B. Vredeling Directive

The so called 'Vredeling Directive' was a draft Directive on informing and consulting the employees of undertakings with complex structures, in particular transnational undertakings.[14] This draft Directive was linked to the first proposals for the European Works Council Directive. First proposed in 1980[15] and amended in 1983[16] the Vredeling Directive appears to have been abandoned because of a failure to reach political agreement as to the organisation and scope of employee participation.[17] It did not gain sufficient support among the Member States or the social partners.[18] The substance of

---

12   See J.J. Du Plessis and J. Dine, 'The Fate of the Draft Fifth Directive on Company Law: Accommodation Instead of Harmonisation' (1997) *JBL* 23–47.

13   See European Commission Medium–term Social Action Programme 1995, and Communication on Worker Information and Consultation COM(95) 547 final, 14.11.1995.

14   For commentary see J. Pipkorn, 'The Draft Directive on Procedures for Informing and Consulting Employees' (1983) *CMLR* 125 and W. Kolvenbach, 'EEC Directive on Information and Consultation of Employees (Vredeling Proposal)' (1982) *International Business Law* 1.

15   1980 [OJ C297/3].

16   1983 [OJ C217/3].

17   *Communication from the Commission on Worker Information and Consultation,* COM(95) 547 final, Brussels 14.11.1995: the Commission stated its intention to withdraw the Vredeling Proposal but 'believes that it should not be withdrawn until a comprehensive solution to the whole problem has been found' (p. 4). See also Hildegard Schneider, 'The European Works Council Directive' in Jan Wouters and Hildegard Schneider (eds), *Current Issues in Cross Border Establishment of Companies in the European Union* (Maastricht: MAKLU, 1995) 185, at p. 187.

18   Schneider, *ibid.* The Directive was subject to lobbying by multinational companies (see Palmer's *Company Law* (Sweet & Maxwell, London, Issue R.58: January 1996) at p. 16103, para. 16.304) and the UK was particularly opposed to it: see eg Press Notice issued by the Department of Trade and Industry, 9 November 1983. See also Schulten who remarks on the change in the political climate across Europe from Social democrat towards a new type of neo–liberal political hegemony which had a

the draft Directive was that the head offices of companies should be required to inform and consult employees in subsidiaries or separate establishments through local management. The parent company was to give to its subsidiaries general information relating to the activities of the group and specific information relating to the activities of that subsidiary. Employee representatives would then receive this information from the management of the subsidiary concerned. Those employee representatives would also be consulted on decisions to be made concerning the whole or a major part of the parent undertaking or of a subsidiary in the Community which were liable to have serious consequences for the employees. This draft Directive recognised the growth of complex corporate structures but perhaps highlighted the problem rather than offer any real solutions to it. Bercusson, for example, observes that the draft Directive was concerned with decisions taken by the parent undertaking of a group but that the reality is often that decisions are made not just at the centre of the organisation but across it.[19] Thus, a decision taken by a subsidiary could have implications for other parts of the group. The draft Directive does not address this problem.

C.   Directive Attached to the Proposed Regulation for a European Company Statute

The proposal for a European Company Statute has two parts: a draft Regulation for a European Company based on Article 100A and an accompanying draft Directive on employee involvement based on Article 54.[20] Although the draft Regulation and Directive would form a composite whole the different national rules relating to employee participation present a

---

significantly negative influence on the fate of the proposal: Thorsten Schulten, 'European Works Councils: Prospects for a New System of European Industrial Relations' (1996) 2 *European Journal of Industrial Relations*, 303 at p. 310.

19   Further, Bercusson also notes the problems raised by sophisticated legal structures of business organisation: Brian Bercusson, 'Workers, Corporate Enterprise and the Law' in R. Lewis (ed.), *Labour Law in Britain* (Oxford, Blackwell, 1986) 134 at pp. 141–142.

20   First proposed in 1970 [OJ C124/1] later proposed in 1989 [OJ 1989 C263/41]; amended proposal 1991 [OJ C176/1, 8.7.91]. See also COM (91) 174. Latest draft Regulation 1996: see DTI Consultation Paper, *The European Company Statute* (Doc Ref: URN 97/786) July 1997.

need for the flexibility which a directive could offer.[21] The draft Directive came into focus again after the adoption of the European Works Council Directive.

Under the proposal Member States are free to restrict the choice of model available to a European company which has a registered office in its territory. Although this would appear to contradict the objective of a trans–European company, it appears that this will be the only possible basis for reaching agreement. The Directive sets out models similar to those in the draft Fifth Directive. In this way Member States may adopt one of three possible models: worker representation on the management board or the supervisory board; a consultative council; collective agreement which must at least provide for information and consultation rights to be granted to the consultative council. Employees should be consulted on a number of matters including: major company proposals; development and organisation of vocational training within the European company and its subsidiaries; and matters affecting health and safety. There should be at least one employee representative from each State in which the company has an establishment proportionate to the number of employees they represent. Adoption of one of the available models is a prerequisite for forming a European company. The proposed Regulation and Directive have been stalled for several years due to the differences over the proposed worker participation requirements.

An expert group was set up in 1996 to discuss the worker participation issue and to propose solutions. The Davignon Group issued a report in May 1997 recommending negotiations between the social partners, supported by a single reference framework of arrangements which should apply if negotiations fail. The reference framework includes: a right for workers' representatives to occupy one fifth of the seats on the board or supervisory board and at least two seats, and the worker representatives should have equal status and voting rights to other board members; an obligation on the board of the European Company to inform the workers' representatives regularly and in good time of matters liable to have implications for their situation and of the progress of the company's business; a right for the workers' representatives to ask the management to provide information on any question significantly affecting the affairs of the company, to have sight of all documents laid before the general meeting and to receive advance notice of the agenda of board meetings; a right for workers' representatives to deliver opinions and to meet management with a view to reaching an agreement on questions significantly affecting workers' interests; an

---

21 It has been suggested that a Directive might also be more appropriate than the
    Regulation given that successive texts have left more and more detail to the national
    states: see Palmer's *Company Law*, above note 18, 16216, para. 16.421.

obligation for the workers' representatives at European Company level to inform those in its subsidiaries and establishments of the outcome of information and consultation procedures; and additional rules on the protection of workers' representatives; the resources to be allocated to these processes; the right to consult experts; and the protection of confidentiality.

Latest reports suggest that the negotiations between the Member States have arrived at a stalemate because the opposing forces – the UK and Germany – are both 'sticking to their guns'.[22]

3.   A LABOUR LAW PERSPECTIVE

A.   The European Works Councils Directive

In view of the consistent failure of the company law initiatives for employee participation in corporate decision–making it may appear surprising that the Commission should have proposed further measures for industrial democracy in the form of works councils. As Hall remarks, any systematic or institutionalised employee participation has been blocked consistently because of incompatibility with national laws and practices as well as through political and ideological objections.[23] However, the new context of the Single Market and the 'new approach' to directives, allowing flexibility and room for national diversities, provided encouragement for fresh initiatives.[24] Then, with the Maastricht discussions, subsidiarity and proportionality gained serious recognition and led to the creation of 'framework' directives.[25] The new Protocol on Social Policy which was added to the Treaty on European Union introduced the possibility of adopting directives by eleven of the then twelve Member States, excluding the UK, and also made possible negotiation of the Works Councils Directive, using works councils already established and operating as an example.[26]

---

22   Simon Coss, 'UK and Germany Sink Latest Formula for European Firm', *Glasgow Herald*, 3 November 1997.

23   Mark Hall, 'Behind the European Works Councils Directive: The European Commission's Legislative Strategy' (1992) 30 *BJIL* 547, at pp. 547–8.

24   *Ibid.*, at p. 547. See also Commission White Paper, *Completing the Internal Market*, (COM (85) 310 final) which makes reference to 'new approach' Directives. See further, Chapter 1 of this book.

25   See Chapter 1 of this book.

26   Works Councils have existed in Germany since the end of the last century. They also became compulsory in many European countries during the 1940s and were given extended rights during the 1960s and 1970s. For a useful survey see Joel Rogers and

Furthermore, on the transnational level there was a clear lack of participation by employees and their representatives in corporate decision–making, reinforced by information and consultation practices being confined to the national level. This difference between transnational and national practices needed to be reconciled. The solution was unlikely to come from national laws, as these were not concerned with helping employees in trans–national companies.[27] The logical result of this lack of co–ordination would be unequal treatment of employees affected by corporate decisions taken by higher–level management in a different country.[28] The solution to the problem of bridging the divide between national laws and trans–European practice came eventually from the Economic and Social Committee which, favouring the views of the ETUC, stated in an Opinion the need to provide a Community framework for information and consultation of employees' representatives at European level but based on national arrangements.[29]

The Directive was first proposed in 1991 and was finally agreed in November 1994.[30] The requirements set out in the Directive include: the establishment of a Works Council in Community scale undertakings or groups of undertakings which have 1,000 or more employees, including at least 150 employees in each of two or more Member States, and where employees and/or their representatives request this. The Directive may also apply to enterprises with head offices outside the European Community, in

---

Wolfgang Streeck (eds), *Works Councils* (University of Chicago Press, Chicago, 1995). See also Thilo Ramm, 'Worker's Participation, the Representation of Labour and Special Labour Courts' in Bob Hepple (ed.), *The Making of Labour Law in Europe: A Comparative Study of Nine Countries up to 1945* (Mansell, 1986) and Gustav J.J. Heerma van Voss, 'The Directive on European Works Councils in Community–scale Undertakings. The Introduction of 'Double Subsidiarity' in European Labour Law' (1995) 2 *Maastricht Journal of European and Comparative Law* 339, esp. pp. 339–340. See also Mark Hall, who discusses the 'prototype' works councils which gave authority to the trade union case for works councils: 'Behind the European Works Councils Directive: The European Commission's Legislative Strategy' (1992) 30 *BJIR* 547, esp. pp. 551–554.

27 See Heerma van Voss, *ibid.*, at p. 341.

28 Hall, above note 23, at p. 550.

29 Economic and Social Committee *Opinion on Social Consequences of Cross–Frontier Concentrations between Undertakings* (Brussels, 18 October 1989). See also Hall, above note 23, p. 551.

30 For a brief discussion of the history of the Directive see Hildegard Schneider, 'The European Works Council Directive' in Jan Wouters and Hildegard Schneider (eds), *Current Issues of Cross–Border Establishment of Companies in the European Union* (Maklu, Maastricht, 1995) 185.

which case the Directive would have to be complied with by the representative agent or with the management which employs the highest number of employees within the Community.

Once established, the works council may deal with matters which concern the whole undertaking or group or at least two of the establishments within the group situated in different Member States. The works council has the right to meet with management annually, to be informed of the progress and prospects of the undertaking or the group and to be consulted on proposals which are likely to have serious consequences for the employees, being able to request a further meeting on these issues. The cost of operation of the works council is borne by the undertaking's central management.

4.   COMPANY LAW VERSUS LABOUR LAW?

The above descriptions show that the 'industrial democracy' initiatives by the Commission have had more success for DGV than for DGXV and its predecessor. Why have the Directives adopted in the labour law area been more successful than those attempted under the company law programme when they appear, essentially, to be concerned with the same issue?

A number of possible explanations exist for the relatively successful[31] progress of the labour law directives in comparison with the company law directives. The two spheres of labour law and company law tend to be divided between social and economic goals.[32] Generally, labour law is more concerned with social goals, aiming to regulate the relationship between employer and worker. Of course, this has economic implications since it imposes costs on businesses but, primarily, labour law aims to protect employers and employees from potential abuse of the employment relationship. In particular, the lack of balance of power between employer and employee has the consequence that the employee needs more protection. Company law, on the other hand, focuses more directly on economic issues and on the relationship between managers and shareholders. The traditional company law discipline of profit–maximisation, as Bercusson remarks, 'goes to the heart of the economic system'.[33] In correspondence with these general

---

31   The level of this success may be qualified by the insufficient implementation of the Directives by some Member States: see eg Case C–382 and Case C–383/92 *Commission* v *UK* [1994] ECR I–2435, 2479, in which the ECJ found the UK's implementation of the Acquired Rights Directive and the Collective Redundancies Directive to be inadequate.

32   Brian Bercusson, above note 19.

33   *Ibid.*, at p. 144.

distinctions, the European Directives also tend to be categorised as social legislation in the labour law field and as single market (ie economic) provisions in the company law field. Therefore, many labour law directives are derived from Europe's social law programme. Thus, the Acquired Rights Directive and the Collective Redundancies Directive, which both give employees rights to information and consultation, were enacted under the social provisions in the EC Treaty.[34] The European Works Councils Directive has as its legal basis Article 2(2) of the Social Protocol of the Maastricht Treaty.[35] By contrast, most of the company law directives, including the draft Fifth Directive, the draft Vredeling Directive, and the draft Directive accompanying the draft Regulation for a European Company Statute are based on Article 54 EC Treaty, which promotes the freedom of establishment, provided by Article 52. This Article has much closer links with the economic aspects of the internal market, its primary objective being to serve the purposes of the EC Treaty laid out in Article 2, which, as noted earlier in this book, are 'establishing a common market and progressively approximating the economic policies of Member States to promote throughout the Community a harmonious development of economic activities, a continuous and balanced expansion, an increase in stability, an accelerated raising of the standard of living and closer relations between the States belonging to it'.

For some commentators this theoretical division has a practical effect. For example, Welch notes the gulf between the two systems of company law and labour law as being as wide as ever. Whereas the company lawyer is interested in the formal framework of the board of directors and the shareholders, the industrial relations adviser concentrates mainly on the management and the workforce.[36] Moreover, it is suggested by some that employee participation is strictly a matter for labour law and not for company law and that such provisions should not be 'intermingled' with company law.[37] As Welch states:

---

34 Both Directives were based on Article 100a which, although not strictly falling within the Social Provisions section of the Treaty (those being Articles 117–122), has been used to introduce measures of a social nature because they have a direct effect on the functioning of the Common Market. Nevertheless, the two Directives are still recognised as social measures rather than as economic measures. See Stephen Weatherill and Paul Beaumont, *EC Law* (Penguin, Harmondsworth, 1993), Ch. 20, 'Social Policy', 541, at p. 564.

35 See discussion by Hildegard Schneider, above note 30, at pp. 189–191.

36 Jane Welch, 'The Fifth Directive – A False Dawn?' (1983) 8 *ELR* 83 at p. 84.

37 See House of Lords – Nineteenth Select Committee Report, *The European Company Statute* (HL Paper 71, 1990) p. 21, para. 64.

Each knows little of the environment in which the other operates and each tends to regard 'employee participation' as his exclusive preserve. For one employee participation generally means employee directors on the board; for the other it may mean works councils at plant or unit level.[38]

The division suggests a reluctance to trespass in areas where there may be less understanding even where issues coincide. Consequently, progress made in one area will not necessarily be translated into other areas. Thus, while it may be argued that the labour laws have been more successful than the company laws in the field of employee participation, at least to the extent that they have been adopted, in reality they do not necessarily offer too much optimism that similar progress will be possible in the company law field. Still, this distinction does not explain why employee participation should be acceptable in the social sphere but not in the economic sphere, when the reality is that measures adopted in the social sphere will have an impact on the economic sphere.

Critically, it could be argued that the labour laws themselves do not really allow for employee participation that could be identified with workplace democracy. This is because, first, the device of the employment contract actually denies the worker membership in the company. David Ellerman, for example, suggests that the employment contract enables the employee to rent his or her services to the employer, who effectively buys a part of the employee's services. Having purchased the services of the employee, the employer then obtains control over the employee within the scope of the employment contract and, rather than being a delegation of authority, the right to govern the employee is transferred or alienated to the employer. Thus, the employment contract puts the employee at a distance from the decision–making centre of the company and the employer acts in his or her own name.[39] Secondly, the Directives in the labour law sphere are much more limited than the company law proposals. They focus on information and consultation, not on employee decision–making nor even on employee influence upon decisions or corporate policies or strategies. Participation may be defined in many ways[40] but for the purpose of

---

38   Welch, above note 36.

39   David Ellerman, *The Democratic Worker–Owned Firm* (Unwyn Hyman, Winchester, Mass., 1990) at pp. 59–60.

40   Pateman surveys these as well as the suggestion by Likert and McGregor of a continuum of situations which may involve a little or a lot of participation: see Pateman, above note 2, Ch. IV. See also: R. Likert, *New Patterns of Management* (McGraw Hill, New York, 1961) at p. 243; D McGregor, *The Human Side of*

democracy it must at least have the capacity to influence decisions and policies and not just to signify passive receipt of information or attendance at meetings. As Pateman suggests, 'the whole point about industrial participation is that it involves a modification, to a greater or lesser degree, of the orthodox authority structure, namely where decision–making is the 'prerogative' of management, in which workers play no part'.[41] This observation may help further to explain the 'success' of the labour law provisions and the 'failure' of the company law proposals. The Works Councils Directive is concerned with information and consultation within defined limits and in limited circumstances.[42] In reality, this may be perceived as workplace 'humanisation' rather than as workplace democracy.[43] Indeed, as McGlynn suggests, the Works Councils Directive succeeded because it provides a compromise, focusing on protection rather than on participation in decision–making.[44] From this perspective, such form of participation may be regarded as a managerial device which makes employees feel included but does not truly emancipate them.[45]

It is through such protective legislation that current corporate structures may be maintained. In this way, Bachrach and Botwinick argue that rights contribute little to the dismantling of the corporate hierarchy and its replacement by a democratic mode of decision–making.[46] Thus, although consultation might be considered at least as a lower level of participation and even potentially as a first step to workplace democracy, the Works Councils Directive, as a protectionist rather than a participatory measure, is politically more acceptable, because it does not actually challenge the existing balance of power in the company. Achieving full workplace democracy seems unlikely through this protective rights route.

Enterprise (McGraw Hill, New York, 1960) at pp. 126–7. Eric Rhenman suggests that there are four stages of participation: taking the initiative; formulating the goals and norms; problem–solving; making the final decision: Eric Rhenman, *Industrial Democracy and Industrial Management* (Tavistock, London, 1968), at pp. 61–66.

41 Pateman, above note 2, at p. 68.

42 Clare McGlynn, 'European Works Council: Towards Industrial Democracy?' (1995) 24 *ILJ* 78.

43 This distinction is discussed by Peter Bachrach and Aryeh Botwinick, *Power and Empowerment: A Radical Theory of Participatory Democracy* (Temple University Press, Philadelphia, 1992) at p. 75.

44 McGlynn, above note 42.

45 Pateman calls this 'pseudo participation': above note 2, at p. 69. See also L. Stephens, 'A Case for Job Enlargement' (11 October, 1962) *New Society*. Another term used for this form of protection is humanisation of work: See eg Bachrach and Botwinick, above note 43 at p. 75.

46 Bachrach and Botwinick, above note 43, at p. 171.

192 *European Company Law – Towards Democracy?*

In this light, company law is, contrary to the views expressed in the House of Lords Select Committee Report on the 1972 draft,[47] precisely the correct area for employee participation to be introduced, since company law is directly concerned with corporate structures. Not surprisingly then, the company law proposals are much more radical than the labour law provisions. The proposed Fifth Directive would bring into question some fundamental concepts in UK company law. The House of Lords Select Committee Report highlighted a host of issues arising from the proposals including: the impact on the contract under which capital was subscribed or purchased if employees were to be placed onto the board of directors; thus, could the employees block the declaration of a dividend? Would the supervisory board be entitled to override the General Meeting on the question of whether the company should be voluntarily wound up? How would conflicts between the supervisory board and the management board be resolved? What would be meant by interests of the employees as well as the shareholders? Would employee directors be removable by their constituents only? How would confidential material be handled? Thus, from the House of Lords Select Committee's point of view, the boldness of the proposals of the draft Fifth Directive was problematic. The involvement of workers in the enterprise would require an 'updating of the company law's conceptual equipment'.[48] Similarly, Dine argues that the move to worker representation on boards would cause a shift of power away from the shareholders and could entrench incumbent management, resulting in a problem for majority shareholders.[49] Even if not technically, then at least politically, these proposals were perhaps asking too much of company law in one swift move. As Conlon stated: 'the Commission is attempting in one comprehensive step to restructure company law when a series of smaller steps would seem more appropriate.'[50]

These responses to the company law proposals may reflect a lack of political or doctrinal willingness to accept employee participation. In company law, employees are treated as outsiders,[51] their relationship with the company being an issue for their employment contract, rather than as

---

47   House of Lords Select Committee Fifty–Fourth Report on the European Communities, *Draft Fifth Directive on Company Law: Two–Tier Boards and Worker Participation* (HL Paper 308, Session 1975–76).

48   Bercusson, above note 19, at p. 139.

49   'Why Not Employee Participation in the European Community Context?' (1995) 16 *Company Lawyer*, 44 at p. 49.

50   Thomas Conlon, 'Industrial Democracy and EEC Company Law: A Review of the Draft Fifth Directive' [1975] 24 *ICLQ* 348, at p. 358.

51   Bercusson, above note 19.

members who are integral to the economic enterprise. Despite company law being the most appropriate in which to introduce employee participation it is clearly also a very hostile ground for such radical steps to be made. What is it about companies that makes them so incompatible with employee participation?

5. COMPANIES AS NON-DEMOCRATIC ASSOCIATIONS

As has been noted, traditionally the *raison d'être* of the company has been profit maximisation,[52] mostly as a short-term objective;[53] a view which naturally favours the shareholders over other potential stakeholders.[54] This philosophy encourages employers to seek to maximise their profits, resulting in a conflict of interests with their workers. This leads to an adversarial and hierarchical relationship in which employers seek control of the employees' working conditions.[55] This argument also coincides with the conflict or dichotomy theories of the firm and industrial relations, which regard workers as having their place outside the company. For example, Clegg's position was that the real guarantee of democracy is the existence of a legitimate opposition to the holders of power. At the level of the company trade unions have the role of legitimate opposition and they must maintain their independence from management. Organised labour should not participate in the decision–making process of enterprises as this would lead to double–loyalties and co–optation.[56] Similarly, Dahrendorf sees the danger of representatives of the subjected becoming agents of the dominating group.[57]

The structure of companies presents a 'barrier to democratic control'.[58] Their hierarchical structure emphasises discipline and obedience with economic policies imposed from the top levels downwards.[59] Furthermore,

---

52   Clive M. Schmitthoff, 'Employee Participation and the Theory of Enterprise' (1975) *JBL* 265, at p. 265.

53   Peter G. Xuereb, 'The Juridification of Industrial Relations Through Company Law Reform' (1988) 51 *MLR* 156.

54   *Ibid.* See also *Parke* v *Daily News Ltd* [1962] Ch. 927.

55   Alan Gewirth, *The Community of Rights* (University of Chicago Press, Chicago, 1996) at p. 266.

56   H.A. Clegg, *A New Approach to Industrial Democracy* (Blackwell, Oxford, 1960).

57   Ralf Dahrendorf, *Class and Class Conflict in Industrial Society* (Routledge & Kegan Paul, London, 1959). Both Clegg and Dahrendorf are discussed in detail in Steve Minett, *Power, Politics and Participation in the Firm* (Avebury, Aldershot, 1992).

58   *Ibid.*, at p. 138.

59   W. Ebenstein, *Today's Isms*, 3rd ed. (Prentice Hall, 1961) at p. 162.

the 'owners' who are provided with voting powers do not exercise that power democratically. Shareholders are given votes which they are able to sell in the market place, thereby allowing voting rights to be held by a small section of the business, since not all shares carry voting rights. As Pennington notes, it is more possible in England than in the rest of Europe for an individual or small group to control even a large company.[60] This shareholder structure provides little incentive for investors to alter their traditional apathy towards the company's annual general meeting.[61] Such apathy might also be explained by the fact that shareholders delegate management to the directors and trust in them to manage the business on their behalf. Furthermore, shareholders do not constitute a homogeneous group. Generally, institutional investors have much more power than individual shareholders, which also presents obstacles to democracy and serves as a further disincentive for individual shareholders to act positively to influence company policies. Recent examples of the power of institutional investors against individuals include the British Gas case where most individual shareholders voted against the pay rise of the executive directors but were outvoted by the institutional shareholders.[62] Similarly, the institutional shareholders of Shell successfully withstood proposals by other shareholders for the publication of environmental accounts.[63] These observations suggest that the company is not concerned with and is not designed to be compatible with democracy.

6.   CONCLUSION

The problem for the company law programme in introducing industrial democracy is clear: employment democracy challenges the traditional concept of companies as hierarchical organisations, whose control over the employee is legitimated by the employment contract. The labour law

---

60   R.R. Pennington, 'Company Law Reform in Great Britain' (1963–4) 1 *CMLR* 58–77 at p. 67. Dunleavy, comparing interest groups to firms, also suggests a poor quality of democracy in firms, contrasting shareholder democracy with interest groups 'where there is no possibility for group voting to be controlled by a few vote–owners, who have amassed large resources': Patrick Dunleavy, *Democracy, Bureaucracy & Public Choice: Economic Explanations in Political Science* (Harvester Wheatsheaf, Hertfordshire, 1991) at p. 73.

61   Brian R. Cheffins, *Company Law: Theory, Structure and Operation* (1997, Clarendon Press, Oxford) at p. 240, and n. 125.

62   'British Gas Ballots Fail to Draw Investors', *Daily Telegraph*, 2 June 1995.

63   See eg Robert Corzine, 'Shell wins on environmental monitoring' *Financial Times*, 15 May 1997.

provisions may be viewed as protective rights rather than as participatory measures. These do not challenge the hierarchy in the same way as the employment democracy proposals in the company law sphere.

Current efforts appear to be following the labour law route. The European Commission is considering the future of the company law employee participation proposals. The Works Councils Directive has given a fresh impetus for the proposals to come back onto the near future agenda. Success so far has been at the limited level of information and consultation of employees and only at the trans–European level. Moreover, the Commission is considering deleting the employee participation aspects from the draft Fifth Directive, and has indicated its intention to withdraw the Vredeling proposal. The Commission is considering three options: maintain the status quo; adopt a global framework for employee information and consultation or involvement; or take immediate action to bring about the European Company Statute.[64] Recently, Padraig Flynn, the social affairs commissioner, published a consultation document proposing that all companies in the European Union should be required to set up information and consultation committees for their workers.[65] The Report of the Davignon Group on the European Company proposals suggests a compromise position which seeks negotiation between management and workers' representatives, and if no agreement is reached there would be rules to include information and consultation and provision for worker representatives to have membership of the board or supervisory board.[66]

By accommodating those Member States who are more opposed to employee participation (and even employee protection!) the European Community leaves itself open to continued problems in the area of company law.

A number of issues remain outstanding in company law harmonisation. The existing labour law provisions will not close the gap between the German co–determination perspective and other corporate structures. These affect corporate governance issues and directors' duties. These issues will have to be resolved if trade collaboration is to be developed further. The next chapter will consider the arguments for participation in further detail and will explore what opportunities might exist for achieving this.

---

64 Commission, *Communication on Worker Information and Consultation*, COM (95) 547 final, Brussels, 14 November 1995.

65 See Robert Taylor, 'Brussels: EU may use social chapter to impose works councils', *Financial Times*, 4 June 1997.

66 *Report of the High Level Group of Experts on European Systems of Workers' Involvement*: see DN IP/97/396, 13 May 1997. See also DTI Consultation Paper, above note 20.

11 Towards Participation in Company Law?

1. INTRODUCTION

The previous chapter focused on the obstacles to democracy in company law and the structure and arrangements of corporate relationships. Some theoretical obstacles to introducing democracy into companies may also be identified. For example, David Held notes the utilitarian claim that politics is to be regarded as 'a distinct and separate sphere in society, a sphere set apart from economy, culture and family life'.[1] According to Held, in the liberal tradition politics means, above all, governmental activity and institutions. This emphasises the representative sphere of democracy, leaving issues of 'organisation of the economy to be thought of as an outcome of "free" private contracts in civil society, not as a political issue or a matter for the state'.[2]

This separation of economic life from political life may, however, be criticised on a number of levels. Business organisations influence political decisions and in so doing shape social organisation. The interaction between economics and politics is indeed strong and government and business have an interdependent relationship.[3] For example, the decisions of whether or not to fund social welfare programmes or to build new schools are not only political decisions but they are also both economic and social decisions. More specifically in relation to companies, economic enterprises, according to Dahl, are a source of political inequality: 'ownership and control contribute to the creation of great differences among citizens in wealth, income, status, skills, information, control over information and propaganda, access to political leaders... differences like these help in turn to generate significant inequalities among citizens in their capacities and opportunities for participating as political equals in *governing the state*.'[4] The connection between economics and politics was seemingly recognised in the establishment in Germany of co-determination. Markovits and Allen note that 'only through the complete democratisation of economic life could

---

1   David Held, *Models of Democracy* (1987, Polity Press, London) at p. 69.
2   *Ibid.*
3   For an interesting discussion of the relationship between business and politics, see Wyn Grant, *Business and Politics in Britain*, 2nd ed. (Macmillan, London, 1993).
4   Robert A. Dahl, *A Preface to Economic Democracy* (University of California Press, Berkeley, 1985) at pp. 54–55, emphasis retained.

capitalism conform to a more equitable and more socially oriented society... The installation of co–determination at all levels of society, from shop floor, firm and industrial levels, through chambers of commerce and industry, up to public institutions ... would give macro–economic direction to the economy'.[5]

This chapter will put forward an argument for introducing democracy into the company and will consider the relevance this may have for the company law harmonisation programme and how it might contribute to an improvement of European representative democracy. It will also explore the opportunities which currently exist for democracy within company law and, more particularly, the company law programme. Finally, it will suggest that more fundamental changes are required for the concept of company law, including a clear identification of the stakeholders and how their interests might be balanced. Moreover, the key problem in both company law and labour law is the focus on the role of the managers and their relationship with the shareholders and the employees. Company law should concentrate more on the relationship between the employees and the shareholders.

2.   THEORETICAL ARGUMENTS FOR DEMOCRACY

The previous chapter demonstrated that there are a number of practical problems standing in the way of employee participation in corporate strategic decision–making. For example, the hierarchical nature of the firm encourages decisions to be made from the top and imposed below, which normally translates practically into decisions from managers imposed on employees. The structure of the firm also favours control in the hands of the shareholders rather than the employees, and the emphasis on profit maximisation is at odds with employee and consumer interests. However, there exist some clear theoretical arguments in favour of such participation.

A.   The Employment Relationship

In any employment situation the employer has power over the workers by deciding what work to give and to whom, by giving orders on when and how the work must be done. The employer is backed by the sanction of discipline

---

5   Andrei S. Markovits and Christopher Allen, 'Trade Union and Economic Crisis: The West German Case', in Peter Gourevitch *et al.* (eds), *Unions and Economic Crisis: Britain, West Germany and Sweden* (Allen & Unwin, London, 1984) and quoted by Peter Bachrach and Aryeh Botwinick, *Power and Empowerment: A Radical Theory of Participatory Democracy* (Temple University Press, Philadelphia, 1992) at p. 77.

or dismissal of the worker.[6] This power of control given to managers has become less justifiable with the growth of firms and the advance of technology, which have created gaps in competence of managers.[7] The managers are often less skilled in particular workplace operations than the workers, who are themselves better able to take practical control in a given situation. It was ironic that Sir Rocco Forte, on leaving the large hotel chain and starting up a new chain, said recently: I now know how to work the photocopier![8] Indeed, the larger the firm the more detached the managers are likely to be from the actual grass–root jobs within the enterprise.

While the transfer of control to the employer may be true of any employment relationship, there is a particular problem in the company because the manager has to balance a clear conflict of interests between the employees and the shareholders, which arises from what Archer calls the 'variability of labour power'.[9] The effect of this conflict is that the capitalist owners will want the workers to do more work than they actually do in order to maximise their profits. As Archer notes, a gap exists between what the firm acquires under the employment contract and what it wants from the contract.[10] The manager, in balancing these conflicting interests, generally favours the shareholders as the company's 'owners'.[11] The effect is to place power into the hands of the 'owners'.

B. Employees as 'Subjects of Authority'

Entrepreneurs might be commended for their 'risk taking, their inventiveness and their investment through which firms are sustained and expanded'.[12] However, from a democratic perspective, ownership does not by itself justify

---

6   See Gewirth, *The Community of Rights* (University of Chicago Press, Chicago, 1996), at p. 266.

7   Steve Minett, *Power, Politics and Participation in the Firm* (Avebury, Aldershot, 1992), at p. 187.

8   Christopher Price, 'Forte Plays Piano', *Financial Times*, 25/26 October 1997.

9   Robin Archer, 'The Philosophical Case for Economic Democracy' in Ugo Pagano and Robert Rowthorn (eds), *Democracy and Efficiency in the Economic Enterprise* (Routledge, London, 1996) 13–35 at p. 22. See also Robin Archer, *Economic Democracy* (Oxford University Press, Oxford, 1995).

10   *Ibid.* (1996) at p. 22.

11   This claim is asserted by Dahl in Robert A. Dahl, *A Preface to Economic Democracy* (University of California Press, Berkeley, 1985) at p. 109.

12   Michael Walzer, *Spheres of Justice* (Blackwell, Oxford, 1983) at p. 294.

democratic power.[13] The most basic definition of democracy, as was noted in the introduction to this book, is 'government by the people'. In a representative democracy, the representatives should base their decisions on and act in accordance with the interests of those who are affected by their decisions, in particular those who are the subjects of their authority,[14] those who are governed. The same principles might apply to companies, especially large companies. If democracy should be considered applicable to companies, then, because of their size and possible multiple geographical locations, the appropriate form of democracy would have to be the representative form of democracy. Indeed, large companies do arguably have both representatives and parties who are affected by the decisions of those representatives and are subject to their authority. In the company, the representatives are the managers or the company directors and there are various interested parties. These include the shareholders, employees, consumers, creditors, suppliers, local residents etc. Shareholders, consumers, suppliers and locals are affected without actually being governed since they are not subject to the authority of the managers. Generally, though not always, shareholders, consumers and suppliers can choose easily to stay or leave. By contrast, the employees are governed by the decisions of the representatives and therefore may be regarded as the subjects of their authority.[15] Walzer quotes the 'decisive words' of R.H.Tawney to illustrate this point:

> What I want to drive home is this, that the man who employs, governs, to the extent of the number of men employed. He has jurisdiction over them. He occupies what is really a public office. He has power, not of pit and gallows... but of overtime and short time, full bellies and empty bellies, health and sickness.[16]

In accordance with democratic theory the employees, who are subject to the authority of the company's managers, should exercise direct control over the authority of the representatives. The other interest groups, such as

---

13   Nor indeed from a moral perspective argues Walzer, *ibid.*

14   Archer (1996), above note 9 at p. 15.

15   See eg David Ellerman, *The Democratic Worker–Owned Firm* (Unwin Hyman, London, 1990) at p. 44; Alan Gewirth, above note 6, at pp. 276–7.

16   J.M. Winter and D.M. Joslin (eds), *R.H. Tawney's Commonplace Book* (Cambridge, England, 1972) pp. 95–96, quoted in Walzer, above note 12, at p. 293.

shareholders or suppliers, should have only indirect control by way of a combination of 'exit'[17] or veto power and government regulation.[18]

The reality in the UK is, however, that a combination of employment law and company law permits only the reverse by giving power to the affected 'non–subjects': power is placed in the hands of the corporate managers on a day–to–day management basis[19] and the 'owners', who vote on corporate policy decisions at the general meeting. This turns corporate 'democracy' into a form of personal property and denies its collective and social aspects.[20] It also leads to the situation in which the managers act as agents for the owners. As noted above, they typically act on behalf of the owners and in their interests, with the employees' interests as secondary to those of the shareholders. The employees, however, by their employment contract are excluded from the company's decision–making process. This is anti–democratic in the light of the definition of democracy provided above, and can be objected to on a practical level, since, among all the company's interested parties, the employees, especially in recession and when jobs are more scarce, are often not able to 'exit', since the cost of leaving may be too high, and under their employment contract they have to provide a period of notice before leaving, although, in practice, this notice period is rarely enforced by employers.

Although they provide the capital, the shareholders are often, in reality, more outside the company than inside it. In particular, individual shareholders display a considerable apathy towards company meetings[21] and show little interest in the information produced by the company. For example, a recent report published by the Institute of Chartered Accountants for England and Wales suggested that private investors are not interested in receiving detailed information about the company's financial status, preferring to receive summarised financial statements, and that their primary interests are profits, share dividend and performance rather than corporate

---

17   Exit as understood in the thesis of Alberto Hirschman, *Exit Voice and Loyalty* (Harvard University Press, Cambridge, Mass, 1970).

18   Both Ellerman, above note 15, and Archer (1996), above note 9, suggest this conforms with democratic theory.

19   See Table A, Article 70.

20   According to Gewirth, 'economic democracy cannot be the personal property of a given individual but is a collectively available social condition': above note 6, at p. 262.

21   See eg Brian R. Cheffins, *Company Law: Theory, Structure and Operation* (Clarendon Press, Oxford, 1997) at pp. 488–89, noting that less than one per cent of shareholders attend annual general meetings in person and the proportion of votes cast on most resolutions does not exceed 20 per cent.

governance and board policies.[22] Furthermore, most investors are unlikely to have daily contact with the company short of checking the value of their shares in the company in the financial pages of the newspaper. The employees, by contrast, provide the work that contributes most to the productive process. The reality of the employees' more dedicated and consistent involvement with the company compared with the role of the shareholders has been recognised by changing theoretical views of the company. Minett, for example, notes that the original conception of the company was as owner–manager but industrialisation made the bond between the individual and the enterprise progressively attenuated, especially after the emergence of institutional investors. So now employees make a personal life–time commitment to an enterprise while the 'owners' behave like 'impersonal rational maximisers flitting from firm to firm in search of the best return'.[23] Collins suggests in this respect that the company could be regarded as a productive organisation of which the employees are members.[24] Indeed, employees are dedicated members, having daily contact with the company and their livelihoods depending on the company and its future. From Collins' perspective, employees as members of the organisation 'should be treated with respect, so that corporate plans should be discussed and a social programme to help with the consequences of redundancy formulated and observed'.[25] However, this theoretical observation has not been transposed into the company laws, which still give precedence to the interests of the shareholders. In the UK, for example, although section 309 of the Companies Act 1985 imposes a duty on directors to consider the interests of the employees, that comes secondary to the interests of the shareholders and it does not provide employees with a strong mechanism for pursuing their interests.

C.   Participation and Efficiency

The search for the 'best return' by the shareholders emphasises the economic priority of the company. If the company does not make sufficient profits the shareholder will place his or her investment elsewhere. The previous chapter

---

22   Institute of Chartered Accountants of England and Wales, *Summary Financial Statements – The Way Forward* (ICAEW, July 1996).

23   Steve Minett, above note 7, at p. 186.

24   Hugh Collins, 'Organisational Regulation and the Limits of Contract' in J. McCahery, S. Picciotto and C. Scott (eds), *Corporate Control and Accountability: Changing Structures and the Dynamics of Regulation* (Clarendon Press, Oxford, 1993) 91–100.

25   *Ibid.*, at p. 99.

suggested that profit maximisation as an overall goal was at odds with the concept of economic democracy, and more particularly with employee participation. However, profits may act as a measure of efficiency. The fact that efficiency may be improved by participation therefore promises at least a potential for greater profits, thus challenging the claim that economic democracy is not compatible with the profit maximising goal.

Many observers note connections between employee participation and efficiency. Blumberg, for example, surveys a number of experiments which suggested some correspondence between participation and increased productivity and efficiency.[26] This claim is also made by Bowles and Gintis who observe that where workers participate they have direct residual claims on the business, and there is mutual monitoring as well as wage incentives.[27] Gewirth surveys a number of these claims and while he notes that there is also evidence which counteracts the claims as well as some theoretical economic arguments against improved productivity and efficiency, such as the 'free rider' and the 'additional worker' problems, his overall conclusion is that the results are 'sufficiently copious to establish as highly plausible that there is a causal connection between economic democracy and increased efficiency'.[28] Sisson also notes that direct participation 'offers the prospect of ever–increasing levels of productivity, plus the opportunity to exploit sources of competitive advantage other than cost, such as the education and skills of the workforce, to produce high quality goods and services'.[29] More importantly he observes that the management of most organisations that have introduced direct participation 'believe it has had beneficial performance effects'.[30] Moreover, there is a case for arguing that hierarchical structures are themselves more likely to obstruct productivity and efficiency.[31] While it cannot be denied that the evidence available is conflicting with regard to the link between participation and efficiency, and that it is difficult to isolate the

---

26 Paul Blumberg, *Industrial Democracy – The Sociology of Participation* (Constable, London, 1968).

27 Samuel Bowles and Herbert Gintis, 'A Political and Economic Case for the Democratic Enterprise' in David Copp, Jean Hampton and John E. Roemer (eds), *The Idea of Democracy* (Cambridge University Press, 1993) 375–399, at pp. 390–2.

28 Gewirth, above note 6, at p. 285.

29 Keith Sisson, *Closing the Gap – Ideas and Practice: Direct Participation in Organisational Change* (Office for Official Publications for the European Communities, Luxembourg, 1996) at p. 10.

30 *Ibid.*, at p. 19.

31 Sisson notes that 'many commentators have concluded that traditional hierarchical structures are inefficient in separating decision–making from doing, and extremely expensive in adding several tiers of managers who add little value': *ibid.*, at p. 9.

effects of one change in the environment from others, overall the existing evidence suggests that, at the very least, employee participation is unlikely to be wholly incompatible with the shareholders' interest in profit maximisation.

One explanation for the evidence of increased efficiency which results from participation lies in the psychological benefits of participation. Pateman, for example, suggests that participation by workers may increase efficiency, on the basis of their increased job satisfaction.[32] By participating, the worker exercises control over his or her job and work environment. Where the worker lacks control this is accompanied by lack of satisfaction and thus affects morale, productivity and efficiency. Both Patemen and Blumberg refer to the Hawthorne experiments which suggested a strong link between participation and job satisfaction.[33] Blumberg concludes that 'there is hardly a study in the entire literature which fails to demonstrate that satisfaction in work is enhanced or that other generally acknowledged beneficial consequences accrue from a genuine increase in workers' decision–making power'.[34]

D.   Participation and Politics

These psychological benefits may also provide an explanatory link between workplace democracy and improved representative democracy at a wider political level. The introduction to this book and the last chapter put forward the suggestion that the wider political system might be improved by the introduction of workplace democracy. How may such improvement be achieved? Pateman indicates that the psychological benefits of participation, which has an integrative function, allow not only job satisfaction but they also lead to 'non–servile' and 'non–passive' behaviour.[35] The workplace is

---

32   Pateman, Participation and Democratic Theory (Cambridge University Press, Cambridge, 1970), at p. 68.

33   See Elton Mayo, *Human Problems of an Industrial Civilisation* (Macmillan, New York, 1933) discussed by Blumberg, above note 26, in chapters 2 and 3, see also Pateman, above note 32, at pp. 64–5.

34   Blumberg, above note 26, at p. 123. However, Pateman observes the strong criticisms of the Hawthorne Experiments made by Carey and suggests that it seems dubious to cite the Hawthorne experiments in support of a thesis about participation. Nevertheless, Pateman still agrees with Blumberg that there is empirical support for the claim that participation has positive psychological effects. See also A. Carey, 'The Hawthorne Experiments: A Radical Critique' (1967) 32 *American Sociological Review*, 403–16.

35   Pateman, above note 32, at p. 45.

regarded by Pateman as the appropriate forum for participation because work is both a productive and a collective activity. Even what Pateman describes as 'partial participation' which influences decisions at the workplace may lead to a feeling of empowerment which carries over into the wider political sphere. However, a 'higher level of participation' or 'full participation' is required for participants to become familiar and confident in using political machinery and procedures.[36] Ultimately, the key argument is that participation at work is likely to encourage participation in wider politics at least to the extent of citizens demanding that representatives become more responsive to their views.

However, against this claim it could be argued that economic democracy has the reverse effect and may actually suppress democracy at a more general level. Gewirth identifies this problem as follows: 'while economic democracy in its particularist or internal stage in the particular firm goes far toward securing the equal rights of all its worker–members to freedom and well–being, in its universalist or external stage it may have a quite adverse impact on those rights of non–members, including workers in other worker-controlled firms, and for society at large.'[37] The problem is based in the fact that self–managed firms or workers' co–operatives may themselves behave like capitalist firms. This problem leads Gewirth to argue for a 'universalisation' of economic democracy. He suggests that economic democracy needs to be applied on two levels: at the particularist level of the firm and at a general level of organisation 'whose function is to see to it that the particular firms continue to fulfil their individual workers' rights and that they do so in ways which promote the freedom and well–being of others'.[38] He prefers this approach to that of leaving the economic relations of separate firms to the 'anarchy' of the market, which could force them into capitalist behaviour, leading to inequality.[39] A general organisational level of support for democracy is required.

E. The Experience in Mondragón

Gewirth suggests that it is possible to achieve such a general organisation and turns to the example provided by the Mondragón co–operatives in the Basque region of northern Spain. Before considering the merits of this

---

36   *Ibid.*, chapter III.
37   Gewirth, above note 6, at p. 294.
38   Gewirth, above note 6, at p. 295.
39   *Ibid.*, at p. 295.

argument it is necessary to provide a short description of Mondragón.[40] This system grew out of a technical school started by a Basque priest, Father Jose Arizmendi. Under the Mondragón system the enterprise is owned and controlled collectively by the workers and each worker is entitled to one vote, though not to marketable shares. The system comprises a network of approximately one hundred worker co–operatives and has more than 20,000 members, with a financial centre in the Caja Laboral Popular, which is a co–operative bank with approximately 180 branches. The system contains educational facilities through a technical engineering college and a postgraduate and professional management training institute. Additionally, there is a research institute and a social service and medical support co–operative which serves the co–operators and their families. Gewirth describes the Mondragón system as 'socialised entrepreneurship' and argues that the success of the Mondragón system[41] lies in its Supportive Organisation, which is a formal network arrangement that supports the activities of the co–operatives and their members by providing training and central banking facilities. Dahl also suggests that the successful democratisation of enterprises would require other support systems and, in making reference to the Mondragón system, suggests that the absence of similar supports has caused the failure of other attempts to introduce democracy in the workplace.[42] It could be argued that the Mondragón system is unique and is unlikely to be achieved on a wider scale. These arguments may be based on the fact that the Mondragón system exists in a very small geographical region of Spain, that each co–operative is only a small unit which may be more amenable to democracy, and that it arises from a particular unity of ethnicity and culture of the Basque people. While all these claims are accurate it is possible to answer each of them. The geographical limits of the Mondragón system and the small size of its units are not necessarily an obstacle to its expansion. As Gewirth observes, the units might be small but the system has many units and itself is fairly large. This provides at least the

---

40   See eg Henk Thomas and Cris Logan, *Mondragón: An Economic Analysis* (Allen and Unwin, London 1982); W.F. Whyte and K.K. Whyte, *Making Mondragón* (ILR Press, Ithaca, NY 1988).

41   Between 1956 and 1983 there were 103 co–operatives created in Mondragón and only three had to go out of business, whereas in the United States it is often claimed that only 20 per cent of all firms survive for five years (Whyte and Whyte, p. 172 and p. 3). Today the figures are approximately 106 co–operatives in Mondragón: see David Ellerman, *The Democratic Worker–Owned Firm* (Unwin Hyman, Boston, 1990), at p. 100.

42   Robert A. Dahl, *Democracy and Its Critics* (Yale University Press, New Haven, 1989) at p. 332.

principle that the system could be extended to a whole national or even international economy.[43] More importantly, claims to Mondragón's cultural uniqueness may be answered by an institutionalised and rational experience of solidarity, which Gewirth considers possible by appealing to moral and human rights justifications.[44] Principally, Gewirth considers it possible to universalise economic democracy.

3. OPPORTUNITIES FOR DEMOCRACY IN THE COMPANY LAW PROGRAMME

Gewirth's argument for universalisation provides a role for the company law harmonisation programme. Company law itself is concerned with the structure of companies and, in particular, the relationship between managers and shareholders. The structure of companies could effectively be altered through company law. To universalise the effects of these laws the European company law programme could be employed. This programme has had an important impact on the company laws of the Member States as we have seen already. The company law harmonisation measures apply to companies throughout Europe and seek to co-ordinate the national laws. At the same time, the European company law provisions are designed to have both an enabling function and a protective function.[45] These functions could assist in both developing and sustaining a democratic corporate environment.

Although the company law programme has not expressly stated an intention to introduce democracy into the company the programme itself is part of a larger agenda which includes democracy. Article 2 EC Treaty concerns economics but within a democratic framework. There are some aspects about the programme that may help to develop a democratic corporate culture. For example, among the prerequisites for any form of democracy are availability of information and appropriate procedures for attaining democracy. Both these aspects represent major characteristics of the European company law programme. Both features are also relevant to democracy.

---

43   Gewirth, above note 6, at p. 302.

44   *Ibid.*, at pp. 305–7.

45   R. Drury, 'The European Company Law Harmonisation Programme' (1992) 24 *Bracton Law Journal*, 45–51.

A. Information

Democracy depends on the provision of information. A number of theorists regard it as an essential condition for democracy. For example, Saward argues that for responsive rule there are a number of logically necessary conditions among which feature freedom of information and a constant and formal process of public notification of decisions, options, arguments, issues and outcomes.[46] Similarly, Dahl claims that a criterion for a democratic process is enlightened understanding in which each citizen has adequate and equal opportunities within the time permitted by the need for a decision for discovering and validating his or her preferences on the matter to be decided.[47] Harden and Lewis also make the point that '[W]ithout freedom of information – subject to the standard set of exceptions in the interests of, for example, national security – democratic government is a contradiction in terms'. They note a foreword by David Steele MP which contained the words of an Australian Senate Standing Committee: 'The essence of democracy lies in the ability of the people to make choices: about who shall govern: or about which policies they support or respect. Such choices cannot be properly made unless adequate information is available.'[48] Effective participation also requires access to information. In this regard, Likert observes that the giving and sharing of information is an essential step in the process of participation.[49]

The company law directives are mostly concerned with the disclosure of information. The First Directive, for example, makes clear the need for company or commercial registers in each Member State. Primarily the commercial register is a source of information for the public as well as providing help in setting up companies. Indeed, as Sánchez Calero observes, the Spanish 1989 reforms aimed to bring the institution much closer to the public and to bring the registries technologically up to date.[50] In this way the register enables the public who deal with the company to make informed decisions about their dealings with the company. The First Directive also contains a section requiring formal disclosure of certain documents and

---

46   Michael Saward, 'Democratic Theory and Indices of Democratisation', in David Beetham (ed.), *Defining and Measuring Democracy*, 6–24, at pp. 16–7.

47   Dahl (1985) above note 4, at p. 59.

48   See Ian Harden and Norman Lewis, *The Noble Lie: The British Constitution and The Rule of Law* (Hutchinson, London, 1986) at p. 262. David Steele's foreword appears in D. Wilson (ed.), *The Secrets File* (Heinemann, 1984).

49   R. Likert, *New Patterns of Management* (McGraw Hill, New York, 1961) at p. 243.

50   Fernando Sánchez Calero, *Instituciones de Derecho Mercantil* (Civitas, Madrid, 1995) at p. 66.

information. The Fourth and Seventh Directives are concerned with disclosure of financial information. This may enable shareholders to evaluate and decide on the distribution of dividends or on proposals for expansion of the business or for a rights issue to be made.[51] The provision of financial information encourages participation not just by shareholders but by many parties, through the promotion of discussion of the data and debates on performances.[52] For example, employees will also be interested in the economic situation of their employers and the provision of such information may improve bargaining mechanisms.[53] In this sense, Chuliá suggests that the objective of the accounts directives is to enable the commercial sector to progress towards democracy and justice as well as the country's economic development.[54] While that claim might be rather optimistic it can be said that the provisions provide at least a starting point for effective participation.

B. Procedures

Procedures are also relevant to democracy. Gewirth claims, for example, that 'to focus on the procedures is to take democracy seriously in the most direct way'.[55] Against this claim it might be argued that procedures alone do not guarantee a democratic outcome: it is possible for draconian laws to be created out of apparently democratic procedures. However, the democratic importance of procedures is that they offer an opportunity for citizens to 'develop their own abilities as productive agents'[56] and take issues up for themselves. Procedures give to citizens an opportunity to participate in politics: they provide access to the political system. The company law programme is also compatible with this approach. For example, the Second Directive contains procedures in connection with decisions concerning the share capital such as reduction or increase of capital, the Third and Sixth Directives contain procedures for various parties to participate in the decision for the fusion or division of companies. The draft Thirteenth

---

51 See especially, Christian J. Meier–Schatz, 'Objectives of Financial Disclosure Regulation' (1986) 8 *Journal of Comparative Business and Capital Market Law* 219–248.

52 *Ibid.*

53 *Ibid.*, at pp. 233–4.

54 Vicent Chuliá (1987), 'Las Cuentas Anuales' in Angel Rojo (ed.), *La Reforma de la Ley de Sociedades Anónimas* (Civitas, Madrid, 1987) 225–292, at p. 292.

55 Gewirth, above note 6, at p. 346.

56 *Ibid.*, at p. 347.

Directive provides for shareholders to participate in the decision of accepting or rejecting a take–over bid.

4.   LIMITS TO THE COMPANY LAW PROGRAMME

There are, however, limitations to these optimistic claims for the universalisation of economic democracy through the company law programme. For example, the information requirements are regarded by some as a costly burden rather than as a form of democratic assistance.[57] One problem is that some of the information requirements appear to be arbitrary and to lack a clear agenda. For example, the need to state whether a company is a limited company or a public limited company on all notepaper and at all trading premises may add little to the protection of third parties but increases significantly the company's administrative costs. Sealy graphically points out the huge cost of 'labelling' to distinguish between public and private companies 'for reasons of Eurocratic tidy–mindedness'.[58] These burdens may serve to alienate the enterprise from certain democratic objectives if their costs outweigh the alleged benefits, though this may be a subjective comparison. Furthermore, the procedures established by the Directives do not always recognise the potential interests of some relevant groups. In particular, the Third and Sixth Directives, while providing for participation by the shareholders and creditors in the company's decision to merge or divide, make reference to the protection offered to employees through the Acquired Rights Directive, which gives to employees only a limited right to information and consultation rather than a full opportunity to participate.

The most devastating charge against the company law programme's potential links with democracy must be that it was the company law programme which tried and failed to establish economic democracy through the proposals for employee participation. The draft Fifth Directive and various attempts at the European Company Statute sought to provide employees with a role in the company's decision–making process. The previous chapter made clear the doomed existence of these proposals. Their potentially radical effect on the structure of companies appeared to be politically too strident to be acceptable. They met opposition from the left

---

57   See the strong criticisms of Professor Sealy in Leonard Sealy, 'The Disclosure Philosophy and Company Law Reform' (1981) 2 *Company Lawyer* 51–56.

58   *Ibid.* See also L.S. Sealy, *Company Law and Commercial Reality* (Sweet & Maxwell, London, 1984) esp. pp. 22–29.

and the right. Nor were the proposals accompanied by suggestions for support mechanisms for maintaining democracy once introduced.

A. Companies and Conflicting Interests

One barrier to the hopes for the company law programme's potential for introducing democracy and a possible explanation for the failures of its efforts to introduce democracy to date perhaps lies in the conflictual nature of the corporate entity and its internal structure. The alleged separation of ownership and control[59] which has dominated corporate theory during the twentieth century has been described by some commentators as 'financial feudalism' which presents both an obstacle to democracy and to commercial co–operation.[60] From this perspective, the company consists of disparate and competing interests which remain distrustful of each other and require constant bargaining and giving of favours or concessions in return for benefits. This appears to be recognised in Article 54(3)(g) EC Treaty which provides the basis for most of the company law programme and refers to shareholders *and* third parties. The drawback is not only that Article 54(3)(g) does not define the term 'others' or 'third parties'. More importantly, rather than seek to challenge this competitive structure of the firm, Article 54(3)(g) simply accepts its presence. The existing Directives seek to protect shareholders and third parties in an equivalent way but they do not, apart from ensuring to them more information from management, alter their bargaining position against management, nor indeed against each other. Both the draft Fifth Directive and the draft Directive which accompanies the proposed European Company Statute Regulation are based on Article 54(3)(g). Their failure to be adopted may reflect the fact that Article 54 does

---

59   As expounded by A. Berle and G. Means, *The Modern Corporation and Private Property* (Harcourt Brace & World, New York, 1932/1968).

60   This was a term used by Garrigues in his interpretation of the Berle and Means concept of separation of ownership and control. Interestingly, the term is referred to by Garcia de Enterria in his discussion of corporate control and take–overs. He quotes from Garrigues: (my translation) 'this financial feudalism destroys all democratic principles that they aspire to and especially the fundamental principle of proportionality between participation in the company's capital and participation in management', from Garrigues, *Tratado de Derecho Mercantil*, tomo 1, vol. II (Madrid, 1947) p. 625; quoted by Javier García de Enterría, 'El Control de Poder Societario en la Gran Empresa y la Función Disciplinar de las OPAs' (1992) 47 *Revista de Derecho Bancario y Bursátil* 665, at p. 668, his note 8.

not equip them adequately for challenging the corporate hierarchical structure.

B. Difficulties in Universalising the German Example

Some of these problems may lie behind the failure to introduce the co–determination system which operates in Germany and which influenced especially the character of the proposed Fifth Directive. To introduce co–determination into the UK corporate environment would require changing the company's internal structures, in particular, by creating two–tier management boards and by altering the position of influence of the employees. This appears to be incompatible with the UK approach. A brief history of the UK's reaction to the draft Fifth Directive will illustrate this point.

When the UK joined the EEC in 1972 the first draft of the Fifth Directive had already been published. The fairly strict two–tier structure proposed in that first draft was very different to the structures established in UK company law. This was a dramatic proposal and, as Schmitthoff observed, it would have altered the power position in many public companies with some impact on the capital market and the economy.[61] It comes as no surprise, then, that UK opposition to the draft was strong.

In 1977 The Bullock Committee published a Report[62] which had been instigated as a reaction to the draft Fifth Directive. The terms of reference were 'accepting the need for a radical extension of industrial democracy in the control of companies by means of representation on boards of directors and accepting the essential role of trade union organisations in this process to consider how such an extension can best be achieved'. Thus, the Report started out on the basis of a recognition of the need to include workers or their representatives in corporate decision–making.

The Report had both a majority and a minority view. The majority view came out in favour of a formula for recognising employee representatives on a unitary board: 2x+y. Basically, the formula meant parity between shareholder and employee representatives on the board of directors with three independent directors co–opted by agreement between the other two groups. The minority Report emphasised the importance of effective participation

---

61   Clive M. Schmitthoff, 'Employee Participation and the Theory of Enterprise' (1975) *JBL* 265, at p. 265.

62   Bullock Committee of Inquiry on *Industrial Democracy*, Report, Cmnd 6706 (HMSO, London, 1977).

below Board level, maintaining the view that employee representatives should be on a Supervisory Board.

The other recommendations of the Bullock Majority Report were: the Companies Act (then of 1967) to be amended so that boards would be required formally to take account of the interests of workers as well as shareholders; worker participation in companies with 2,000 or more employees in a mandatory form for the existing boards, but at the option of the workers and trade unions; the initiative in exercising the option should come from recognised trade unions but all workers should vote on the question; worker directors to be chosen by the workforce; all directors to have the same legal responsibility to pursue the interests of the company including the interests of both workers and shareholders, and the companies legislation should reflect this duty; an Industrial Democracy Commission to be established to arbitrate the co–option of independent directors and generally to promote and supervise the introduction of the new system; establish a fund by the government to provide training for workers and trade unions. Overall, the view of the Report was that collective bargaining and board level participation were interdependent and could be made compatible with each other.[63]

Many of these recommendations were supported and proposed also by the British Institute of Management.[64] The CBI, however, while not completely opposed to the notion of employee participation, saw the majority report as about trade union control of industry.[65] It criticised the Report on this basis pointing out the likely disadvantages for overseas workers and non–unionised employees. The CBI did not support the Report. Its view was that the proposals would remove the ultimate control of shareholders and pass that control to the board and that the proposals would change the free enterprise system. The Trade Unions were not altogether supportive either. They feared that a conflict of interest would push the worker directors to a

---

63 This view is countered by for example: K. Coates and T. Topham, *The Shop Steward's Guide to the Bullock Report* (Spokesman, Nottingham, 1977); Otto Kahn–Freund 'Industrial Democracy' (1977) 6 *ILJ* 65.

64 British Institute of Management, *Employee Participation: The Way Ahead* (October 1977). This pamphlet noted that there are different degrees of participation and these should be used in different circumstances. It also suggested we build on experience gained by tripartite committees already in existence, but that the worker participation provisions being proposed should complement collective bargaining, possibly as a mixture between participation agreements and unstructured participation. The BIM also pointed out the need for clear and accurate information rather than too much information.

65 Confederation of British Industry, *In Place of Bullock* (London, May 1977).

distance from their membership who they were supposed to be representing. In this way they were keen to see a distinction in the duties of directors on the board which would reflect the reason why the workers were actually a part of the board.

In the previous chapter the political and structural problems were highlighted as was the conflict theory perspective, most predominantly represented by Clegg, who regarded employee membership of the management board as undermining the role and independence of the trade unions. Clegg's views have been both criticised and supported by other commentators in the industrial democracy debate. Both Pateman and Blumberg, for example, while generally supporting the principle of employee participation do not consider that Clegg's insistence on democracy through opposition is an appropriate solution. Pateman suggests that Clegg's analogy with the company as a form of state government is inaccurate since a state is governed by leaders who are subject to removal on a regular basis unlike the directors of a company who are neither elected by those they govern nor are always subject to removal.[66] Blumberg also suggests that the independence of trade unions prevents them from being part of the management group even if trade union representatives appear on the board.[67] On the other hand, Bachrach and Botwinick, who regard co–determination as a conservative approach to economic democracy, purport to confirm Clegg's predictions suggesting that within Germany's co–determination system there are oligarchal tendencies in the union movement and evidence of aggrandisement and monetary self enrichment by trade union and employee representatives who become board members.[68]

A number of practical problems would also arise from such a system. These lead to many of the current objections by Member States, including the UK, to participation beyond Pateman's low level or partial level of information and consultation granted by the Works Councils Directive. For example, board membership for employees would present a conflict of directors' duties. In UK law, for example, a director's duties are to the company and not just to the employees. Worker directors would thus face a dichotomy between their political loyalties and group allegiances and their legal duties. Employees may also lack management expertise and, at least in the earlier, more formative years of co–determination, they would be at a disadvantage against the more experienced directors on the board and therefore not be able to pursue their interests as effectively as those represented by other directors. Another problem would be that employees

---

66   Pateman, above note 32, at p. 72.

67   Blumberg, above note 26, 142–152.

68   Bachrach and Botwinick, above note 5, at p. 78.

would still not have enough members on the board and so could be outvoted in board decisions. Indeed, in Germany the Chairman has the casting vote, which arguably reduces the potential influence of the employees. Some experiments in the UK whereby corporations had worker directors did not confirm that this would be the best form of employee participation.[69] It may be possible to resolve some of these practical difficulties by providing appropriate legal safeguards but the ideological problems are more deep-rooted.

For the European company law harmonisation programme there is an extra problem of searching for some unity between the contrasting systems in the sphere of employee participation and economic democracy. Both the German system and the UK system are united at least to the extent that theoretically, and practically, the company is treated as an autonomous entity separate from its members. However that is the limit to which the two systems coincide. A closer examination of the characteristics of the laws in each system may explain why the German system has been able to accommodate the concept of co–determination and why this would be very difficult to establish effectively in the UK. The German system regards the company as an autonomous enterprise with a public and social dimension which entails a diversity of interests to be recognised by the management of the firm and indeed to be represented on the management board.[70] While co-determination may, in reality, be what Pateman might call *partial* or *low*

---

69 The CBI referred to the experiment by the British Steel Corporation which initially had 'mixed results'. The CBI also pointed out the problem of employee representatives becoming alienated from the people they represent unless relationships are properly defined: CBI, *In Place of Bullock*, above note 65, at p. 27. Bercusson refers to a number of studies which concluded that the representatives 'had relatively little impact upon the outcome of company board discussions' and that 'such form of worker participation would not lead to radical changes in management behaviour': Brian Bercusson, 'Workers, Corporate Enterprise and the Law' in R. Lewis (ed.), *Labour Law in Britain* (Oxford, Blackwell, 1986) 134, at p. 148 citing: E. Batstone A. Ferner and M. Terry, *Unions on the Board: An Experiment in Industrial Democracy* (Oxford: Blackwell, 1983); P. Brannen, 'Worker Directors – An Approach to Analysis: The Case of the BSC' and E. Chell, 'Political Perspectives and Worker Participation at Board level: The British Experience' both in C. Crouch and F. Heller (eds), *Organisational Democracy and Political Processes*, Volume 1, *International Yearbook of Organisational Democracy* (Wiley, Chichester, 1983).

70 John Kay and Aubrey Silberston, 'Corporate Governance' (1995) *National Institute Economic Review*, 84–97, at p. 86; Paddy Ireland, 'Corporate Governance, Stakeholding, and the Company: Towards a Less Degenerate Capitalism?' (1996) *Journal of Law and Society*, 287–320, at p. 297.

level participation, to the extent that workers, through their representatives on the supervisory board, may do no more than influence the decisions of directors on the management board this has at least provided workers with a voice.[71] The managers must listen even if they ultimately choose to ignore. The social enterprise concept makes this possible since the employee's interest is a part of that social enterprise. The UK system, by contrast, is filled with tensions and contradictions which would undermine the role to be played by employees on a management board.

5.   UK COMPANY LAW TENSIONS

UK law acknowledges the theoretical autonomy of the company.[72] However, this conception, together with the notion of separation of ownership and control has met with a number of problems. The separation of ownership and control theory brings with it a suspicion of the 'managerial revolution' as providing managers with an opportunity to pursue their own interests rather than the interests of the 'owners'. The shareholders, having been 'expelled'[73] from the enterprise, remain outside it with little control over the behaviour and activities of the managers. This problem has dominated debates on corporate governance and executive pay during the late 1980s and 1990s.[74] Empirical evidence in the economics field also suggests that managers may pursue their own interests before the interests of shareholders or others in mergers and take–overs.[75] Such concerns have led to searches for justifications for managers' independence, giving rise to agency and fiduciary rules. The shareholders, legitimised by the property oriented thesis of company law, regard the directors as their agents.[76] This has its own difficulty, because the analogy with ownership for shareholders is not

---

71   Pateman, above note 32, at p. 70.

72   *Salomon* v *Salomon* [1897] AC 1 firmly established the principle of separate personality.

73   As described by Ireland, above note 70, at p. 301.

74   See eg Thomas Sheridan and Nigel Kendall, *Corporate Governance: An Action Plan for Profitability and Business Success* (Pitman, London, 1992).

75   For a useful review of the economic literature see: Pauline O'Sullivan, 'Governance by Exit: An Analysis of the Market for Corporate Control' in Kevin Keasey *et al.* (eds), *Corporate Governance: Economic, Management and Financial Issues* (Oxford University Press, Oxford, 1997) 122–146.

76   Mary Stokes, 'Company Law and Legal Theory', in W. Twining (ed.), *Legal Theory and Common Law* (Basil Blackwell, Oxford, 1986) 155–183.

entirely accurate,[77] which in turn leads to tensions about who the managers should serve. There exists a mixture of views all of which have some legal authority.

These range from the managers having to serve the company and not any third parties. Such a view is voiced in the *Tomorrow's Company* report.[78] An alternative view is that the managers should act principally on behalf of the shareholders. This view is often expounded by managers themselves and some company law rules support this. For example, as was observed above, section 309 Companies Act 1985, while requiring the directors to take into account the interests of the employees, states that this is subordinate to the interests of the shareholders. Another suggestion is that the managers should serve a variety of interests. The Court of Appeal in *Brady v Brady*[79] indicated that the predominant interest to be considered would depend on the financial circumstances of the company. The stakeholder theory also suggests that there are a number of participants with a stake in the corporate entity. This theory also supports the claim that companies have social responsibilities as well as profit maximising objectives.[80] The stakeholder theory has gained considerable support. However, if we look more closely at this theory it reveals a number of significant problems.

6. STAKEHOLDER THEORY AND ITS LIMITS

The first hurdle for the stakeholder approach is to identify the different interests and to balance them effectively. Rhenman defines stakeholders as 'the individuals or groups dependent on the company for the realisation of their personal goals and on whom the company is dependent for its existence'.[81] From this definition Rhenman identifies as stakeholders: employees, owners, customers, suppliers, creditors and managers 'as well as many other groups'.

This initial list is much too crude to be able effectively to take into account the variety of interests in the firm. Shareholders, for example, are not a homogeneous body. There is a huge difference in character, influence and interests of private shareholders and institutional investors. The short–

---

77 See the arguments in Kay and Silberston, above note 70, at pp. 87–8.
78 RSA, *Tomorrow's Company: The Role of Business in a Changing World* (1995).
79 [1988] 2 WLR 1308.
80 See eg discussion in J. E. Parkinson, *Corporate Power and Responsibility: Issues in the Theory of Company Law* (Oxford University Press, Oxford, 1993) Ch. 9.
81 Eric Rhenman, *Industrial Democracy and Industrial Management* (Tavistock, London, 1968) at p. 25.

term and long term interests of shareholders may also be different. Similarly, consumers can be divided into many different groups. For example, domestic consumers of energy companies will have very different needs to industrial consumers. Suppliers of a company may range from monopoly suppliers to suppliers in a very competitive sector. The level of influence on the company would differ significantly between these two categories. Employees may also have a number of categories each with different preferences and needs. For example, a more professional level worker might seek to exercise control over his or her work in different ways to the shop floor worker. Some employees are themselves managers while others may be part–time and casual workers, who would, in turn, have different needs and requirements to their full–time or permanent colleagues. The potential influence of each such category will also differ enormously. This kaleidoscope of interests is likely to present very great difficulties for managers in a company with a stakeholding philosophy. Added to these problems is the fact that sometimes the different identities of stakeholders may overlap. For example, an employee might also be a shareholder. The employee might also be a customer. Similarly a shareholder may also be a customer.

At the very least, the stakeholder theory calls for a clarification of the identities and the roles of these different stakeholder participants. Even the managers fall into different categories with different roles which would require them to focus on different specific interest groups. For example, the personnel director would have closer contact and may have to consider more closely the needs of the employees against other interests, whereas the finance director might be particularly concerned with the interests of the creditors and the shareholders. Similarly, the publicity director will be especially interested in customer views. The Securities and Investments Board's recent call for management to issue a statement of management structure and systems which would clarify lines of responsibility so that they are held accountable for failures in controls[82] is to be welcomed because such a declaration would force managers to clarify not only their responsibilities but also to whom those responsibilities are owed. This should improve accountability by publicising to third parties what the specific role of each manager entails. However, directors also have an overall responsibility to the company, and it may prove difficult, in reality, for a director to identify specific interests in the company within this proposed blanket legal rule. Yet, without clarifying the director's general and specific responsibilities, the danger is that the managers will be accountable to no–

---

82   Securities and Investments Board, *The Responsibilities of Senior Management*, SIB Consultative Paper 109 (London, 1997).

one and such a criticism may be led against the stakeholder theory generally.[83]

The potentially insurmountable problem for the stakeholder debate is, argues Ireland, the deceptive notion of autonomy of the company in a competitive market place. Although the shareholders are placed outside the organisation and they welcome that position in terms of their protection from full liability and freedom to pursue other activities, they are regarded as insiders in company law generally and their interests are, in practice, protected because the managers submit to the disciplines of the market through competition and take–overs. The survival of the company in this context demands that the shareholders' interests are protected since their great potential for 'exit' allows them to hold that threat over the company.[84] Germany does not have such a strong take–over culture so there is more room for other interests to flourish. In the UK these are significant problems for the stakeholder theory. These problems force us to search for an alternative.

UK company law also tends to have overlapping terminology which may perhaps only appear to be a semantic issue but which may also present some conceptual difficulties. In particular, industrial relations theory speaks in terms of subordination of labour to capital or of employee to employer. Sometimes the employer means the company and sometimes the employer means the manager. Capital may also mean either the company or the shareholders or the company's funds. This creates a difficulty for the employees and their representatives. Who is their dialogue to be with: the company, the managers, or the shareholders?

7.   AN ALTERNATIVE SOLUTION

An alternative approach to the problem of employee democracy in the context of UK company law and markets might be to suggest that if a balance or compromise cannot be found between the competing interests in the company, it may be that the inherent conflict in the relationships within the company structure is unavoidable. This conflict needs to be addressed by providing legal support to those parties who are in a weaker position, not simply by protecting them as the labour law provisions have sought to do but by providing them with a platform to put their views forward and, more importantly, to participate effectively in making the decisions.

---

83   Ireland, above note 70.
84   Although managers sometimes pursue their own interests first: see above, note 75.

Clearly, the board of directors is not in a position to uphold the employees' interests when they are in conflict with the interests of the shareholders since the structure and background context of UK company law forces the board to protect the shareholders' interests first. In this respect it might be asked if it is appropriate for employees to appear on the board of managers? On one level, this would help employees by bringing them into the company and regarding them as 'insiders' rather than keeping them at arm's length and outside the company for negotiation purposes, as collective bargaining appears to have done. This has been exacerbated by the replacement of a permanent and full–time workforce with a more casualised and flexible labour force. But this would be the limit of board participation: it would establish a partial participatory form. However, if the company is to be regarded as a 'productive organisation'[85] and the employees are to be fully integrated and treated as members of that organisation, they should be allowed the opportunity of a share in the control of the company.

Pateman speaks in terms of *full participation*, which signifies that 'each individual member of a decision–making body has equal power to determine the outcome of decisions'.[86] From this perspective employee participation entails 'a group of equal individuals who have to make their own decisions about how work is to be allocated and carried out'.[87] In this way, the employees are able to make their own decisions about their work and how that work is to be done. There are, however, a number of problems with this suggestion. First, it ignores the real environment of the company and views workers on each shop floor in isolation from the rest of the company and the rest of the competitive market in which it operates. To pursue Pateman's approach would risk the long term future of the workers who are forced to compete with companies not necessarily just in the same town but also with companies world–wide. By taking control of their own jobs fully there is a high risk that workers would be beaten by these competing forces of which they may not have adequate knowledge or even information. Some of these problems may arise from Pateman's failure to consider in detail the role of the shareholders who have an influence on the workplace in reality. Such problems make Pateman's approach ultimately unattractive. A more realistic and constructive approach is to provide employees with the opportunity of participative control in which they share the decision–making with shareholders and managers in work decisions and in corporate policy decisions. For example, by establishing a participative debate within the

---

85   As suggested by Collins, see above note 24.

86   Pateman, above note 32, at p. 71.

87   *Ibid.*, at p. 71.

company. Part of the role of the managers and shareholders would be to confront the workforce with these external constraints.

Currently in the UK, company law concentrates on the relationship of the managers and shareholders and labour law concentrates on the relationship between the managers and employees. The effect of these combined legal fields is that management acts to protect and favour the shareholders over other interest groups. The shareholders are shielded by their position of strength from the combined force of company law and the nature of capital markets and competition and by the fact that in labour law their role is largely ignored.

The shared control of company decisions might offer a possible solution to this conflict. In this way a new role for company law could be to facilitate a direct dialogue between the employees and the shareholders with the voices of each respective group carrying equal weight. This dialogue should be combined with other forms of employee participation so that participation is carried out at several levels. The first level would involve employees sharing with managers control over their immediate tasks by deciding jointly with management their work allocation and methods of work. The second level would be management, which would also be shared between managers and workers, by which worker representatives and managers would discuss terms and conditions of work such as working environment and facilities to be provided for doing the work. The third level would concern corporate policy decisions such as where the company should go for its supplies, or merger or take–over decisions, the elaboration of corporate strategies or vision statements. It is this third level at which the dialogue with shareholders should be made possible, with employees holding votes which are as effective as the votes held by shareholders and with equal access to the board of directors.

There are many important practical implications in this proposal. A number of obstacles may be placed before the possibility of dialogue between workers and shareholders. Larger companies, in particular, have dispersed shareholders and these are a variety of individual investors and institutional investors. As has been noted, individual investors are often not interested in the policy decision–making aspects of the company, preferring to leave the decision to the managers. Their vast numbers and their dispersed locations may create problems for a dialogue to be arranged between them and the employees. The institutional investors have a multiplicity of interests in their own firms and generally do not use the company meetings for influencing directors in their managerial decisions. They prefer to deal with managers more discreetly and directly, which could keep employees outside of the discussions. Another problem is the lack of informed discussion, each side protecting its own interests and not holding all the relevant information necessary to come to informed decisions. A further problem occurs where there are multinational companies or indeed, companies with numerous branches or subsidiaries. There may be practical difficulties in arranging meetings between shareholders and employees in these situations. Some of these problems could be resolved relatively easily such as by the provision of legal requirements for the same information to be passed by the managers to employees and shareholders. Others may need some more thought before this potential solution could work effectively. For example, if meetings cannot be so easily arranged perhaps this provides a role for the trade unions and the employers' organisations with a return to a modern form of corporatism.[88] However, although there may exist practical difficulties, the principle itself does at least appear to be supported by the discussion pursued in this chapter.

8.   CONCLUSION

The arguments in favour of employee participation demand a radical approach to the subjects of company law and industrial democracy. Archer suggests establishing employee democracy on a step–by–step basis[89] but, arguably, this would not sufficiently meet the requirements of the democratic philosophy within the firm. The competing interests of shareholders and employees have to be dealt with directly rather than offering the employees a consultative role or a position on the board of directors and no more. Industrial activity is political. As Pateman argues, the relationships of superiority and subordination make industry the most political of all areas in which ordinary individuals interact and the decisions taken there have a great effect on the rest of their lives.[90] Perhaps the key point is that made by Walzer: 'what is important is that we know it to be political, the exercise of power, not the free use of property.'[91]

---

88   I wish to thank Neil Kay for discussing these ideas with me.
89   Archer (1996), above note 9, at p. 31.
90   Pateman, above note 32, at pp. 83–84.
91   Walzer, above note 12, at p. 302.

12 Conclusion

European company law has reached a critical point in its development. The European Commission has expressed concern that in recent years there have been few discussions on company law within the Community institutions. In the Commission's view, the lack of any discussions or mutual contact brings with it the 'risk that a common view of the usefulness of existing or future Community legislation in the company law field might become blurred or even disappear altogether'.[1] This brings into question the future of the company law programme.

The theoretical benefits of harmonisation include: freedom of establishment and freedom of enterprise by eliminating restrictive barriers between the Member States; reduced costs; more certainty when conducting business abroad or with an overseas trading partner; and stronger cultural and legal ties across the Community.[2] The practical outcome, however, has been rather different. While the experience of the UK and Spain reveals that the company law programme has had a significant impact on the national company laws, important differences between those national laws still exist to the extent that freedom of establishment may continue to be inhibited. In addition, many of the administrative and formal requirements created by the company law Directives have led to considerable costs for companies; the complexity of many of the rules has increased uncertainty at national and transnational level; and the small take-up of some of the benefits offered by the company law programme, such as the economic interest grouping entity, might suggest that cultural and legal ties across the Community have not actually been strengthened in reality. The development of the company law programme also shows that whilst many decisions may have moved into the remit of centralised regulation, the detailed provisions have been extended more and more to the Member States, allowing their differences to continue.

---

1   European Commission, *Consultation Paper on Company Law* DGXV, D2/6017/96en (Brussels, March 1997).

2   See Jacob S. Ziegel, 'Harmonisation of Provincial Laws, with Particular Reference to Commercial, Consumer and Corporate Law' in Ronald C.C. Cuming (ed.), *Harmonisation of Business Law in Canada* (1986, University of Toronto Press, Toronto) 1–76, at p. 4.

1.   FOUR GENERATIONS OF DIRECTIVES

The company law directives appear to have progressed through four distinct generations which have increasingly moved towards leaving more to the discretion of the Member States. The First and Second Directives, which represent the first generation, are very precise, leaving Member States with little opportunity to deviate from their provisions and requirements. The second generation, most clearly represented by the Fourth and Seventh Directives, reflects a greater diversity of views with the German dominance less strong. These Directives are characterised by optional provisions, and exemptions and exceptions for small and medium–sized undertakings. The third generation of directives, represented by the Eleventh and Twelfth Directives, displays even more flexible provisions and they are shorter in length with a number of discretionary provisions for Member States to decide upon. The fourth generation of directives is represented by the draft Thirteenth Directive which is framed by the policies of proportionality and subsidiarity which underlined the Maastricht Treaty negotiations. The result of this approach is a draft Directive on take–over bids containing minimalist contents and expressing statements of principle whilst leaving the technical details to be decided by the Member States.

Some of the provisions do not fit easily into these generational categories, such as the supranational legislation, in particular the Regulation on the European Economic Interest Grouping. However, the generational categorisation may help to predict the likely developments of some of those outstanding measures, some of which were originally proposed as early as 1970, such as the proposal for the European Company Statute. They appear to have progressively accommodated the views of the Member States. As the Community has grown in size the variety of views and opinions has increased so that the only practical compromise between those views is to make the provisions more flexible. That appears to have been the direction of the successive drafts of the proposed Thirteenth Directive and also of the European Company Statute. The 1989 draft of the Thirteenth Directive was 23 Articles and the latest draft has only 12 Articles. Similarly, the draft European Company Statute had 137 Articles in its 1989 draft, 108 Articles in its 1991 draft and only 69 Articles in its 1996 draft. These have also moved towards leaving more issues to be decided by the Member States.

2.   LAW–MAKING PROCESS AND REPRESENTATIVE DEMOCRACY

These generational categories may also be identified to some extent by the successive legislative procedures by which the company law programme has been developed. The first two generations of directives were adopted under the consultation procedure, the third generation by the co–operation procedure and the fourth generation by the co–decision procedure. The company law programme serves as an example of the complexity and lack of transparency which characterises these different procedures.

The procedural problems cause some difficulty for the European Community in its claims to democracy. The weight of the Community's influence on economic activity compels it to justify the powers of its institutions and their decision–making processes. Democracy serves as a justification for the European Community's activities. For example, democracy featured as a primary focus of debate in the 1997 Intergovernmental Conference.[3] Official publications of the European Communities also claim democracy as an achievement of the Community.[4] Yet, for democracy to be effective it must exist at all levels of Community activity, in policy formation, in the law–making processes, in the implementation of those laws at Member State level, and in the practical application of the laws.

One criticism of the institutional arrangements is the lack of balance of power between them. The Commission and the Council are perceived to have too much power and the Parliament too little power. The introduction of the co–operation procedure and, later, the co–decision procedure promised to alter this lack of balance but the experience of the company law programme's development does not suggest that any dramatic shift in the balance of power between the legislative institutions has been achieved. Ironically, despite attempts to strengthen the Parliament's position, the reverse appears to have been achieved. The Member States, formally represented by the Council, appear to have gained an increasingly stronger voice but the influence of the Parliament on the legislative provisions does not appear to have gained much strength. Certainly, under the co–operation procedure there was no clear evidence of extra influence. The example of the Twelfth Directive's development does not indicate that the co–operation procedure achieved any improvement for the Parliament. Moreover, it was not easy to establish precisely who or which institution influenced the legislation produced under that procedure, because a number of the internal Community documents were marked as restrained. From this perspective, the expressed intention of the Commission and the Council for more openness is to be welcomed. It is perhaps too early to conclude on the results of the co–decision procedure, at least in the company law context. The latest amended draft of the Thirteenth Directive indicates that the Commission has been prepared to take on board

---

3   See introduction, note 13 and surrounding text.
4   See introduction, note 10.

the Parliament's opinion, albeit not fully. However, the ambivalence of the Member States towards the 1996 proposal, with a split of approximately 50–50 for and against the draft, suggests that the Parliament's strength remains to be tested by this proposal. The steps taken by the UK and the Take–over Panel may alone bring the negotiations to a halt, indicating that the Member States' views can be strong enough to prevent the Parliament from having a voice at all.[5] On the other hand, the UK's objections have not resulted in the proposal being abandoned, and the latest draft does not appear to have tried too hard to come into line with the UK's views.

The form of democracy at European Community level is representative democracy. However, the quality of that representative democracy is influenced by what degree of participation in decision–making is possible. In reality, participation in the legislative process is confined formally to the Member States. Interest groups and citizens participate by voting and lobbying. The level of interest in European elections is very low so that voting does not appear to be a hugely effective form of participation. Lobbying is often of poor quality, tends to be sporadic and allows interest groups, rather than citizens, to put their views forward. These small opportunities for participation coupled with the procedural complexities and lack of openness indicate that commentators are correct to conclude that the Community suffers from a democratic deficit.

The level of quality of democracy may be reflected by the degree of quality of the legislation produced. This may be measured by how the legislation is received by the Member States who have to implement it and by those whose actions are regulated by it.

3.   MEMBER STATE DIFFERENCES

The main emphasis of the company law directives is disclosure of information and establishment of protective procedures. The directives also contain both political and technical details, including valuation rules, extension of benefits to certain undertakings such as limited liability to single member companies and publicity exemptions to small and medium–sized companies. This displays a relatively limited subject matter, which may, to some extent, explain the continuing differences between the national company laws.

Even the aspects of company law covered by the directives remain different in many ways. The First and Second Directives, which represent the first identifiable generation, are relatively prescriptive and one might expect

---

5   See Robert Rice, 'Defending the Code', *Financial Times*, 4 November 1997.

these to have achieved more uniformity across the Member States. However, there are still some important differences between national laws concerned with the First Directive's provisions. For example, the role of the Registrars are quite different in the UK and Spain. Other examples include differences in minimum capital requirements – in Spain a minimum capital is required for private companies but this is not required in the UK; and there are different rules on aspects such as the valuation of non–cash payments for shares required by the Second Directive. Later generations of directives have also left differences between the laws of the Member States. For example, the Fourth and Seventh Directives are notable for their large number of options with regard to valuation methods and to presentation of accounts granted to Member States and companies, which have resulted in different forms of regulation. The UK provisions appear to be more liberal that the Spanish provisions. Indeed, the Accounts Directives do not alter the different approaches to responsibility of auditors. For example, in Spain auditors may be held liable to third parties, but this is not strictly the case in the UK.[6] The Twelfth Directive, which falls into the third generation of Directives, was implemented in different ways by the UK and Spain. The UK adopted very minimalist regulations and Spain was more comprehensive both formally and substantively, extending the concept to public as well as to private companies, and there are differences with regard to sanctions for failure to comply with the provisions. Finally, the draft Thirteenth Directive on take–overs, which represents the fourth generation of directives, promises even less proximity between Member States' laws, since it leaves to the Member States their own mechanisms for regulating take–overs. The result of the European directives and the implementation measures leaves the impression that the UK and Spain tried to get the reforms to fit into their structures rather than to alter their laws fundamentally.

---

6 The basic position is that there should be a relationship of proximity between the auditor and the claimant. See *Caparo Industries plc* v *Dickman* [1990] 2 AC 605; *Berg Sons & Co Ltd* v *Adams* [1993] BCLC 1045; *Anthony* v *Wright* [1995] 1 BCLC 236; cf: *Peach Publishing Ltd* v *Slater & Co* [1996] BCC 751; *ADT Ltd* v *BDO Binder Hamlyn* [1996] BCC 808; *Morgan Crucible Co plc* v *Hill Samuel & Co Ltd* [1991] Ch. 295.The Commission is working with the accountancy profession to deal with such issues: see Commission Green Paper, *The Role, The Position and the Liability of the Statutory Auditor within the European Union*, COM(96) 338. See also for a report of the Commission's plans to co–operate with the accountancy profession and to study possibilities for a single regime for auditor liability in the EU: Jim Kelly, 'Brussels spells out vision for auditing', *Financial Times*, 10 December 1996.

There are a number of explanations for these continuing differences. For example, different official language versions could have led to different interpretations of the Directives' provisions.[7] Further, the different entry dates of Member States into the Community means that some Member States have had an opportunity to be involved in Community negotiations for the creation of its laws while others have not. This could affect their attitude towards and their interpretation of the Directives, leading to different approaches to implementation. For example, the UK's involvement in the negotiations for the Accounts Directives could explain her relatively painless implementation of those Directives in comparison with the mess she made of implementing the validity of obligations provisions of the First Directive, the negotiations for which she took no part. Some States have a more supportive attitude towards Europe, thereby encouraging a more energetic response. Spain has been regarded generally as a pro–European State. She had to invest much to gain entry into the Community and this may explain why some of her reforms go beyond the requirements of the Directives. The comparisons in this book have revealed that, generally, the Spanish laws have been more extensive than the UK laws. By contrast, with the exception of its implementation of the Second Directive, the UK has tended to adopt a minimalist approach, at times almost to the point of appearing contemptuous of the European provisions. Additionally, national political characteristics could affect the approach of the Member State towards the Community provisions. For example, the existence of a written constitution in Spain, with strong democratic claims, may have encouraged her willingness to address a wider range of interests in her company law reforms. The UK system has no written constitution, unlike her continental partners. The UK company law is based on proprietorial and contractual notions whereas the continental emphasis is on third party security.

The extent to which many of these differences present a barrier to business between the two countries, however, is probably minimal. Yet, without the European legislation the differences between the two systems in these respects would perhaps have not been a significant obstruction to collaboration either. Empirical research might provide an answer to confirm either of these possibilities. However, there are further problems with the Directives. The low take–up of some provisions suggests that the company laws do not reflect accurately what is needed at the European level. The Directives themselves appear not to have dispelled the differences between

---

7   See eg Hans Claudius Ficker, 'The EEC Directives on Company Law Harmonisation' in Clive M. Schmitthoff (ed.), *The Harmonisation of European Company Law* (UKNCCL, London, 1973) 66.

the Member States. However, uniformity between the national laws would have been impossible and was not the intention behind the programme. On the other hand, the programme does seek 'harmony' through co–ordinated laws and protections, which could be regarded as equivalent. The compromise obtained in the Accounts Directives moves towards establishing more comparable accounts although their complexity may reduce that possibility. The information requirements in the Directives perhaps also increase transparency and therefore confidence in cross–border business relations, although not all the information is very helpful and sometimes the cost of providing that information may outweigh the benefits. Some of the provisions have little relevance in practice. For example, the EEIGs have had a low take up.

More seriously, the Directives, while not offering great practical advantages to the business community, may impose cost burdens or create new problems. This is the view, for example, of the UK Take–over Panel in relation to the draft Thirteenth Directive. Ironically, this proposal is charged with being contrary to European law because, while subsidiarity and proportionality are recognised, the very need for this legislation is questioned by the fact that national provisions allegedly work effectively already.[8] The development of this proposal so far verifies the claim by Du Plessis and Dine that accommodation does not necessarily lead to harmonisation.[9] The Directives are perhaps also noticeable for what they omit. Taxation still presents large barriers to cross–border trade though work is continuing on the development of harmonised taxation. Other issues which perhaps need still to be addressed include directors' duties and shareholders' remedies. These are issues of corporate governance which the Commission regards as a potential area for reform and has consulted on this point.[10] Perhaps the most significant barrier to cross–border trade is the variety of approaches to employee participation. This is perhaps also the greatest threat to the future of the company law programme.

4.   EMPLOYEE PARTICIPATION

From a very early stage in the development of the company law programme employee participation has been a controversial issue. The debate has

---

8   See Rice, above note 5.

9   J.J. Du Plessis and J. Dine, 'The Fate of the Draft Fifth Directive on Company Law: Accommodation instead of Harmonisation' (1997) *JBL* 23–47.

10   European Commission, *Consultation Paper on Company Law*, DGXV, D2/6017/96en (Brussels, March 1997).

intensified with time and currently presents a barrier to the progress of the proposed European Company Statute, the draft Tenth Directive and the draft Fifth Directive. This may ultimately be a threat to the future of the company law programme as a whole. Alternatively, if a solution were found that could serve to bring the cultural and business ties more closely together, then theoretically, it could also contribute to an improvement of the democratic quality of the Community.

The final part of this book presented the problems for introducing employee participation in the company law context and the limits of labour law for the possibilities of employee participation. Labour law offers protective legislation which, at most, may provide employees with a partial or low level of participation. Under the labour law provisions employees are offered information and consultation. However, this level of participation does little to challenge the corporate structures which place decision–making power into the hands of the directors and the shareholders. The combination of labour law and company law serves to keep employees outside the organisation rather than treating them as members of a productive organisation.[11] However, company law, which focuses on the structure of companies and the balance of relations in the company, holds the potential key to release democracy into the corporate organisation.

Presently, the stakeholder theory has gained considerable popularity. Its attraction lies in the recognition of a multiplicity of interests in the company including shareholders, directors, employees, consumers, suppliers, creditors and local residents. This at least diverts attention away from the focus on the relationship between managers and shareholders. However, at least in the UK, this is not enough to give the other stakeholders a strong voice in the organisation. In the UK the autonomy of the company in the context of a competitive market place ensures that the shareholders' interests are considered first by the managers, although sometimes they are also charged with pursuing their own interests before those of the shareholders. Most importantly, the interests of other stakeholders are deferred as a result of the UK company law perspective and business environment.

While the stakeholder theory appears to promise major changes to company law, this seems over optimistic. It is also evident that changes are required in favour of employee participation. Democratic theory justifies the need for employees to participate fully in decisions of the company at all levels where they are both affected by the decisions and where they are

---

11   Hugh Collins, 'Organisational Regulation and the Limits of Contract' in J. McCahery, S. Picciotto and C. Scott (eds), *Corporate Control and Accountability: Changing Structures and the Dynamics of Regulation* (Clarendon Press, Oxford, 1993) 91–100: see Chapter 11 of this book.

subject to the authority created by the decisions. Democratic theory suggests that employees should have priority over other stakeholders in making corporate decisions and that those other stakeholders be protected by a combination of government intervention through legal protections and the possibility of exit.

Since labour law does not promise them this role employees must turn to company law which, while seeming to be hostile to the concept of employee participation, is concerned with corporate structures and therefore may provide employees with a place inside the corporate structure as members rather than outside it as mere associates. The European company law programme offers some support for these changes. The primary demands of the programme are the provision of information and the availability of effective participatory structures. These need to be focused on the establishment of employee participation and the possibility of exit for shareholders and other stakeholders such as creditors and consumers. Currently, the information requirements concern a large number of irrelevant issues. They fail to take into account the interests of stakeholders and the realities of globalisation. For example, the accounts directives do not include the provision of social or environmental accounts which are of interest to a variety of interest groups. The international developments of accounting and the growth of global trade also present new challenges to the European Community, some of which are being tackled by the European institutions. New legal information requirements should also be relevant for informed dialogue between shareholders and employees. The procedural requirements should not just concentrate on shareholder votes but should also give to employees voting opportunities with the shareholders.

The current debates on the European Company Statute and the recommendations of the Davignon Report do not suggest that full participation for employees will be possible. The UK government's view is that while information and consultation rights are acceptable, a higher degree of participation will not be welcomed. The culture in the UK of take–overs and the use of single–tier boards creates practical and conceptual difficulties for employees to be granted a higher level of participation in the company. Yet if the UK is to make claims of democracy, employee participation in corporate decisions is required.

Furthermore, the theoretical discussions also suggest that employee participation is a potential key to the improvement of political democracy at the representative level. This is of interest to the European Community which is charged with a democratic deficit but which desires a democratic underpinning to its activities. Without having achieved effective employee participation across the Community's Member States it is impossible to confirm the accuracy of these theoretical claims. However, many commentators have provided evidence of a link between local participation and national participation in politics on the basis of the educative function of local level participation. In the company this educative process may benefit all sides through direct dialogue between the employees, the managers and the shareholders. Shareholders and managers may educate workers about the processes of the market place and in the long term this may protect the employees and their jobs. Employees may be also be educated about politics and political processes by acting politically at the level of the workplace. At the same time shareholders and managers might be educated by employees through direct dialogue and may be encouraged to think in terms beyond profit–maximisation. If, ultimately, these local participative processes bring about improvements to national level politics then logically, if employee participation is established across the Community, this ought to have some effect on the political activities of the European Community.

These theoretical suggestions give rise to a potential role for trade unions. Trade unions could represent workers in the discussions with managers and with shareholders or with shareholder and industry representatives such as the CBI. By including them in the discussions with shareholders this could prevent trade union representatives from allowing a conflict of interests to weaken their representation on the board of directors. Furthermore, the information requirements for these discussions could be channelled through the trade unions who could provide information to the employees about European law and political activities as well as about the company.

The arguments in this book present a first step and more research is needed to arrive at the practical steps necessary to achieve what democracy and democratic theory appears to justify. It might not be possible to guarantee democracy through legal rules. Furthermore, companies vary enormously in size and type and legal rules may well only set out a principle, with the details to be worked out at company level. However, the creation of laws may at least provide a framework for implementing the principles in practice. In any event, without providing an answer to the problem of employee participation the future of the whole company law programme is under threat.

Subject Index

Spain, 205–7
New Approach Directives, 28, 29,
46, 186
discretion to member states, 21,
28–9, 46, 48–9, 224
draft Thirteenth Directive, 49–
50, 106–8, 159, 162, 209,
224, 225, 227, 229
Eleventh Directive, 46–7, 224
European Commission White
Paper *Completing the
Internal Market*, 29, 46
fourth generation of directives,
29, 48–9, 51, 105–6, 224,
225
third generation of directives, 29,
46, 51, 97, 224, 225
Twelfth Directive, 47–8, 98–103,
152–6, 159, 162, 164, 167,
168, 171, 224, 225, 227
Nullity Of Companies, 31, 33,
134–5
First Directive, 31, 33, 134–5
Spain, 134–5

Participatory Democracy, 7–11, 12,
179–96, 198, 202–4
class struggle, 10
corporate structure, 191, 192,
193–4, 195–6, 197, 198, 221
employee participation, 10, 11,
19, 24, 62, 63, 181–5, 191,
192–3, 195, 197–222, 229–
32
labour law, 180, 186–8, 189,
190, 191, 195–6, 210, 214,
221, 230, 231
MacPherson, C. B., 7n, 9, 10,
180
Pateman, C., 7n, 10, 179, 191,
204, 205, 214, 215, 220, 222
relationship to politics, 7, 8, 9,
10, 11, 179–80, 204–5, 222,

230, 231–2
workplace democracy, 10–11,
179–96, 197–222, 229–32
see also democracy
Politics
relationship to participation, 7, 8,
9, 10, 11, 179–80, 204–5,
222, 230, 231–2
representative democracy, 7–11,
179, 198, 231
Private Limited Companies, 32, 47,
119, 139, 152, 154, 163–4, 166
Germany, Gesellschaft mit
beschränkter Haftung
(GmbH), 23, 25–6
Spain, sociedad de
responsabilidad limitada
(SRL), 122, 123–4, 138,
154, 163–4, 166
UK, 119, 139, 152, 163–4, 166
Profit And Loss Account, 43, 46,
148, 169
accounts, 42–6
draft Thirteenth Directive, 49–
50, 106, 107, 229
Fourth Directive, 43, 148, 169
fourth generation of directives,
48–9, 104–5
Proportionality, 48–9, 104, 105,
229
Seventh Directive, 46
Protection Of Employees, 40, 41,
50, 144
as opposed to participation, 191,
195, 230
in labour law, 191, 195, 230
Protection Of Share Capital, 35,
141
Second Directive, 35, 141
Protection Of Shareholders, 32, 34,
36, 40, 41, 42–6, 49–50, 135–
6, 141–6, 165–6
interaction of labour law and